Collected Wisdom

American Indian Education

Linda Miller Cleary

University of Minnesota, Duluth

Thomas D. Peacock

University of Minnesota, Duluth

Allyn and Bacon

Boston   London   Toronto   Sydney   Tokyo   Singapore

Series Editor: Frances Helland
Series Editorial Assistant: Kris Lamarre
Sr. Marketing Manager: Kathy Hunter
Sr. Editorial Production Administrator: Susan McIntyre
Editorial Production Service: Ruttle, Shaw & Wetherill, Inc.
Text Design and Electronic Composition: Denise Hoffman
Composition Buyer: Linda Cox
Manufacturing Buyer: Suzanne Lareau
Cover Administrator: Suzanne Harbison

Copyright © 1998 by Allyn & Bacon
A Viacom Company
160 Gould Street
Needham Heights, MA 02194

Internet: www.abacon.com
America Online: keyword: College Online

Library of Congress Cataloging-in-Publication Data
Cleary, Linda Miller.
    Collected wisdom : American Indian education / Linda Miller
Cleary, Thomas D. Peacock.
        p.   cm.
    Includes bibliographical references and index.
    ISBN 0-205-26757-2
    1. Indians of North America—Education.   2. Multicultural
education—United States   3. Indian students—United States—
Psychology.   4. Intercultural communication—United States.
I. Peacock, Thomas D.   II. Title.
E97.C63 1998
370'.8997—dc21   97-1212
                                                          CIP

Printed in the United States of America
10   RRD   08 07 06

*To the sixty teachers of American Indian students
who contributed their words and wisdom.*

*To all students everywhere who deserve good schools and good teachers;
to Jed and Sarah Cleary and Brady and Beau Peacock,
for their support of everything that is important on this earth;
Tom Peacock especially dedicates this to his granddaughter Alex,
who will inherit all the problems this generation
hasn't solved or has created,
and to the memory of his daughter Becca.*

*In my dark horse dreams
I dream of you
In my dark horse dreams*

Contents

3 What Has Gone Wrong: The Remnants of Oppression 59

4 Creating a Two-Way Bridge: Being Indian in a Non-Indian World 97

Issues of Native Language   123

6 Ways of Learning   151

7 Literacy, Thought, and Empowerment   175

 8 What Works: Student Motivation as a Guide to Practice   201

9 Epilogue: Full Circle   247

Preface

Collected Wisdom is for everyone who has an interest in American Indian education. Although this book will be important to researchers and graduate students who study American Indian education (learning, language, and literacy), it is written for those who need it the most, the practicing and prospective teachers who teach or will teach in schools in which American Indian students are enrolled.

In addition, the collected wisdom herein will be useful for administrators who serve these students; for local, state, and national policymakers; and for Indian school board members. Because the U.S. educational system has not been successful in preparing a very high percentage of American Indian teachers, many non-Indian teachers work with American Indian children. They are important to American Indian children, and we hope this book will help them to begin or continue their work.

Acknowledgments

For their assistance in helping us to set up the research, we would like to thank Joane Bercu, Manny Begay, Beatrice Bivens, Mary Bray, Martin Coyle, Norm Dorpat, Wayne Newell, Linda Rudolph, and Brian Smith. For the hours of tedious work that becoming immersed in the data takes and for insights provided along the way, we thank Catherine Long, Anna Ahlgren, Anna Wirta, Bonnie Laakkonen, and Liz Mouw. For readers who gave generously of their time, advice, counsel, and commentary (and occasionally witty sarcasm) on the book, we thank Terrie Shannon, "Sonny" Peacock, Joyce Kramer, Liz Mouw, Harriet Gott, Lou Lipkin, Alice Jean Schleiderer, Charlin Diver, Clifton Rabideaux, Brady Peacock, and Amy Bergstrom. We would also like to thank Ines M. Chisolm, Arizona State University West; Catherine McCartney, Benidji State University; Adelaida Santana, Northern Arizona University; Robert E. Vadas, University of Akron; and Carlos J. Vallijo, Arizona State University for their insightful reviews.

Introduction

The Teacher as Learner

Several years ago, when I, Linda Miller Cleary, entered teacher Tom Ketron's art room in a public high school located near the border of two reservations in the Southwest, I was aware that I was in the presence of a non-Indian teacher who accomplished remarkable things with his American Indian students. Scattered on tables around the clay-dusted room were rust-red sculptures, up to three feet high, which were covered with wet rags to slow down the clay's drying. As Ketron uncovered a few of the forty or so sculptures for me to see, I was astounded at the skillful entwining of representations of kachina and animals and people. Ketron found a cloth and dusted off two tall stools for us. I turned on the tape recorder and started to collect the wisdom that was in his stories. During that and three subsequent preparation periods conjoined with lunch, he jolted me into deeper understandings of cultural difference, of the ways a teacher might interact with those who have been oppressed and whose ancestors have been oppressed, and of the charm, distress, and reward of working with American Indian students. Tom Ketron was a teacher who was a learner; he had learned a lot from his students and his teaching situation, and I, in turn, learned from him.

In this book we have collected teachers' wisdom about American Indian education: about how it has been, how it is, and how it might be. Writing this book has asked us as the authors, and, in reading, will ask you as readers, to see beyond our

own initial perspectives to the complex nature of the collision of two cultures, the one culture barely dented and the other almost crumpled. *Collected Wisdom* is dedicated to seeing clearly, and if we have learned anything in its writing, it is that this business of seeing clearly takes some courage. When we begin to see clearly, we must leave previous comfortable ways of thinking and contemplate how we must do things in the future.

A Chapter Road Map

The purposes of this chapter are introductory, and Tom Ketron will help us with the introduction. We would like to acquaint you with how we collaborated to collect the teachers' wisdom that will be presented in this book. We begin by examining stories as a way of knowing; we tell the stories that led us to this work, and we tell the story of our research, showing you how we went through this process with Tom Ketron. Finally, we introduce the issues that have emerged from this research, using stories that Tom Ketron told of his work teaching American Indian students.

Collected Stories: A Way to Make Sense of American Indian Education

Many American Indian people learn their way in life through stories. So in being consonant with our topic, much of our material is introduced with stories. This is a different presentation from what many readers are used to, but we have stuck to it, even when some of our early readers asked us for our conclusions up front. We ask you to learn from the stories initially, but we have included chapter summaries for readers who want solid conclusions from the stories.

We have collected many stories in this text—the stories of teachers who teach American Indian students. Among the most compelling voices are those of American Indian educators, those who have been teaching so long that they have much to tell and those who are so new that they have vivid recollections of being on the other side of the desk. The book also tells the stories of courageous non-Indian educators who have entered schools to work in sometimes uncomfortable situations; who have worked hard to understand; who, in many cases, have done admirable work; and who have had the courage to reflect, learn, accept, and teach. All of these teachers have important stories to tell.

Clifford (1986) said, "Any story has a propensity to generate another story in the mind of its reader (or hearer), to repeat and displace some prior story" (p. 100). As Clifford suggests, "convincing" or "rich" stories can be almost metaphoric. They can lead you, as readers, to patterns of associations in your own experience, combined with which you will generate your own unique meanings. The stories in this book cannot help but become part of the rich collage of the future stories we all will tell, and we will not all make the same meanings of these stories, nor should we.

Teachers tell stories in this book, and, as authors, we pose questions and problems along the way so that you, as readers, will work actively toward your own understandings of the educational issues the book explores. Thus, though teachers-as-soloists are featured in profiles, and the rest of the sixty teachers will come in with a chorus of quotes, and though we as authors will respond antiphonally with questions and conclusions, all of us—teachers, readers, and authors—will take part in composing meaning from this material. And through this composing, we will all construct a new base of knowledge from which to act.

The Story of Our Research

This book is based on interviews that we have done with more than sixty teachers, American Indian and non-Indian, on or near nine reservations (in the Northeast, Southeast, Southwest, Northwest, and Midwest) and in two cities with high American Indian populations. Although this book is based on the collected wisdom of these American teachers, we also interviewed another fifty teachers of indigenous people in Australia and Costa Rica, allowing us to understand some of the universals in indigenous education. This learning was rich and the patterns unsurprisingly similar, given the colonization involved in each setting. Indeed, certain dynamics were clarified when we recognized similarities or discrepancies in very different environments. We only call on an occasional voice from abroad in this work. The strong voices of American teachers will speak out through the pages of this volume, strengthened by the broader base of interviews. The teachers speak about their joy and frustration in working with American Indian students; their insights weave answers to problems in American Indian education.

To illustrate how we went about this research and to introduce issues the research raised, we have already introduced one of my early interviewees, Tom Ketron. Ketron was one of the participants in the study who decided he wanted to keep his own name. Others felt more comfortable in giving a pseudonym or in being designated only by the area of the country in which they taught. We have been careful to preserve anonymity when teachers requested it.

We chose Ketron to help introduce our research procedures because he was the kind of teacher that we came to especially admire as we continued this work. He was a teacher who was a learner, a teacher committed to learning so that he could work well with his students.

At each reservation, we gained official permission to do these interviews. At some schools, the research had to be approved at the tribal office level; at Ketron's school, the principal gave his permission. Ingrid, a curriculum coordinator/ English teacher, helped me generate a balanced list of teachers teaching different subjects, American Indian and non-Indian, experienced and inexperienced. We realized that some of these contact people had an interest in connecting us with their best teachers. So, while collecting material from the very best teachers (not bad wisdom to collect), we also looked for teachers who were less positive about their work with American Indian students. Some we have quoted with explanatory text. We interviewed four administrators because of their prior rich and varied teaching experience.

Most teachers were interviewed on three occasions, each interview lasting between sixty and ninety minutes. We also spent time in the schools in informal observations and conversations so that we might understand the context of what the teachers were telling us. For instance, it was easier to understand Ketron's frustration with changing administration when I listened informally to other teachers bitterly joking about navigating their work with yet another principal.

The basic open-ended questions for each of the interviews were: (1) Tell me about what led up to the teaching you are now doing; (2) Tell me about your teaching right now on or near American Indian reservations; and (3) What meaning/ sense do you make of the teaching you have done in these schools? We followed up with other questions, as we led the teachers to talk deeply about their experience of working with American Indian students.

Willingness on the part of the interviewee was essential, so I found Ketron in the hall in front of his classroom between classes and shouted above the noise to see if he would be willing. We arranged a time for the first interview. Tom Ketron began his first interview with:

◆ I am an artist who teaches art. I teach sculpture here. I had heard a lot about the Indian kids from my cousin who was the physical education director here, that they were really good at art. So I came here and interviewed, and I've been here for nine years.

Many teachers were most comfortable when given some follow-up questions, but Ketron had already done a lot of thinking about his work, and his words came easily. He had worked hard to understand his work, and he deepened the clarity with which we saw the complexities of teaching American Indian students.

After four hours of interview time over three sessions with Ketron, making for fifty-six single-spaced, transcribed interview pages, times sixty interviewees, we amassed a great deal of interview material, which we needed to analyze. The analysis (see Appendix 1 for a fuller description of the interviewing and analysis process) led us naturally to the emerging themes in our research.

One such theme, "Teacher as Learner," we chose to cover in this first chapter. Though this theme emerged first in Ketron's interviews, it was echoed by the teachers who clearly enjoyed and were interested in their work. Teachers who seemed to last in schools serving American Indian students and who seemed to get the most out of their work were teachers who were learners. In the quotes that follow, we have woven sections from the interviews with Ketron and with others, so they can introduce the issues that we raise in the book.

An Emerging Theme: Teacher as Learner

Sitting in his clay-strewn classroom, Ketron plucked a mask off the wall and said, "You see this is how the mask is made. The skin is made out of rabbit skin; the inside is made out of rawhide." Ketron proceeded to tell me what he had to learn about local art and about how to work well with his students.

◆ There are [times] as a teacher when you don't know the things you need [to know], and you better get them someplace else. So I have kids teach me things about art; they know that I'm trying to pass it on to the next group. I may be the teacher, but I need to learn something too. It is guaranteed that you will make mistakes, so if you try to bluff your way through, you are not going to make it. Sometimes, if you are smart enough, you will go for help. I think if you come from a white [background], it's easy to get yourself in this spot on a reservation and maybe say and do [offensive] things that you don't realize that you're doing.

If teachers, American Indian and non-Indian alike, come into schools that serve American Indian students thinking of themselves as learners, they will learn ways of being and teaching that will benefit their students. They will come with an attitude that will keep them where the students need them. A chorus of teachers joined in on this theme. Linda, a non-Indian from the Northeast, said:

◆ Some people here are the most introspective people, and the most able to understand the depth of their issues. The people who live in this community are

human beings who have given me as a learner more exciting, deep, and wonderful questions than I've gotten anywhere else. They're not afraid to just ask a question and let it sit. I think one of the reasons I'm so comfortable here is because I like to ponder. And since I came here, I've learned a lot about the power of listening. I came here to learn and to share. I didn't come here to save [people]. And . . . a major problem in Native American communities is the "rescue" operation.

All told, the most important endeavor for teachers in Indian schools and in schools where Indian children are served is to see themselves as learners, learners who are open to understanding the reasons the children and communities are the way they are, learners who are willing to discover and consider the differences between the cultures of the school and the home of the child, and learners who are willing to change their ways of teaching so that the children have a better chance in school and a better chance to have purpose and hope in their lives thereafter. We challenge you to be learners, researchers in your own right, as you read this book and as you enter or reenter classrooms with American Indian students.

Ketron's Stories Introduce the Emerging Themes in the Research

As Ketron talked about what he learned, he raised issues that were echoed by other teachers; our book has taken on its structure from some of these issues. We have not done this structuring casually; it has been based on rigorous analysis of thousands and thousands of pages of interview material. From that mass of data the following themes emerged, demanding chapters of their own. Ketron's words will provide an introduction to these themes.

Learning about Cultural Differences

Ketron learned the hard way about the importance of recognizing cultural differences:

◆ I was a brand new teacher, and I didn't know. There were a couple of ladies who I was doing some pots for, and they belonged to the snake clan. They wanted a snake on the pot because there was some batter they stirred up on the morning for some ceremony. [When I was doing this work in my classroom], a kid from another tribe looked in some *National Geographics,* and he put a cobra on a pot and took it home. Couple days later, the mother came in. She wanted me fired; she was taking her son out of the school. When he brought that pot home, it cost them about $500 to hire a medicine man to destroy the pot, and they weren't a very wealthy family. The boy came back to school one day with bruises up and all down his neck where they had some ceremony and pulled the snake bones out of him. She was pregnant, and she thought I was trying to kill her unborn child. So now I don't allow snakes on anything no matter what clan or tribe I think the student is from. For one clan the snakes are okay, but for another tribe, it's a big no no. So it's very easy to degrade or insult, even when you're not trying to. How many things, things that you don't even think may be abusive, do you do every day? In your culture, you might not think about it, but when you take it somewhere else. . . . And the problem is, there are differences between tribes, and within a tribe there's a lot of variety, and even within a community, depending on how traditional or how contemporary people are, there is variety. There is no "Native American way." As a teacher, you have to learn.

When there are strong differences between the culture of a child's home and the culture of the school, school can be confusing to a child. As educators we need to learn to see these differences clearly if we are to transact them in the educational setting. Ketron worked hard to understand both the obvious differences and the more subtle ones that include different perceptions of time, values, world views, and ways of expression, learning, and aspects of being such as humor.

◆ Finding their sense of humor helps. I learned how to joke with them. We joke when I'm teaching them to do kachina; "Well, what tribe do you belong to?" they ask. "Well, I belong to the honky tribe: tall, big, and ugly." But I've had them even ask me would I let my son marry an Indian girl. Or if I wasn't married, would I marry an Indian girl. Testing, testing. And I say, "My son? Only if she's a volleyball girl, 'cause I used to coach volleyball, and they were real classy girls." Humor works, but not to insult or to degrade. And I'll poke fun at myself. Like the Friday before vacation—and I was really tired. I'd been up late several nights doing my own art work, and I'd stagger out of the bed and came to school, and the third hour the kids are saying, "You trying to make a new fashion statement, Ketron?" "What are you talking about?" "Well, look at your feet." I had one shoe on one foot and one from another pair on the other foot. And I wondered why my hip was bothering me because one of them was higher than the other. So you can't be wrapped too tight. And you joke with them, but you got to let them laugh and joke at you, too. In this setting, it's got to go both ways.

Teachers who are unaware of these differences may find themselves alienated from Indian students or parents. Chapter 2 is dedicated to helping teachers see cultural differences more clearly.

Issues of Oppression

Ketron talked frankly about working in communities suffering from complex problems brought on by historical oppression. He showed how these problems surface in multiple related and unrelated ways.

◆ Native Americans are very suspecting because in BIA [Bureau of Indian Affairs] days terrible things got done to them. All kinds of stories. The parents don't have a real good feeling toward the school system, so they are cautious. But once they trust, they are your friend for life. One time parents walked in my room, and they said, "But you're not Indian!" They were just genuinely surprised. The kids are color blind if they like you. Other teachers too have come here and thrived, adapted, and learned new things, and have a respect for things.

Teachers have a lot of rewards, but it is a hard job. Sometimes a girl comes to me, "I'm pregnant." The parents don't know. Why does she come to me? Well, I talk to her. [So I] go get the guy out of the class, take [them] down to the social worker, talk to the social worker, the social worker gets the parents. At high school level, these kids have lots of needs; you can't just be an art teacher, you can't be a math teacher. If you don't take care of these kinds of problems, then how can you teach them? So you play a lot of roles. You really know them, and when they do well, you are happy, and if they don't, it gets to be draining. But when things go well, there are things that you can't get paid for. To give you a classic example, when I first came here, there was a boy that was a holy terror—drugs, fighting. I've had him curse me up and down, and [I'd] teach him art. I'd get him supplies to take home, and then, when he was in trouble, I'd be up one side of him and down the other. He lived in the dorm and got kicked out, and I got him put back in the dorm. [At one time] this kid hated my guts. But he turned out to be one of the best art students I'd ever had. He came back three years later, and he wanted to show me his new son, and he'd named him Tom. So there are things like that. These kids emotionally can suck you dry. You need one or two once in a while to say thank you, or you need to know that they're doing well, to keep you going.

Principals at the high school last fourteen months average; superintendents two years. So, see, there's a lot of turmoil; you have to be adaptable. Sometimes principals are fired because they are not good; sometimes it's politics. One year I argued with the high school principal and got sent to the junior high school. I had a ball for one year. That principal is now the superintendent. He wrote in my last evaluation: "This is the most unorthodox guy I've ever seen in my life, but it is working well, so leave it alone."

Some of the kids quit trying, quit coming; then they have to be referred to the court system, which takes it out of our hands. Till eighteen their parents are responsible for them. So then the judge wants to get involved. His options are: [I can] send the parents to jail, I can fine the parents, I can take the student away from the parents, or I can send the student to one of these reform places. That's why I'm chewing on some of the kids so hard in class now. Look at what some of the alternatives are. "You guys are messing up, and once it goes there [to court], then it's out of our hands. It'll already be too late."

I take it [this work] seriously. The kids here haven't learned all the bad habits yet. There's still hope. They're starting to, but it's something you can turn around. I figure things I'd done in their life had to be a little worthwhile. Like other kids, they need tough love—knowing you care.

Teachers talked about what happens when a people are removed from their traditional way of being, when they see little purpose in their lives and a lot of hopelessness in their communities. Chapter 3 addresses these remnants of oppression. It offers the reader a sense of the enormity of the problems confronting Indian students, the barriers to their success, and the subsequent challenges to teachers of Indian students and to the communities.

Do Students Need to Bridge Two Worlds?

Teachers puzzled over what their students needed for their futures. Ketron looked out for his students' futures by connecting his students with their cultural background, establishing pride and self-esteem, while teaching enough skills so that they could make a living in the other world.

◆ One year we did wooden flutes; another year we stretched canvasses. We're trying to make them multimedium, multisubject artists, to broaden the base with as many techniques as possible, so that if they want to do something when they get out, they have it.

The most remarkable examples of those who possess the necessary skills and attitudes to move in and out of both worlds are the American Indian teachers in the book. They demonstrate success in the majority culture's academic and work environment while retaining their Indian cultures, values, and, often, languages. They provide most of the insight for Chapter 4.

Native Language and Cultural Issues

When Ketron talked a second time about the mother who was so distressed about the cobra her son put on a pot, he alluded to the great loss of culture and language that has occurred for many native people.

◆ Like this mother [who came in], we are very good friends now. She said she realized they were a very traditional family, but they hadn't taught their kids anything. And I was a brand new teacher, and I didn't know. [Now] I say, "You've got to go home and talk to your parents. I don't have [the cultural knowledge]. You want to learn it from the library like I do? Well, that's ridiculous. You better go to the dances and the ceremonies." So we have an understanding between us. "There are some [times] that I don't know what you need, and you better get them someplace else." And the same with language. Some of these kids have real language problems. Like the kids we have now in our lower grades. Kids used to translate from [their home language] in their mind to English. That's not so much the problem anymore. The problem is now they have no English, no language, because some of their parents were young enough that when they were going through the school, trying to learn English, they were losing their language. And while they were losing their language, they didn't learn English well enough, so their children didn't learn either one. So when they test the kids, they have no solid language. They have no language base from which to learn. They're [trying to] undo what the BIA did all over the United States. Same with culture.

Ketron presents just a glimpse of the process of loss, recognizing that native culture and language were ripped away from children in the boarding school era and that this loss is perpetuated in our modern world. Chapter 5 looks at the desperate state of native language and the disparate ways in which schools are dealing with it.

Ways of Learning

◆ I don't know, they're always saying Indian kids are right-brained learners, whatever that is. . . . I don't understand all that. Your style [just has to] change with different kids. I demonstrate a lot. Constantly showing them, showing them. You know everything can be explained very simply, and everything is shown, continually shown until they understand it. Nobody gets left behind. And what's nice in big classes like this, because there's such a range of students, they learn from each other. They see other people doing other things. I just think that if you have a teacher [that] is tough and works really hard and has high expectations and does whatever, technique-wise, it takes to get them there, that kids can do well in any area, any time. You have to think hard about how they best can learn. I basically believe all kids want to learn. Some days these kids are just trying to stay alive, and we're trying to worry about educating them? But when you stop and think: These kids are pretty tough. When you look at their background and things they have to deal with and how well they're doing, they don't have a lot of the pluses and bonuses, and they do well anyway. You ought to have a high opinion of them.

Ketron and other teachers challenge learning style stereotypes of American Indians. Significant research has been done in the last twenty years on learning "styles" of American Indian children. Chapter 6 reviews that literature and contributes to it with the perceptions of sixty teachers who are in the field working with Indian students.

American Indian Literacy, Thought, and Empowerment

Teachers were mostly confused about how to work with their Indian students in reading and writing. They luxuriated in some of the creative strengths students had in writing but had difficulty understanding other problems with literacy. But their confusion and the discoveries they had made about what worked led me to an emerging theory about the strengths American Indian students can bring to acts of literacy.

Ketron was an art teacher, and aside from being aware of the problems his colleagues face with establishing literacy, he thinks little about it. But he does touch on another aspect of Chapter 7, empowerment. Ketron orchestrated ways that students might use the skills he taught to feel hopeful and purposeful in their lives.

◆ You hear about problems on the reservation about reading and writing, but it's like I died and went to heaven. These kids have some natural talent, but it'll only take them so far. If they're going to [make it], they have to have technique, and they have to know why they need it. I'm trying to teach them new things, enough things. A drawing is a dime a dozen, but there's a shortage of three-dimensional artists. And stone is starting to get hot in the Southwest and spreading to the rest of the United States, so what I picked were mediums to get the kids started early and get them into areas that would get them into galleries. I'm trying to teach them new things. [I'd like] to get some of these people who are [already] successful artists, then bring in some young kids and let them spend some time, [let them] teach them jewelry.

Chapter 7 explores issues of literacy in ways similar to the way Ketron explores issues of art and empowerment.

Things That Work

Ketron managed to find teaching methods and modes of interaction with students that worked for him:

◆ At the beginning of the year, when we get new kids, I start cutting hunks of clay and start throwing it around the room, "Work, get your hands in it. Don't worry about the small stuff; we'll get into that later." And that's the other part of my technique. It's called guaranteed success. You don't know the lunch hours I spend, "Here fix this [sculpture's] broken nose, patch this arm," but it reaches a point, success brings more success. When they feel success, that kid over there who made that sculpture [points to a three-foot-high, re-markable sculpture he has shown me], we just talk art. I don't even touch his projects anymore. In fact, he's getting better than I am. And then I bring in my Chinese ink paintings; they know I do art at night and on weekends.

In the first weeks I roughed out 130 sculptures for the kids. Quicker success. They get to that quality faster, but you have to decide when to help and when to say, "No." They get withdrawal symptoms because they are used to me doing it, so we start, and then "You work on it a while, and then I'll come around." And I give lots of demonstrations and lots of models, and they get successful faster. It's like a director; you have to know when to be kind, when to reward, when to help, or not to help.

One year in the commons area, I had a chain saw, and we were cutting logs; we were going to carve big totems. And other teachers were upset be-cause of the gas and the fumes and the floor. And the principal came down, and he saw what I was doing, so he had some custodians come in and lay down some plastic and wood around the edges. At lunch time every day, I had seventy to eighty curious kids, pounding and carving, taking turns. That's the way I've done things here. Whatever I do, I need supplies. When administra-tors see results, they generally get what I need. If teachers are really working for the kids, and everything is based around the kids, teachers have power that new teachers have no idea they have, no idea how they can use it to be more successful with the kids. The most powerful person in the whole educa-tional system is the schoolteacher. If you're working hard and you're doing a good job, no school board or principal or superintendent's going to mess with you. Because the bottom line is parents love their children, even though sometimes they don't know how to deal with them, and maybe they've turned over too much of their education and responsibility to the school systems. But if you're doing your job, parents know somebody's doing a good job; they won't stand for anybody messing with them. The seeds I'm planting may take years to even sprout, then mature, but at least they are planted.

In Ketron's words, we can see some methods and teacher behaviors that work: the need to build trust; to connect with the community; to establish cultural relevance in the curriculum; to tap intrinsic motivation for learning; to use humor; to establish family support; to provide situations that yield small successes; to make personal connections with students; to use highly engaging, activity-based learning and, in some cases, cooperative learning; to provide role models; to be flexible, fair, and consistent; and to provide real audience and purpose for student work. Chapter 8 collects what more than sixty teachers agree with in working effectively with American Indian children.

Why We Collected These Stories

As researchers, we acknowledge the difficulty of seeing clearly. Though we listened carefully to teachers, taped and transcribed what they said, and analyzed these interview data meticulously, inevitably some of our own ways of thinking (the theories of the world in our heads that we have woven from our past experience) and our own interpretations seep into our conclusions. We value our own experience and have worked hard and long to make our conclusions true to the data, but we acknowledge that our own experience influences this book. This was one reason that we thought it valuable to have both an American Indian and a non-Indian collaborate in its writing; it is also one reason we have included so much text directly from the teachers—raw data, as researchers might term it. Those data remove us, to a degree, so that as readers and teachers, you can be researchers of and learners from these stories. Nevertheless, we believe it is important to let you hear our own stories, so you can better perceive the ideas we bring to this work.

Beginning the Study: Linda Miller Cleary

It was the October before I interviewed Tom Ketron that this book really started for me. A former student of mine came to tell me that she couldn't use what I taught her. "If I use much other than workbooks, I get into situations where the Indian students call me a 'white bitch.'" And I was forced to listen carefully to my own incompetence playing itself out in classrooms far removed from the university. I, an idealistic, middle-class woman of Northern European heritage, had warned my prospective teachers repeatedly against the too-easy use of workbooks and canned curriculum, especially with students who weren't successful. I had studied the complex issues of race and schooling, and I thought I had prepared English teachers to work well with "minorities." But sitting in my office on that October day, I came to the humbling realization that I needed to know more.

During that same month, three other occurrences lined up to show me that there was much I needed to learn. First, I was asked by a former Ojibwe student if I could recommend candidates for the English position that had opened up by his sudden promotion to principal of his reservation school, and I was forced to admit to myself that I could recommend no recent graduates as being fully ready for the challenging problems of that work. On the following day, Amy, then my only Ojibwe student, came to me in despair because she had failed the examination required to make her, officially, a prospective teacher in the eyes of the Minnesota State Department of Education. She was also distraught because of a paper returned to her with more red ink than black. Finally, in the next week, I received evaluation forms back from a conference I had organized at which an Ojibwe man had presented his ideas for working with Ojibwe writers. Several evaluations of his presentation deeply concerned me: One local practicing teacher wrote, "Good ideas, but he's just a 'Show Indian,'" and another wrote, "I don't know who his students are, but his ideas are just not going to work with my lazy Indian students." The succession of these events posed challenges for me: I wanted to know how to prepare students for the challenge of teaching in reservation schools; I wanted to know more about literacy so that I could help Ojibwe students such as Amy, who I knew would become a fine teacher, through the perilous maze of academia; and I wanted to know what experiences to give prospective teachers so that they wouldn't cave in to the negative attitudes expressed after the writer's conference that I had been unaware were so prevalent.

By late October, I knew what I needed to accomplish in my upcoming sabbatical year. I wanted to find out what I needed to know to make me better at my work. I set out to collect wisdom from teachers of American Indian children, those who are often the last to be consulted about their work's joys, difficulties, and accumulating successes.

Early in my interviewing for this book, a Northeast American Indian teacher asked me, angrily, "Why are you doing this?" We were sitting at a picnic table next to his house on a lake. I was facing the lake, looking at some ducks at that moment, and I wished I were floating out there with them instead of feeling the anger from this man. I had felt anger before from people who saw me, I was realizing, as yet another white woman do-gooder. But I had already learned enough to understand where it came from. I gave him the truth as it was when I began the research: "In northern Minnesota I prepare English teachers who will teach Ojibwe students, and I feel I haven't been doing a very good job. For my sabbatical I decided to find out from teachers who work with American Indian students more about what my students need to know."

It was a pat line I had used before, but when his question came so angrily this time, saying it didn't soothe me. As usual, as I listened carefully, as he began to trust me, his anger dissolved. At the end of the third interview, he asked again, earnestly this time, "Why are you doing this?" The interviewer was being interviewed. I got closer to the truth that I was beginning to understand, and I muttered something about having experienced a bit of oppression myself as a woman and about hating to the core the fact that oppression existed and especially that it existed today, in the schools of a supposedly democratic nation.

And after that final interview with him, I had to flee to the coast for a few days to reflect on the discomfort that I had continuously felt in this research. Beach hopping my way north, with hours spent staring introspectively at waves, I realized more fully that I was representative of a part of the larger dilemma. I was a non-Indian person, carrying the aura of a missionary and burdened with generations of well-deserved mistrust.

I also realized that what began as a quest to do better work had grown into outrage. As I traveled from reservation to reservation, I began to understand the depth and complexity of American Indian education. I had to work myself past successive stages of shock, guilt, shame, and anger, so I could get down to the really hard work of listening and analysis. And while staring at waves that weekend, I realized how wrong I was to think that I could do the research alone. I was experiencing what men encountered in doing women's studies. Additionally, having recognized some of my own naivete and misassumptions during the early days of this research, I knew I might make serious misperceptions unless an American Indian mind joined me in analysis of the material I collected. I returned inland to finish off the first part of my sabbatical work, knowing that I needed an American Indian perspective on it. I had learned, for myself, more than I thought I would to improve teacher preparation, but to complete anything worthy to share, I knew I had to collaborate with someone who had been through our educational system as an American Indian student, someone who would listen to what I had already taped, who would do interviews as an American Indian interviewer, and who would help make sense of our mutually collected data.

For years the University of Minnesota at Duluth had been generating funds for an Endowed Chair of American Indian Education, and while I was on sabbatical, fund-raising was completed, and the position was filled by Tom Peacock.

The Story of My Involvement:
Thomas Peacock

I drove back home to the Fond du Lac Reservation in northern Minnesota from Boston in May of 1988, after only dreaming of it for many years. My brother Skin had flown out to the East Coast just a few days earlier to help me pack, to fix the muffler on my old Indian car (with a coffee can and wire), and to share the driving. It was necessary that he be with me because the journey home after so many years

brought back a flood of memories, and he was there to listen. I think he knew that. The roads that led me away from the rez only to return there many years later had taken me many places. For much of that time I'd lived on the Leech Lake Reservation in north central Minnesota. More recently I had lived in Boston while attending graduate school. Now home again. Home to the hills and river and pasture of my childhood. This place would again wrap around me like a living blanket, like an Indian grandmother holding her grandchild. There is the crest of a hill several miles out of Superior, Wisconsin, on Highway 53 from which I could see Lake Superior. The lake invokes a powerful spiritual presence to so many of us Ojibwe people. It has such an overpowering collective spirit. Gitchi Gummi, my ancestors called it. Home of the Anishinabe. Home for a host of brothers and sisters and cousins and aunties. My thoughts: *I'm home. I'm finally home.* Then I became overwhelmed with the changes in my life that had occurred in all those years of being away. So coming home has meant many early evenings of walking the hills and pastures of my childhood.

Sometimes we get involved in things because we need a sense of purpose, or because we have a responsibility to get involved. Sometimes we do things simply to keep from going insane. Often it is all of these things. So it wasn't hard to get involved again in my reservation community. It didn't take long to notice that things had surely changed. People had changed. I had also changed a great deal, but there are unspoken bonds and a sense of responsibility among people who have grown up together and shared the same sense of community. It felt wonderful to be back home again. I had left right out of high school and for many years returned only to visit relatives. Gone to college. Gotten married. Taught some GED and college classes. Become a high school principal on a northern Minnesota reservation. Gone back to school. Now home again.

I had become a professional Indian educator, and both my professional and life experiences led me to see the need to improve American Indian education. There had been dozens, possibly hundreds, of situations and experiences that served to remind me that most of the schools purported to teach American Indian students knew little, if anything, about American Indians, both in terms of what was taught about American Indians and about how to teach children of their backgrounds.

My own schooling had reminded me that American Indians were a neglected part of the American story. My Minnesota history was the history of non-Indian settlement. American history began with the landing of Columbus. During Thanksgiving we decorated our classrooms with pilgrims, turkeys, and Indians. That was the only time it was good to be an Indian. There were no American Indian teachers, teacher aides, or bus drivers. There wasn't even an American Indian janitor. Once I got on the bus for school each morning it was like taking a trip to

16

another country, a place that bore no resemblance to my own world. It was as if American Indians were invisible. We didn't count. We weren't important.

Like most of the other rez kids who attended the local public school, I faced racism on a daily basis. We seemed to be singled out for more and firmer discipline, more special education, and more suspicion. This made me hypersensitive about issues of race, and sometimes I reacted to non-Indians with anger. But most of the time I would say nothing, thinking: *This shall pass. This shall pass.*

But it wasn't all bad. I had more than my share of supportive teachers, and a few to whom I remain indebted because they pushed me to do my best, encouraged me to finish what I started, and most important, treated me like a human being. All of those experiences, good and bad, made me a stronger person. Maybe all of that anger from the bad things came out of me in the writing of this book. But I doubt it, because when I look around me I see my own children experiencing the same issues. The story of American Indians is still missing in most school curricula. My nephews and nieces and my own children are still singled out for more and firmer discipline, more special education, and more suspicion. Our communities suffer from the same ills I remember as a child. It is as if this great cycle of pain is repeating itself over and over and over again.

Being the high school principal in several northern Minnesota schools had reminded me that the problems facing Indian children went far beyond simply integrating the curriculum with American Indian content, increasing parent involvement, and hiring more American Indian teachers and administrators. Surely these were part of the solution, but there were also issues of both institutional and overt racism, topics neither schools nor society seem to want to confront in any proactive way. There were issues of anger on the part of teachers, parents, and children. As a principal, I dealt with angry people on a daily basis. There were issues of internalized oppression in our communities, which go unresolved whether the people are neglected or the target of social programs. There were issues of cultural loss and change. I had come to the conclusion that Indian education needed a good solid kick in the ass. That we were acting like drunks in denial because we weren't dealing with these issues head-on. That we were codependent enablers because we needed to do interventions in our schools and communities, and with our children. That we needed to do something about all of these issues.

I spent four years on my reservation as the tribal school superintendent, but when the opportunity came to teach at the university, I was more than ready for it. No more program administration for this rez warrior. No more real children to break my heart because now they would exist only in journal articles, books, and theory.

On my first day of university work, I met Linda Miller Cleary, who would become my collaborator on this research and in the writing of this story. I was think-

ing she was in need of an Indian to help her interpret the subtleties of the tribal world. When I began working with Linda, I immediately saw that for both of us to see more clearly, we needed to balance each other's naivete and misassumptions. I see and interpret reality from one angle of the forest of reality, as Linda does from hers. Add to our perspectives the collected voices of sixty other teachers, and our collective view is an infinitely clearer and broader picture of the reality of the education of American Indian children.

What I may have contributed to this work will answer for some people why it is that our Indian children have had such a difficult time with life in general, and school specifically. To detail, from the voices of teachers who work with our children on a daily basis, what works and what does not. To answer those questions.

So this is one of those circle things. It's about coming home. It's about helping and about responsibility. It's about finding some answers. It is about sharing them. It's about all of these things.

An Only Partially Resolved Problem with Language

In the fall of 1995, I, Linda Miller Cleary, sat in on a session on Native American Literature at the National Council of English Teachers Conference in San Diego. The speaker made the mistake of using the word "squaw" in her presentation, and Debbie LaCroix, who was attending, pointed out, very politely I might add, that the word "squaw" was popularized by white settlers. In the language it was drawn from, it meant "cunt."

This incident made me poignantly aware of just how offensive, even wounding, words can unintentionally or intentionally be. We have struggled with language in this book and still find that words we have chosen are inept at getting across the meanings we intend.

Rarely have we been able to identify people or places by tribal names, though we are fully aware that American Indian people prefer to be called by tribal names rather than by any generic term available. We realize the term "American Indian" refers to hundreds of distinct cultural systems, even though they are sometimes subtly distinct. We have found ourselves in this position because we offered anonymity to our interviewees, and a number of people wanted that anonymity. Though some participants in our study requested to speak under their own names, others have taken on a self-chosen pseudonym. We also believed that we were in a position in which we needed to protect groups of people and schools while still allowing teachers to speak freely. To act with integrity, we have had to use generic words that we would prefer not to use.

In naming those people who were present in North America before Europeans came to the continent, we rejected the terms Native American, indigenous, native, Indian, and chose, in the end, the legal term, "American Indian." We also rejected the term *white* and have used *non-Indian* because it is the least pejorative and most inclusive way to describe those who do not have American Indian blood. We were tempted by the word *Eurocentric* to fill our need to describe the "usual" schools or culture out there, but in the end opted to use the words *mainstream* or *dominant* in the adjective position as less inflammatory. It is useless to blame Europe when blame surely lies by now in this continent.

In truth, all words by their nature tend to support generalization or marginalization, and words are more powerful in their ability to injure when used in relation to anyone out of the "stream." Within quotes we have let words stand that we ourselves have declined to use because there are shades of meaning tied to the words that the interviewees chose to use, as they were telling the truth as they saw it.

How to Read This Book

As authors, we know full well that not every reader will read every word in this entire book. This is why we have given you an overview of what you will find in each chapter. However, we have one wish: As you gather speed, *do not skip the profiles and the quotes from the teachers.* Their collected wisdom is at the heart of this work, and, unless indicated, we have chosen quotes because they indicate good practice. You will find your best teaching tips in these quotes.

Also, remember that this book is a report of interview research; it is not meant to review all the current literature on the topic of American Indian education. We cite secondary research when it sheds light on what teachers have said or when teachers contradict what that literature says. In doing our research, we purposely tried to listen to our participants without prior research reviews in mind, so that we did not unconsciously doubt, taint, superimpose, or substitute what teachers had to say with the conventional wisdom on the subject. To listen carefully to new things that teachers might be saying, we delayed reading or rereading the literature on the emerging themes in our research until our own analysis of our data was complete. We have chosen to let the teachers teach you and have called in prior research only when we thought it important to delve beyond what the sixty teachers said.

Chapters often begin with a story that we, as authors, have to tell that will introduce the chapter's content. We then provide several questions to help you tap your own prior knowledge about the topic. Reading theorists tell us that readers

will comprehend text better if they can link it with their own schemata of experience. In each chapter, we have included a question or two that will help you to do this.

A chapter may include a profile of a teacher who had a lot to say about that theme, and in the process give an in-depth view of the complexity of a teacher's work. In this chapter, we have profiled Tom Ketron to show you how broadly many of the teachers talked; in other chapters, you will see profiles and quotes focused on a specific topic.

Most chapters include a purposely problematic case study (fiction based on fact) that will push you as a reader to a fuller understanding of complex issues by having you put what you have learned from the "collected wisdom" into practice in fictionalized situations. The questions connected with each case will help you think further about the issues raised in the chapter. Finally, each chapter ends with a summary of our research and its implications for practice for those who want a linear lineup of what should be learned from the chapter material. The chapters often start theoretically, but more and more practice emerges as each chapter proceeds and as the chapters accumulate.

While reading this book, you will begin to realize that, though the book is about American Indian students, their schools, their teachers, and their communities, it has much to say to those interested in the education of any oppressed minority. Indeed, the book raises ideological questions for all teachers.

Reference

Clifford, J. (1986). On ethnographic allegory. In J. Clifford, & G. E. Marcus (Eds.), *Writing culture: The poetics and politics of ethnography* (pp. 98–121). Berkeley: University of California Press.

Cultural Difference

Recognizing the Gap into Which Students and Teachers Fall

Many American Indian students live with a sort of dissonance because the culture of their schools is different from the culture of their homes and communities. Whenever there is a profound difference between the culture of students and the culture of a school and of its teachers, there is a gap into which both students and teachers can fall. I, Linda Miller Cleary, glimpsed this gap years ago, but it has only been in collecting the wisdom of many teachers that I have come to understand its depth and breadth.

As it is for many non-Indian teachers, the first time I sat down to talk to an American Indian person was as an educator in an educational setting. In 1985, in conjunction with a different study on writing motivation, I arranged with the Fond du Lac Ojibwe School to interview and work with three eleventh-grade students, and I fell, head first, into the gap. After nineteen trips to the reservation, Tim was the only one who completed our three scheduled interviews; absenteeism was the primary problem. When Tim was there, he was pleasant, bright, and even earnest in answering my open-ended questions, but at the time I couldn't be sure he wanted to be there, even after giving him many chances to opt out. He stared at the table, the windows, and even the wall instead of meeting my eyes during our interview. And as I squirmed in front of his averted gaze, I began a long journey in coming to

understand the gap that cultural difference can make. Tim's teachers told me he lived with an aunt, and I felt sorry for him, not understanding that aunts to him were akin to parents. I understand that Tim, a bright young man who had college aspirations, dropped out of school before graduation and is in jail now.

Tim and the sixty teachers we interviewed for this book have helped me understand the difference between what has been the mainstream culture of the schools that serve American Indian children and the culture of their homes. My partner in this research, Tom Peacock, views the gap from the other side. Today he moves easily between the American Indian and non-Indian worlds, but he has been uncomfortable with the role he has had to "play" in the academic world since kindergarten:

> I first remember that discomfort when Mrs. Bushie asked me to do "I'm a Little Teapot" in kindergarten. And my rez rug was homemade; everyone else had the storebought kind for naps. I started thinking something must be wrong with me because my rug was different. I rode in on the separate rez bus, the oldest bus with the crabbiest bus driver. It's still an uncomfortable ride between the rez and my professional life. In the non-Indian world, it is necessary to look people in the eye when we speak, give a firm handshake, and be able to engage in social chit-chat. Our professional careers depend on it. But my Anishinabe value system taught me that to look people in the eye is to look into their souls. My culture taught me that a firm handshake is a sign of aggression. It taught me not to engage in conversation unless I had something important to say. Actually, I still have periods when I have a great deal of difficulty moving in and out of these worlds, but I have recognized and confronted the reality of it. It involves compromises.

I, Linda Miller Cleary, have undertaken the writing of this chapter because a view of the deep discontinuity between the culture of the home and the culture of the school is relatively new and amazing to me. Nevertheless, as I write this chapter, Tom Peacock has been looking over my shoulder because he began seeing cultural difference in kindergarten. From both sides of the gap, from the juxtaposed perspectives of American Indian and non-Indian, we examine cultural differences as they play out in the many schools we visited.

Finding the Subtlety of Cultural Differences

As Ketron notes in Chapter 1, there are differences between mainstream and American Indian cultures, differences between tribes, and differences within tribes. For obvious reasons, American Indian teachers have built-in understandings if they come from the same community as the children they teach, and they are just the people to go to with questions, if the questions will be perceived as being for the sake of the students and not as prying. In this chapter, we present some differences that teachers discovered between the mainstream culture and the culture of the community in which they teach. But we warn you not to take what teachers relate as North American Indian truths; you will find that wherever you are will present variations and even antitheses to what these particular teachers say. In these descriptions of cultural differences, we may be wrong before we start. Even when what teachers report is in concert with what research has noted, it is possible that some of these statements, though they may be true in many cases, might simply be extensions of what preservice teacher educators and other "authorities" (books by people who do reviews of research, in-service workshop presenters, ethnic studies classes, and others) have passed on to teachers. The last thing we want to do is add to what has been a minefield of stereotypes and generalities. It will be healthy if, as readers, you set out with some questions: Do humans tend to see in their own situations what they have been primed to see? How much of what teachers say is based on real observation and experience; how much on what they are taught to expect to see? We cannot answer these questions, but they act as a caution for all of us.

If you already teach in a setting with a large American Indian population, you will know that there are more than a few differences between mainstream students and American Indian students. And recognizing culture as tenacious, you will begin to see, through reading and through observation, even the subtler differences. In settings in which American Indian families are less traditional, where differences are less obvious, where people are not as concerned about snakes on pots anymore, teachers must work even harder to see why American schooling is difficult for American Indian children and must work harder to make school consonant with and relevant to the children's lives. Each teacher in these settings not only must learn more obvious customs and beliefs of the sort that Ketron tripped over, but also must learn about the culture that is deeper than the surface culture of food, dress, and custom. It takes considerable endeavor. Kevin Ritchie, a teacher in the Northeast, said:

◆ Everything—my whole experience growing up as a white male, the Cowboys and Indians thing, my idea that we were all in a melting pot, that becoming American somehow means your own self melting away and you [taking on a] white European perspective and so on—it all got in the way. I think of myself as kind for the most part, and I don't intentionally demean or be thoughtless to other people. And yet, I can think of so many times when I just—out of ignorance—did or said inappropriate things. Because there was nothing in my own growing up that would lead me to believe that they were any different than I was. I have a sense of difference at work a large part of the time. I need to be consciously aware of how I ask questions and what I'm getting for a re-

sponse if I'm talking to a Native American student. I need to have a clear sense that she and I, or he and I, know what we're talking about with each other. I don't feel like I have a particular affinity [for doing this]. It's been kind of hard-won.

The purpose of this chapter is to help those who teach American Indian children to see cultural differences more clearly, to help them find reasons to narrow "the gap" for American Indian children entering schools. All humans have difficulty perceiving cultural differences because they are so thoroughly acquainted and comfortable with their own culture. It is human nature to assume that our way of being is the way of being for all humans unless we have experienced differences by traveling about in the world and traveling with an inquiring mind. People whose culture is different from the mainstream culture are often forced into early forays into the mainstream culture, but they still may benefit from explicit explanations of difference. This chapter may give American Indian teachers a view of how to hasten the process of understanding for non-Indian colleagues who are confused about their interactions with American Indian people.

Questions to Jump-Start Your Reading

Kevin Ritchie's earliest views of American Indians came from the movies. Before you start reading this chapter, think back to your early views of the culture on the other side of the gap.

1. If you are American Indian, what formed your initial view of mainstream culture?
2. Or if you are non-Indian, what experiences or observations formed your initial views of American Indians?
3. How have those views changed through the years, and what kind of input has changed them?

A Chapter Road Map

In this chapter, we first investigate differences in beliefs and customs, focusing on the importance of harmony and balance in the lives of American Indians. Second, we look at differences in ways of being: eye contact, body language and attention; social discourse; interference versus influence; modes of inquiry; views of success, failure, and shame; issues of time; privacy of teachings and language; humor; concepts of family; competition and cooperation; views of material possessions; and oral and literate backgrounds. Third, we examine how American Indian spirituality is connected to all of the above. After presenting a case study, "Meg and the Hurricane," we move to looking at the challenges of seeing cultural differences clearly. In coming chapters, many of the cultural differences introduced here are discussed in terms of their implications for practice.

Difference in Beliefs

Customs

Tom Ketron, the Southwest art teacher introduced in Chapter 1, has introduced wisdom that many other teachers reiterated: "As a teacher, you have to learn." He learned the hard way that teachers who are unaware of tribal customs may find themselves alienated from American Indian parents or from the community. As Tom Ketron found when he let a student represent a cobra on a pot, every tribe has different customs, and they take these customs seriously. Customs are handed down from generation to generation by culture bearers. If the parents do not involve their children with tribal customs, children may not be able to tell teachers about cultural expectations. Teachers must learn what is important to know so they can do their work effectively with American Indian students. When communities see that teachers are interested in learning about their customs, they usually appreciate those efforts.

Beliefs: Harmony and Balance

Though belief systems vary with every tribe, striving for harmony and balance in life seems central to many American Indians. Though I have understood the quest for harmony and balance to be an aspect of American Indian spirituality for decades, I was less aware of how that quest is intertwined with every aspect of American Indian life.

Part of the dissonance many American Indian students experience in school is related to their need for harmony and balance in their lives. Harmony and balance is the American Indian belief in interrelatedness and connectedness with all that is natural. The concept not only explains the interdependence of humans with other animates and inanimates in the world, but it also recognizes the need for individual wellness—of the interdependence of physical, emotional, psychological, and spiritual well-being.

Individuals are considered whole when their physical, mental, spiritual, and emotional selves exist in harmony. If there is something negative going on with one part of the self, it affects the other parts and causes an imbalance in the whole self. For example, if someone grieves, it can adversely affect physical health, and if grief is not effectively allowed to run its course, it can eventually have a negative effect on the spiritual self.

Though this concept is uncomfortable to many non-Indian people, medical research is starting to support these beliefs with hard data. For instance, Candace Pert, formerly chief of the section on brain biochemistry of the clinical neuroscience branch at the National Institute of Mental Health, said when interviewed by Bill Moyers for his book *Healing and the Mind* (1993), ". . . There is a growing body of literature, much of it European, that suggests the emotional history is extremely important in things like the incidence of cancer. For example, it appears that suppression of grief, and suppression of anger, in particular, is associated with an increased incidence of breast cancer in women. This research is controversial, and there are always methodological issues to address—but it's very interesting" (p. 191). In a way it is ironic that I provide research to support what American Indians have known for centuries. In addition to the recent attention to some of these concepts by the medical community, the importance of harmony and balance in the world has been a strong part of the reasoning behind the environmental movement. Protection of endangered species and of the environment speaks to the interdependence of living and inanimate things.

As educators of American Indian children, it is important to extend the concept of harmony and balance to understand how it plays out in schools. If a student experiences dissonance between the ways of school and the ways of home and community, that represents an imbalance. For example, if children's traditional concept of respect for all things is at odds with what they are asked to do in school, a conflict may result, and they may experience a lack of harmony. If in school it is appropriate to dissect frogs or fetal pigs, but children know, based on their traditional teachings and the behavior of their elders, that all things have spirit and that all things must be treated with respect and dignity, then they may experience disharmony. Bruchac shows how reverence for living things is modeled by elders in the following poem.

Birdfoot's Grandpa
Joseph Bruchac

The old man
must have stopped our car
two dozen times to climb out
and gather into his hands

the small toads blinded
by our leaping,
live drops of rain.

The rain was falling
a mist around his white hair
and I kept saying
you can't save them all,
accept it, get back in
we've got places to go.

But, leathery hands full
of wet brown life,
knee deep in the summer
roadside grass,
he just smiled and said
they have places to go
too.

Source: "Birdfoot's Grampa" by Joseph Bruchac from *Entering Onandaga* by Joseph Bruchac © 1975.

After a series of such lessons from relatives and elders, the young person in this poem might well be resistant to or distressed by the dissection of frogs in school.

Students may not consciously know why they feel uncomfortable, resistant, or even rebellious. Even when they have been brought up in a traditional setting, they may not be able to articulate what is wrong when they experience disharmony. As a teacher, you may see resistant behavior that you do not at first understand. Checking out resistant behavior with American Indian teachers or experienced non-Indian teachers may help you understand the discontinuities that children feel so you can build a relevant and comfortable curriculum.

Difference in Ways of Being

Tom Ketron described some obvious differences that can trip up teachers who are not from the tribe of the children they teach—differences in custom. More subtle cultural differences include the different perceptions, values, worldviews, and ways of expression and interaction that we call different ways of being. It is not surprising that many non-Indian teachers enter schools that serve American Indian students without knowledge of these culturally different ways of being because, as

members of the dominant culture, they do not question issues of identity as other nonmainstream groups must. Most American Indians generally share a common sense of how to be and how to interact that is very different from that of non-Indians and, for that matter, different from that of people from any immigrant group that has not assimilated into the dominant culture. For the most part, these different ways of being cannot be labeled good or bad, but rather comfortable or uncomfortable, depending on what was comfortable to begin with.

Eye Contact, Body Language, and Attention

Terri, an American Indian teacher's aide in the Southeast, had worked with many different teachers during her long career. The following is part of my interview with her:

◆ *Terri:* Maybe about ten years ago the kids didn't want to look their teacher in the eye. And there would be times [teachers would say], "Look at me! Look me in the eye!" And kids had a hard time with that, and they would look away. [If] I'd be sitting here and if my aunt was sitting here [across from me], I wouldn't even look at her. I would look somewhere else, or sit like this [next to her] and talk to her.

Linda: Am I making you uncomfortable right now?

Terri: I'm used to it now. I guess they [the teachers] weren't told that some of the kids won't look them in the eye. And that's what they were doing, and sometimes I would tell teachers that: "You know, they're not used to looking at you when they're speaking."

Almost every non-Indian teacher mentioned differences in eye contact, and, as with me, it was often the first difference and the first discomfort new teachers experienced. Some teachers felt irritated until someone like Terri explained the difference to them, and others, such as Ginny Bell, a tutor in the public school that Terri's students went to after eighth grade, felt hurt instead of irritated. Bell said:

◆ At first I thought the kids were scared of me, or they didn't like me. And I was talking to Ms. G. from the rez: "Why do the kids never talk and always look down like they've done something wrong? These kids haven't done anything wrong." She said, "No, that's the way they're brought up; you don't look a grown-up in the eye." But they kind of lost that after a few years of being in school around these white kids. Once I learned that was their way, it was easier for me because I felt it wasn't something they had against me.

As a new non-Indian teacher, it is easy to make a similar mistake in the community. Ingrid was in a Southwest grocery store, a place where teachers often came together with community members:

◆ Not looking a person in the eyes—which whites interpret as a sign of weak character, impoliteness, or lying—to them it's a sign of respect. If you come from a traditional family, you'd never look the grandmother in the eye. I've gone up to women in the store, older ladies, and made eye contact with them, and they looked at me like, "Huh, why did you!" And I didn't understand what was going on. If you watch very traditional people talk, they never look at each other, but everyone listens to what everyone says.

What is important here is Ketron's, Bell's, and Ingrid's ability to "watch," to see beyond their own culture's interpretation of behavior and to understand that respect is intended. For years American Indians have had to deal with the insult of eye contact, and those who have been less exposed to the mainstream culture will still feel its sting.

There are body language differences that are to be discovered by both American Indians and non-Indians. A non-Indian teacher from the Southeast offered the following advice to new teachers: "Pick up on the body language of your students; it's even different at different reservations."

Linda, a principal at a Northeast school, talks about how eye contact, body language, and their links with "paying attention" are not necessarily the same across cultures:

◆ What I'm realizing the longer I'm here [is] that these kids are absorbing all the time. And when we demand that they sit in rows and that they pay attention on our terms, like looking at us in the eyes, something happens to the learning that's not positive.

There is cultural difference in the way that people show they are paying attention and giving respect. And as soon as you begin to notice these differences, you will meet American Indian people who look you comfortably "in the eye" even though they are strongly identified with their home community.

Social Discourse Difference: Respect and Reserve

Before I began interviewing teachers, I had lunch with Rosemary Christensen, an Ojibwe woman who has done important curriculum work in northern Minnesota, but even though I sought to tap her knowledge, I realized that I had talked more at

lunch than she. Later, she sent me some articles that were invaluable, and one by Rosalie H. Wax and Robert K. Thomas (1961), dated though it was, helped me understand why I had jabbered away my valuable lunch time with her when I was seeking her guidance. This is a passage from that article on social discourse:

◆ Social discourse is one of the areas where Indians and whites most easily misunderstand each other. Placed in an informal social gathering, such as a small party where he knows only the host, the Indian will usually sit or stand quietly, saying nothing and seeming to do nothing. He may do this so naturally that he disappears into the background, merged with the light fixtures. If addressed directly, he will not look at the speaker; there may be considerable delay before a reply and this may be pitched so softly as to be below the hearing threshold of the white interlocutor; he may even look deliberately away and give no response at all.

In this same situation, the white man will often become undiscourageably loquacious. A silent neighbor will be peppered with small shop talk in the hope that one of his rounds will trigger and exchange a conversational engagement. If the neighbor happens to be an Indian, his protracted silence will spur the white to ever more extreme exertions; and the more frantic the one becomes the less the response he is likely to elicit from the other.

Ironically, both parties are trying to establish communication and good feelings, but . . . each employs devices that puzzle, alienate, and sometimes anger the other. (pp. 305–306)

I thought of this article when I observed the vocal, energetic children at my first reservation stop in the Southeast and the silent American Indian children in border town schoolrooms thirty miles away. I began to realize that the silence that non-Indian teachers see in some American Indian students is probably a complicated mixture of discomfort, traditional discourse, and maybe even resistance. Greg, a teacher from the closest high school to a Southeast reservation, had begun to think about students' reticence. He sensed that it was born of the fact that they are often strangers to border town schools they attend:

◆ I find that they tend to be almost introverted. It's hard to elicit a response out of them at times. It might come down through generations of feeling out of place. That probably would explain it a bit since they do spend so much time being students on the rez, then all of a sudden they're supposed to be over here, thrown into the melting pot. So many of them tend to be very quiet, withdrawn, and I wish they could be a little more assertive. So it seems that they're kind of held back in expressing themselves vocally.

Many teachers who interpreted the sit-back-and-study-the-situation behavior as passivity were frustrated with it. Karen Brown, a dynamic black teacher in a reservation setting, said:

◆ I've told school board meetings, stop being so nice. We had an educational conference out here in the summer of '91. And I told them, "Stop being so nice. You're too nice. You don't know how to fight for yourselves, and I know that's not in your nature, but you've got to learn to do it. Because if you don't, you're always going to be the doormats." I probably get away with saying a lot of things that most whites can't. Because I'm black, they see me as a victim as well.

What is clear is that some non-Indian teachers, especially those who are new at their work, feel very uncomfortable with some American Indian ways of being. It is hard for them to see how issues of trust, discourse difference, and a history of oppression connect.

Jeb Beaulieu described being on the other side of the desk as an American Indian student in a Midwest, mainstream school setting. Beaulieu felt a stranger in his own school:

◆ I was brought up in an Indian household with my grandparents and parents and that's just the way you behaved. I mean, you were seen and not heard. It wasn't polite to show off. In school I felt really isolated and really alienated and really alone. I just didn't volunteer a lot of information. The Indian way of behaving is: you watch and you observe before you act. You don't want to make a fool out of yourself in front of the group because of the shame culture. You observe, and so once you know what's expected of you, then you act, but you never want to show off because it's not good taste to pound your own drum. I didn't realize why I behaved the way I did until I got into college and took a course that talked about value differences, and then it was like a light bulb going on. I started making the connections.

Once this guy, in a university class I was in, said, "I can't understand why blacks eat by themselves, and other Indians will stay by themselves in the cafeteria." And I said, "It's a comfort thing." Non-Indian people, because this is their educational environment, don't realize how alien it is to somebody that's not from this culture. It's situational; you have to behave like an Indian with Indians and get out your bag of tricks and behave like a non-Indian in other situations. I was probably evaluated poorly on my classroom participation because I didn't participate. Indian kids don't cause any trouble, and they do what they're supposed to do, and the way they respond to conflict is withdrawing. Not saying anything, or just not showing up.

Wax and Thomas (1961) describe the different ways that two cultures deal with anxiety-provoking situations. Non-Indian people are apt to increase their solve-the-problem activity, and try, try again until something is resolved, whereas many American Indian people, who often find schools to be anxiety-provoking situations, are more apt to go into inactivity and to use all of their senses to discover what is "proper, seemly, and safe" before acting with energy.

Some teachers described this difference and had found some positive ways of transacting the gap. Rose Fleming, a non-Indian teacher from the Northeast, talked about how she has worked with these differences in ways of being:

◆ When I arrived here, some of my colleagues would say, "I can't tell whether they're following the discussion." And I said, "Why?" And they said, "Well, they don't look at me when I'm talking." And I said, "That's cultural; that's something I learned years ago." And they said, "Well, they don't ever share responses." I said, "That's cultural, too. I'm willing to bet that in your classroom, the majority of the students that do to the letter of what you ask are from the reservation, and probably don't ask a lot of questions." "Well, yes." I was making a generalization, but it's based on my observations. So I have to work at really getting the students to ask questions and talk. Early in the year, I introduce their own literature. Because once I've made that contact, it seems to have brought more success for me.

In setting up interviews, I often had to keep myself from leaping to conclusions. When Terri, an American Indian teacher's aide whom I especially wanted to interview because there were no teachers from her tribe in the school, seemed to avoid me, I found that I needed to force myself to talk to her. I had to ask her whether she'd be willing to be interviewed, rather than taking her avoidance for unwillingness. She agreed readily, and later, when I asked Terri about differences between her culture and that of the non-Indian teachers in the school, she said to me:

◆ I have a problem with interrupting people. You know, two people are talking and I need to talk with one of them. So I need to say, "Excuse me, but I need to . . ." or something like that. [But] if I see them talking, I just go the other way. That's why, when, that other day, I wanted to go over there and talk to you, but you were talking so I came this way. That's when you found me. I just can't interrupt. And that's why it's hard for me when I'm attending a class; it's hard for me to say, "Wait a minute, I don't understand this."

It is particularly difficult for non-Indian people to differentiate between behavior that is born of discomfort or difference in social discourse and that is passive resistance and, hence, nontraditional. (For more about interethnic communication see Ron and Suzanne Scollon, *Narrative, Literacy and Face in Interethnic Communication.*)

Interference versus Influence

I have come to understand that what is perceived by some non-Indians as passive behavior may indicate a profound difference in the ways that people are willing to influence others. The Minnesota Department of Children, Families and Learning American Indian Learner Outcomes team (1995) talk about noninterference in the following way:

◆ Respect for the Creator, Mother Earth, Community, Family, Age, and Knowledge leads one to value noninterference and to behave in such a way that does not interfere in the choices of others. Adults will go to great lengths to respect the choices of other people without interference. Parenting styles are often a result of the high value placed on non-interference. This is sometimes mistaken for overpermissiveness or lack of discipline. Children are allowed to make mistakes and learn from those mistakes without scolding.

Wax and Thomas (1961) point out that although non-Indians also believe in freedom and minding one's own business, they also give advice freely and act in behalf of another if they feel another is not acting in their own best interest. Traditionally, there were plenty of unwritten rules of conduct in some American Indian societies in which everyone relied on everyone else for survival. There were subtle but accepted ways of intervening, and everyone knew the rules. Today, from a mainstream perspective, American Indian people will not seem to "interfere" or will give subtle messages about a need for change in behavior if they believe their people are irresponsible or are ignorant of a possible bad result of their action. Hence, non-Indians are not aware that active "helping" can be irritating to American Indian people, and American Indian people might not even let a non-Indian person know about the irritation because they might see it as a form of interference.

Mainstream children often learn to influence others at a young age and conscientiously try to improve these skills through schooling and family interaction. Some American Indians are more apt to see any influence as "meddling" and may react to such influence/interference with "bewilderment, disgust, or fear." Often when I was on reservations, people told me that some sort of celebration, festival, or even gathering was going on. I immediately felt left out, but I was told later that

such a statement might have been something akin to an invitation. As a non-Indian person, I would have had to be urged to come to feel like I was not intrusive, whereas an American Indian person might see such urging as interference.

Modes of Inquiry

One day I went with an Australian colleague of mine, Josephine Ryan, to a family gathering in the Melbourne Arboretum. After the picnic, she said, "It's fun to hang around with you because you often ask the questions that it would be impolite for me to ask, but you get away with it because you are American and sincerely curious. But . . . you might want to watch out for that when you talk with Aboriginal teachers." I have learned in traveling that mainstream Americans are known for their questions. I have also learned that with American Indians sometimes you can come to better understandings by commenting and waiting for explanations, rather than asking. Linda discovered a similar thing in her early years as a principal at a Northeast reservation school:

◆ When I went into the board meeting, as we began to discuss the budget, comments came, and more often than not it would be a comment, not a question. [At my first school board meetings] I would interpret comments as people without educational expertise making judgments, making judgments as if they were the evaluator. Now, I understand that comments and observations are the same as questions and concerns.

With non-Indian people, questions can sometimes be comments, and with American Indians, comments can sometimes be questions. Linda discovered one reason American Indian children may not be the first students with their hands up to ask questions in a classroom "discussion." And there are other reasons, which follow.

Shame/Competence

In some American Indian communities, children are expected to behave well: to respect all living things, to respect the land, to respect the community, to honor elders, to show gratitude, generosity, courage, patience, tolerance, and acceptance. The child who does not is accorded what is felt as severe punishment: they are censored or shamed. Furthermore, American Indian children have traditionally been expected to act competently or not to act at all. They are encouraged to observe until they are sure they can do well; to fail is to feel shame. For this reason, some American Indian children do not like to be put on the spot. Most mainstream children, in the "try, try again" mode, are more likely to see failure as a step on the path to success. Kate, an American Indian teacher from the Northeast, talks about the complexity of this issue:

◆ The students don't like to be put on the spot, not even in a positive way. I don't single anybody out. In fact, [praise] can backfire on that particular student. And if they don't want to do presentations in front of the class, I don't require that as much anymore, one or two a year but not as a regular thing. In fact, they're quite comfortable doing someone else's; they'll all trade. If the goal is just to get them used to talking to a group, then what difference does it make if it's their own? But you'll find that sometimes when they do have strong feelings, you'll hear from the really quiet ones.

Knowing about shame and competence can help teachers as they try to help students through disputes. Warner Wirta said:

◆ See, its terribly important not to lose face, so I came up with this: If their feathers were ruffled out, I'd say, "Hey wait a minute now, if you can't work it out, go ahead and fight, but not on the school grounds. But let's come on upstairs and talk it over." Boy, they trek right up there. They still have an avenue left, so we go up and talk, and everything was all fine. See, and that's an old Indian way again. Like the tribal councils, there's always meeting places set up to iron out differences.

Prizes, awards, and successes that bring pride or honor to an entire community are celebrated. Individual awards and success can be seen as shameful. Thomas Smith from the Southwest said:

◆ When I first got here eight years ago, students would tease each other and call each other "school boy" or "school girl" or "scholar." Our National Honor Society is like a secret society. They only use the (initials) NHS, and always in the evening and privately, just the families and the kids come. It's not any kind of honor in front of the rest of the student body.

American Indian children might like the feelings of competence they glean from accomplishing a new skill or gaining new information, but the mainstream system of rewards and awards based on performance may engender shame and may pit the extrinsic rewards of grades and awards against the more intrinsic rewards of feelings of competence. There are cultural differences in perceptions of the importance of test taking and in perceptions of grades and other forms of evaluations. We discuss this further in the last chapter.

Issues of Time

In our study, almost every teacher talked about the cultural difference in perception of time. A non-Indian teacher in a Northeast border town school verbalizes the usual mainstream perspective on time:

◆ At the reservation open house for public school teachers, the eighth graders gave a little skit. They tried to show what they called "Indian time" and why they might have some trouble fitting into the high school schedule. So that was cute, but it's an issue I've had some trouble with. I feel we have to have bells to operate. So I just say, "Look, when the bell rings, you're going to have to be here or else." I don't let anybody get away with that. Indian time is a nice concept. I hate that banks have to open at 9:00, and then we have people trying to get in just as they're locking it, but the world seems to have to operate that way.

When I described "Indian time" versus mainstream time in my first draft, I knew I wasn't making the distinctions well and sent my disk to Tom Peacock for help. Tom inserted a note in caps that I will leave right here:

ABOUT THE TIME THING, LINDA: CONCEPTUALLY TIME IS DIFFERENT BETWEEN SOME TRIBES AND ANGLOS. IN MY TRIBE, THERE IS LITTLE CONCEPTUAL DIFFERENCE BETWEEN THE PAST, PRESENT, AND FUTURE. IT IS NOT LINEAR IN THAT SENSE. SPIRITS CAN EXIST IN THE PAST, PRESENT, AND FUTURE ALL AT THE SAME TIME, AS CAN DREAMS, AS CAN GOD. THERE IS AN OMNIPRESENCE OF TIME. I ALSO WONDER HOW MUCH OF THE TIME THING IS PART OF A NEW STEREOTYPE ABOUT INDIANS ALWAYS BEING LATE. IT IS AN OVERSIMPLIFICATION OF A MUCH LARGER CONCEPT.

And a Midwest American Indian teacher said:

◆ We hurry too much. We have to do CAT tests. So everybody hurries. That's not part of being an Indian. We're slow people. We think about what we do. And the people that we're putting in with the kids are just the opposite. They have to get through three subjects in two hours. And they're just real caught up in this whole thing.

So our challenge, then, as teachers is to more fully understand this difference in conceptions of time so that we can figure out how to be with children in schools.

Some educators worked hard to understand different systems of time. Linda, a non-Indian from a Northeast school, said:

◆ I'm beginning to appreciate the difference. Time has a deep effect on how the children can best learn. I'll give you a really good example that I see in students' work. "I couldn't do homework last night," [a student said]. And the very same student, because it's time, it feels right, the thoughts are there, all of the pieces of his learning come together, all at once—today will sit down at the computer and stay there until all the teachers are gone because now's the time to do it. And time has a deep effect on how a cross-cultural staff can get along with one another. And the white staff will frequently be very concerned because the native staff isn't where they're supposed to be. But if I listen, I learn that native person was involved in an activity with another student or with another staff person that in that person's schema was what needed to happen. And yet, I can also see that it [a different time scheme] would totally disrupt the paradigm of what this school looks like. So it's one of the greatest sources of conflict in this school.

And some American Indian teachers feel the same conflict. They have often been products of mainstream school systems and have to figure out the time thing all over again as they first work with the children of their tribe. Kate, a Northeast middle school teacher, said:

◆ At first I thought, all you have to do is wear a watch, and you'll be on time 'cause I was so used to that from school. And then, when I was more involved in the community activities again, I thought, well, as long as I'm accomplishing what I want to accomplish in my lesson, why does it matter so much if we're not exactly on with the clock. It's not worth the struggle in having them start their class all uptight.

A non-Indian teacher on a Southeast reservation notes that ways of thinking about time are similar and interrelated to concepts of space.

◆ I went out to help build a hogan, and the old fella that we were helping never used a measuring tape on anything, never said anything. He'd just point at a log, and we'd pick it up, and drag, and drop it in a hole. He'd look at it, shake his head. We'd pull it back out and get another one and drop it in, rather than measure them all out and figure out which one's longest, which one's shortest, which one'll work. And one day we got what we could probably have done in an hour, using a measuring tape, done in a day. But if you're not in a hurry, then that's not important.

American Indian children in most schools are caught in the gap between the more linear concept of time and their forbears' view of the omnipresence of time. This conflict will not go away.

Privacy of Teachings and Language

English has become a world language because, as colonizers, the English demanded its use. Most American schools operate with vestiges of European ways for similar reasons. But American Indian people often feel quite differently about the use of their language and culture. An American Indian teacher says:

◆ The hard part about our culture and our beliefs [is] we do not all agree about it. Like even our language, we have not agreed on the one, or even two or three, ways of writing it. People object because if we have our language in writing, then other people who are not supposed to speak the language will speak the language. Stories are not to be told in writing. And there's that constant battling between some of us who feel like the language and stories should be written. The story itself teaches discipline, which we all need to know, regardless of race. We need to know that we should respect one another. We should live in harmony. That's what these stories tell. So I don't see a problem there, where we all learn from it, but I do object to someone else learning my language and speaking my language.

The issue of loss of language and culture and what to do about it takes the entirety of Chapter 5. What the reader needs to understand here is the reverence in which tribal language and culture are held. Those teachers who are trying to help with preservation are sometimes frustrated.

◆ Sometimes I feel that they should just move the tribe deep into the reservation and stay there. There are such deep conflicts in ways of living between the white and the original culture. Ways that I see to breech the difference are not accepted. The chairman here threw out all the tapes that had been made of the elders telling about their ways. There is a deep-felt notion that when native culture and custom is written down, it will become public and, thereafter, diluted. It is a little sad that the people do not teach their children their native ways.

As a new teacher in a school that serves American Indian children, it is important to learn about local language issues and to support the tribe in preservation of language and culture without being naive about strong feelings that tribal members may have.

Humor

It was in the Southeast that I first began to view humor as a factor in American Indian education. I met Therese, a reflective and experienced teacher, who had only worked with American Indian children for a few months.

◆ I'm learning that their interpretations of [things] are much different than mine. And I'm having some problems with things like laughing. I've always thought of the Indians as being brave and strong and gentle and kind. Indians have told me themselves, "Well, you know if an Indian falls down, you laugh at him till he gets up." Our value would be to help the person, encourage. The Indians' value might be, "You're not going to make it if you're not strong enough to survive; therefore, I'm not going to pander to you." I'm trying to be respectful of the value difference, but it affects me as totally unacceptable for any human being to treat another human being in an unkind manner. Like, the kids walked out one day, and quite by accident, they slammed the door into my face. And they stood there laughing, and they had hurt me. It happened to me fairly early on, and I dealt with it more like I would in a white setting. "I just can't believe that you would laugh at hurting someone. I would never laugh at you if you were hurt." And then, a little bit later, I learned that it is typically done, and they don't mean anything by it.

With many more years of work with American Indian students and on the opposite end of the United States, Kevin Ritchie had a door experience, too:

◆ I've always enjoyed their humor, even when I didn't understand it. I still don't half the time. We're in a room, there's three Indian kids and me, and everybody's laughing, and I'm laughing, too. But I'm not so sure what I'm laughing at. What the heck, we're all laughing. There's that easy spontaneity; they're a pleasure to be around. Slapstick. That's what I call it. Physical humor is funny. Humor at somebody's expense. Like, if I turn around and bump into the door, a white kid would laugh and kind of feel guilty, cover up a little bit. But a lot of the Indian kids would laugh, slap their leg. I mean, they wouldn't want me to be hurt, but still, seeing me bump into that door was just awful funny. The humor's intensified for them more. It's hard to describe it without looking like I'm stereotyping, but I feel like the sense of humor is more immediate and more direct. With some involved intellectual joke, the Indian kids will get it, but they don't think it's funny.

My research partner, Tom Peacock, had more to say about what Ketron and Ritchie had begun to say and answered a question that I had about the survival theory:

◆ Laughter is often prescribed as the best medicine for all that ails us. That laughter is good for all parts of the self is an assertion that has proven itself through medical research. Humor is a way of coping with hardship and sorrow. But humor isn't solely a way of survival; it's a way of teaching, and it's part of humility and leveling. Think about it that way and it integrates with a lot of other parts of this chapter.

Tom Ketron, our art teacher from the Southeast, indicated in the shoe incident in Chapter 1 how important it is to let people laugh at you, the function that Peacock identifies as leveling. Hoffman, from the Southeast, adds more about how humor can lessen the distance in teaching:

◆ I'll tell you one thing that I have found about teaching Native Americans: it is very important to learn their social sense of humor—those topics and interpersonal dynamics that allow you to make people laugh. It takes some time to find out their sense of humor and go with it. Teasing was so important when I worked in the Southwest—it seemed almost a necessary communication medium—and without it, folks would simply be less interested in communicating with you. Sometimes in other tribal communities, it seemed less important, but it still worked, and the subtler the funnier. But as often as one would tease, you would have to be able to take it. The more you laughed at yourself, the more at ease people were.

Hoffman's statement cautions us that the ways different tribes use humor varies. As a teacher and learner, you will begin to see how humor can work for you, how you can laugh at yourself and with your students.

Concept of Family

A family in the United States' dominant culture is considered whole if there is a mother, father, and a child or children. When the children are still of school age, if one of these members is not living under the same roof, the family is deemed broken. There are feelings of loss and grief. At a more distant level of family, there are grandfathers, grandmothers, aunts, uncles, and cousins; these people are often depended on, but only if there is some reason the mother and father need help.

In 1986, when I was interviewing Tim about his writing at the Fond du Lac Ojibwe School, I felt sad for him because he was living with his aunt. It was only later that I realized that in American Indian cultures many more relatives (and sometimes even clan members) act as family in the way my people depend on, care for, and love immediate family. This is different in each tribe. For the Anishinabe, for example, conceptually there is no such thing as an uncle, particularly when describing the father's brothers. Their brother's and sister's children are their children. Aunts are often considered to be mothers, uncles are called fathers, and cousins are seen as brothers and sisters. Even clan members are considered relatives, so American Indian cultures are apt to consider many more individuals to be family than non-Indian cultures do. And the extended family supports, disciplines, gives to, and cares for family members in the same way that mainstream mothers and fathers care for their children. It is common in many tribes for grandparents to raise grandchildren. Furthermore, all things on earth might be perceived as relatives, given the interrelatedness of all things (American Indian Learner Outcome Team, 1995).

A northeastern non-Indian teacher, Wilfred, said:

◆ With the American Indians here, you have quite an extended family. It's not uncommon at all for those kids to go from aunt to uncle to grandfather, grandmother. It's not just mother and father; it's extended family where everybody basically has the same position of authority or respect. It's harder and harder today to assume that the kids come from a "normal" family. But with the white kids, you can kind of assume they're not living with mommy and daddy because there's trouble at home; but that's not the case necessarily with the Indians.

Arlene, a Southwest American Indian teacher, talks about how relationships work in school:

◆ [My students] usually ask me my last name, and I find out how we're related, so I know how to treat them. Like there's a little boy who's the same clan as I am, and I told him on more than one occasion, "I will discipline you because I mean more than just [another teacher]." And so, a couple teachers have brought him to me, and I say, "You didn't do this and this and this. I'm taking you home; you're gonna get your notebook. It does not belong at home, and I'll tell your mom. And I'll tell her why I'm mad at you." And so now he doesn't do those things, which is really great.

Even after they graduate from high school, American Indian children may feel tighter bonds with their extended family than mainstream children do with theirs. Kay Lasagna, a non-Indian teacher in the Southeast, expresses the frustration she feels when her students drop out of college because of family:

◆ I had some very talented, wonderful, wonderful kids, and they reacted like any kids I've taught anywhere else. But they rarely lasted more than a couple

41

of weeks in college and then would be home again. And that was very defeating for me as a teacher. I found out that there were intense family ties, students pulled back by their family. That invisible umbilical cord I called it.

Wayne Newell, an honored educator and currently a doctoral candidate, spoke of what it was like to go off to college:

◆ I don't know how I made it [in graduate school], but I did. I think it's because I had made the connection between here and there. I think if I hadn't, I would have probably done [one of] two things, either commit suicide or quit. It really was that heavy. And then I started realizing, wait a minute, I've been on this cliff before. Wait a minute, I know where the footholds are. And my strength comes from a cultural support system. I didn't do well at all in college. I flunked out of two colleges in my bachelor's level. It just didn't click. I still feel it today. When I leave here and go to Boston [for course work], I'm able to monitor how I'm feeling. When I left the reservation, the first place that I went to college was in the city of Boston. And I had never left the reservation, and I ended up in downtown Boston at Emerson College. And how I survived as long as I did is a miracle. I was twenty. Pretty scary proposition. Anyway, I just didn't make it, barely survived it emotionally as well as materially.

The invisible umbilical cord is real and strong. American Indian children may need support systems when they first leave the home. This strong sense of family might confuse non-Indian administrators or teachers. Family responsibility might cause children to stay at home, "absent" as it would be perceived by the schools, to take over child care or to see to other family obligations. All involved must work at being flexible enough to accommodate that cultural difference. As Ketron says:

◆ If you come from a white background, it's easy to get yourself in a bad spot. You have to be careful with these kids, and sometimes as a teacher you make a mistake: "How come you have all these absences and tardies?" and then [you find] there was a funeral at home.

Competition and Collaboration

Non-Indian educators often recognize that American Indian children are less competitive than other children. I can see how the strong ties that children have with extended family extend also to other students, siblings, cousins, or distant relatives within a school setting. In the past, for all to fare well, everyone worked for all. Having just become an educator at a reservation school, Joseph describes how he sees children and competition:

◆ There's absolutely no competition that I can see between kids. And that's the difference for me. In other schools, you'd always have the child that's got all the answers and wants to finish first. That's not in the culture here. I'm sure that came about for very good reasons way back when, probably precluded fighting. But it's not a characteristic conducive to aggressiveness in academics.

As teachers gained in understanding, they saw deeper levels of this behavior. Rachel, a Northeast non-Indian teacher shows how feelings of family extend to other students in a school:

◆ There's a real bond that I don't think is there in white society. We're taught to be independent and self-reliant, but it seems to me that they're more family-oriented and do things for the benefit of all. In a dorm situation, they might have arguments amongst themselves, but they stick up for one another in every situation. There's one student, he was going out with a girl in the dorm, and apparently he slept with somebody on the reservation, so he hurt the girl in the dorm. So then all the kids in the dorm shunned him. They didn't talk to him. But if somebody from outside told the guy he was a jerk, they would have stuck up for him, even though they thought that he was wrong. In our white society that might not happen as much.

Carol Locust (1988) explains this bond as an intrinsic part of Indian culture:

◆ This survival instinct is still present in Indian communities, and it dictates behaviors that are frequently misunderstood by non-Indians. For example, the group's survival depends on everyone's working together and sharing. All members work together and contribute to the group, supporting each other in times of stress, for they know that they will find the same network of support for themselves should they require it. Children are expected to contribute to their group, as soon as they are mature enough to do so. (pp. 327–328)

Teachers can take advantage of some American Indians' propensity for collaborative work, but at the same time, they must be aware that the mainstream's way of

assessing students through competitive test taking and grading may not contribute to student motivation as it does in mainstream schools. These issues are discussed again in Chapter 8.

Material Possessions

In the mainstream culture, status and happiness are, to a certain extent, dependent on possessions. A nation's power and status depend largely on the ability to control and to own.

Traditionally, the person who holds status in many American Indian nations is more often one who shares wealth. For many, there is honor in sharing. If people live in balance with nature, extra is not needed. People accept the world as it is, enjoying it for what it is. Some tribes, the Lakota and Dakotah, for instance, hold celebrations and give away most of their possessions to others as gifts.

Non-Indian people are often unaware of why they offend when it comes to material things. Patty George is concerned about non-Indian teachers who do not understand the difference in values, teachers who feel sorry for children when they do not need to:

◆ And that's what all these non-native people do: "Oh, that poor boy, he doesn't have anything to eat." There's so much anxiety and so much sorrow. I saw a bureau Indian guy speak, and he said, "These people in here, they're still sorry about what they did to the Indian people, and it just overlaps in the classroom." And it's true. I got a teacher over there, she's just so sorry for everybody that she can't even educate them. But this is how I grew up. I mean, you [go] into a house, and there's food all over the place, and to a white person, that's terrible. But that's how I grew up. There's nothing to judge if a kid doesn't see sorrow in that: that's a family. But to those non-Native people, that's sad, [even though] that's not their judgment to make. If they would just come in and say, "Hey, this is cool." I've seen non-natives be successful. Maybe the kid doesn't have a sheet on his bed or parents are drinking, [but] that's not exactly sad to that kid. That's a psychological judgment that we're getting all confused with education.

Or the first thing [new teachers] want to know is, "How much am I gonna make?" And my first response was, "You can't work with these kids if your value system is money." I don't know if it's a spiritual thing, but if you're here because of money, somehow I think the Creator's setting you up to get out of here. I see people who don't care about money, who are giving the kids the 50 cents for a pop, buying kids cleats; they succeed. Not because they're buying the kid out, but if the kids see that, then they're gonna say, "OK. My value system matches." And then all of a sudden, whether they're Indian or non-Indian, those values match.

Teachers feel real concern for children, and sometimes the concern is well-founded. Other times emotional energy is wasted on well-loved children who do not feel deprived. These concerns are based, as Patty George notes, on judgments made from their own cultural perspective.

Oral and Literate Traditions

People differ in the way they make sense of the world, differ in the theory that they have of the world in their heads, and differ in the way they express what is on their minds. A person's worldview is a particular construct of perceptions of the world through what they see, hear, smell, and touch. In more traditional American Indian culture, stories are a medium through which children's theories of the world are, in part, constructed. Words are not seen as records but rather as reflections of events. The tradition of telling stories to teach American Indian philosophy, values, beliefs, and culture is still practiced. It is important not to trivialize the vital role these stories play by calling them myths or fables.

American Indian people generally fear the loss of this oral tradition. Warner Wirta, from the Midwest, acknowledged what is lost when written versions of history and stories are depended on:

◆ Saying history and stuff in an oral way is a lot more positive than having things written. Most people would rather listen, in most cases, instead of trying to read something from a paper. Once it's down on paper, you can't add a little dressing on to it to make it a little more palatable. And this is where oral history has it over something that's written. You lose the harmony that you can give to the story, and I think that we have forgotten how to dress up a piece of history in a colorful attitude. That individual [oral historian], through the abbreviation that comes through the movements of the body and flashes of their eye, [adds to the story], and you never get that off a paper. Oral traditionalists search out what an audience is like and then just put it across. It is a great talent. Most people can write words on paper, but it becomes so bland and so dry.

Dennis Bowen, a man from an eastern tribe who worked with adolescents in the Southeast, said:

◆ In order to make an oral history work, you need a unifying force like our spiritual way of life. Because if you're not spiritual, you are going to forget

things, and that's one of the arguments that modern education has torn at us [with]: "Indians, how can you have an oral tradition and forget things? You have to write it down." And we say, "No."

Teachers who recognized that values, humor, truth, and history are taught through oral tradition were puzzled about how to approach literacy. Linda, a principal at a Northeast school, said:

◆ I'm at the level right now where I believe that the children need to learn to read because society's perception is that intelligent people know how to read. And because they love to read. They love the written page. They love the exploration, but to force the reading at the expense of the richness of their oral community is . . . it's a dilemma for me.

Teachers must understand that oral tradition is part of the essence of life for many American Indians. We delve into the dilemmas that literacy presents to many of those who come from an oral tradition in Chapter 7.

A Non-Indian's View of American Indian Spirituality

In this section, I do not try to definitively describe American Indian spirituality; that would be impossible, first, because as one raised in the mainstream culture, I will never be able to completely understand those beliefs, and, second, because every tribe has its own construct of beliefs. I do, however, describe my own evolving understandings, as a non-Indian person, of some of the common beliefs that many tribes hold and share the perceptions other teachers had about American Indian spirituality.

Educators should know the essence of the beliefs of children they teach (and of course this could be applied to educators of any group of children), for not to understand the beliefs is to risk violating the children's freedom of religion (only granted to American Indians in 1979 when Congress passed the American Indian Religious Freedom Act). To take the most obvious example, children on some reservations are still marked "absent" on days when they are at religious observances because the calendar in most reservation schools is guided by Christian holidays. Though many American Indians are Christians, some have melded several religions, and many practice their traditional tribal beliefs and customs.

There are some American Indian spiritual beliefs that seem to be accepted by many American Indian cultures. For instance, humans are held to have at once a mind, body, and spirit. Plants, animals, and inanimate things are part of the spirit world as well as the physical world. The spirit world intermingles with the world on earth. And as mentioned before, when the spirit, mind, and body are in harmony, all is well.

So as not to be intrusive, our interview questions purposely did not focus on American Indian spirituality, but some teachers talked about ways in which spirituality connected with their work. Non-Indian LeRoux, from the Southwest, had advice for teachers who teach on reservations but who are not of the tribe:

◆ One of the things you have to deal with is [your own] ethnocentric vision, that you are the center of the world. Sometimes you butt heads because these people here are saying, "We're the center of the world," and you're saying, "We're the center of the world." And you can't [both] be! Out here there are two tribal religions. And they're not superstitions. They are the religions of the people. And they are as viable and realistic as Christianity. And that's going to offend some teachers because their entire lives have been spent being told what people [should] believe. And occasionally you have to step back and say, "This tribe has been here for ten thousand years, and they're still alive, and they're still running around and [peaceful]. They're not at war—other than in courts—with anyone." Occasionally you'll get asked to one of the villages to a dance. They'll just tell you where it is. And they won't push you away. The thing they try to stress is when you go to these cultural events, like a dance in the village, it's a religious occasion, and you should act appropriately, as [if] you're going to someone else's church. Of course, when you go to a dance in a village, occasionally they throw gifts out. And when they're throwing tin washbowls, you have to be careful 'cause you could get hit. There are some things that you'd be invited to, and there are some things that you're not invited to. In some way it was made clear to me.

Ingrid, a non-Indian English teacher, talks about aspects of spirituality as it comes into her literature and writing classroom:

◆ I think that our students take for granted that there are intangible things in life, things you can't see and can't touch, that are very powerful, and they understand that implicitly, whereas Anglo kids are trained in the scientific method, where if you can't measure it, it doesn't exist. The belief about the skin walker doesn't faze these kids at all—that there could be some creature running around in the desert that could assume different shapes is not bizarre at all to them. They may or may not actually believe that it exists or have seen one, but the concept is completely acceptable. That's really not true of American mainstream culture. Religion or spirituality is more something

you do on Sunday. Most of our students are as close to living on the land as most people can be these days: you still haul your own water and don't have electricity. My feeling is that they're just in tune a little more with things. And I think they have much more access to their creative energy than most of us do, just more in touch with all of their senses than we are.

There are aspects of my own culture that help me to understand some of the more commonly held beliefs in the 500 or so remaining American Indian tribes, though in no sense do I intend to trivialize anyone's beliefs by making the connections that help me understand. Actually, much in world religions has common ground, especially if words are seen as metaphoric and not narrowly read from religious tracts. The Christian sacrament in which the body and blood of Christ are found in a wafer or in wine and bread parallels the belief that inanimate beings have spirits. That the spirit of Christ and others have existence in the past, the present, and the future also has parallels with the beliefs of many tribes. American Transcendentalism of Emerson and Thoreau in the nineteenth century and its concept of the Oversoul and the divinity of man and nature has similarities.

Part of understanding American Indian beliefs for me has been in seeing similarities with what is familiar rather than in focusing on differences, though I am aware that I shouldn't minimize the differences. I am reminded of a day when my then teenage daughter, who has always been happier outside than inside, came to me with a poem by Emily Dickinson. "This should be in our Bible, Mom," she said.

LVI

Some keep the Sabbath going to church;
I keep it staying at home,
With a bobolink for a chorister,
And an orchard for a dome.

Some keep the Sabbath in surplice;
I just wear my wings,
And instead of tolling the bell for church,
Our little sexton sings.

God preaches,—a noted clergyman,—
And the sermon is never long;
So instead of getting to heaven at last,
I'm going all along!

I think often of LeRoux's reference to humans' propensity for thinking that they are at the center of the world. One way to understand differences between groups' beliefs and ways of being and to respect them, is to see more broadly, even metaphorically, the parallels between beliefs, the commonalities in human existence. Then again, as soon as I draw connections, I run the danger of trying to describe the whole by some discernible parts, its similarities with what I have come to understand.

Seeing clearly does take courage and persistence from both sides, and it takes us beyond seeing ourselves or our cultural group as being the center of the world. It means looking hard to see that which may remain hidden beneath the surface; it involves vigilance in making our own hidden beliefs and values conscious and in regarding the impact that those values and beliefs may have on those around us.

Challenges to Seeing Cultural Difference

While seeing clearly is made easier by having some knowledge of cultural difference, the knowledge itself does not solve all the problems that bicultural situations pose. Both the children in schools and their well-meaning teachers are still met with the challenges we describe in the following sections.

Children's Possible Misunderstandings of Mainstream Culture

Sometimes I have to see things from far away to recognize them at my doorstep. When I went to interview teachers of Aboriginal children in a community called Maree, I had traveled far into central South Australia. Early one morning I traveled through the Flinders Range, at dawn, avoiding the kangaroos, which were busy with their early morning business. Other than these creatures, there was no sign of life for hours. Finally, I arrived at a community with a few buildings, a number of satellite disks, and a school. While the teacher arranged for lunch, I joined his students so I could tell them about Minnesota. An adolescent girl said that she knew someone from Minnesota. The others agreed, "Yes, Miss." I was flabbergasted since I had experienced just how far this community was from nowhere. Then she said, and I can duplicate only the gist of her Aboriginal English, "Do you know her? Her name's Brenda. She doesn't really live in Minnesota anymore; she moved to Beverly Hills, but she talks a lot about Minnesota." I told them that Minnesota and Beverly

Hills were large and heavily populated and quite distant from one another. They were very disappointed that I didn't know Brenda. Later I asked her teacher about this visitor from Minnesota, and he laughed, saying that she was a character on an American sitcom, "Beverly Hills 90210," that came in on satellite, and that he was having trouble getting the kids to understand the concept of actors. As my friends call me "media deficient," I didn't know about the Brenda of Beverly Hills, so it was hard for our worlds to meet. I had misunderstood the worldliness of her knowledge and was at once thrown by the cultural misconceptions she could have. This incident made me realize how easy it is to overlook what students do not know or what they misunderstand.

Some of the teachers that we interviewed in the United States were beginning to see their students' sometimes limited understandings of mainstream culture. Arlene, an American Indian teacher from the Southwest, talked about more subtle misunderstandings:

◆ When they get to the high school level, some of our students have not been out of the community. They don't have the knowledge of what's out there, although we have TVs and radios to expose us. I don't think they truly can understand unless they experience it for themselves. Speaking from my experiences, I didn't realize what I was getting into when I left the reservation to go to school, and I was an adult with three children. They have experienced a different world. And that adds to how they act, and their planning, their decision making.

Although some American Indian children may have less distance between their worlds and the world of the school, others have a long distance to travel even on a short bus ride. Carrie, a non-Indian teacher from a Northeast public school, was beginning to understand the distance between her high school and the reservation only twenty miles away:

◆ It's like they're being displaced to a different area, different time. I can see why some of the apathy is present within some of the students. You grow up on a reservation for eight years [of school], and you are completely absorbed within that, and then you come to a high school. Their freshman year, they've got "ancient civilization" with the whole history course revolving around the Greeks, the Romans, etcetera; but when you walk in the Indian reservation, everything is just focused on their heritage, and their beliefs, their custom. And when you get on that bus, and you get closer and closer to the city, even the way the houses are set up, it just changes. And I don't believe you'll see anything in reference to Native Americans within this entire school. Last month I was invited onto the reservation to meet the eighth graders, and for the first time I felt what it must be like to be an Indian kid stepping into the high school. It's like going into a different world.

There is a mismatch between what might be relevant curriculum and what American Indian students actually experience in many schools. Teachers must stretch out antennae to be aware of misunderstandings that American Indian children might have about mainstream culture, and they must stretch to make their curriculum relevant to these students' lives.

Challenges Teachers Meet in Seeing Cultural Difference

The need to be a teacher and a learner

Teachers said to us, "If you enjoy learning and feel pretty good about yourself, it is hard to find teaching that is more interesting or rewarding." Being able to learn on the job and being flexible enough to adjust seemed to be attributes of those teachers who enjoyed their work. Indeed, Shobothteau, an American Indian principal of a reservation school, said:

◆ I need rubberband teachers. A teacher to me [should be] like a rubberband. It's very flexible, it can be stretched to a point, it can snap back, or it can hold things together. Rubberband teachers are the ones that keep things going. And they come in different sizes and shapes.

But no matter how flexible and willing to learn a teacher is, there are still challenges to the work that teachers have the right to know about. One is that you will not be able to see your teaching situation clearly on the first day of work. You can only hope to learn as much as you can initially and then keep learning the whole time that you teach American Indian students.

The need to analyze stereotypes

Another challenge in seeing cultural difference clearly is distinguishing between stereotypes and differences. Mary, from the Midwest, recognized that stereotypes can become expectations, which, in turn, can actually be lived out by those of whom they are expected:

◆ There's always fun made of Native Americans because they have "Indian time," and I think that a lot of native people, because of hearing that they

weren't conscious of time, weren't conscious of time, or because everyone was going to expect them to be, were late anyway. Some of our native staff are very punctual, and so that is a stereotype. "Indian time" can be an excuse. Some Indian teachers on our staff go way out of their way to be early because they don't want to perpetuate that stereotype, which is exactly what it is—a stereotype.

The need to recognize defensive behavior and mistrust

Teachers reported that seeing clearly is also difficult because of the old patterns of behavior that oppressed people build to defend themselves. Teachers entering schools in which there has been abuse in the past may need to wait out periods of mistrust. Teachers may see behavioral difference, anger for instance, that they first perceive as cultural difference but eventually identify as mistrust. Wilma, a Midwest teacher, said:

◆ I was white, and I was intruding on their cultural boundaries. I guess they assumed that I would be prejudiced against them. I don't know if you call it a reverse prejudice. It's like they were waiting for me to prove that I was there for the money and not to teach them anything. And it was like walking on egg shells everyday. They were always waiting for me to prove that I was prejudiced against them, waiting for me to produce some proof.

The need to be sensitive to how students identify the culture

Another challenge is figuring out just how traditional students are. Each human being is unique. Humans build their identities from influences coming from family, culture, and experiences. In some situations, American Indian and non-Indian teachers do not know what to expect because, though some students come from very traditional backgrounds, others do not. And some who by physical appearance seem to be assimilated might be very traditional in lifestyle. Just as soon as teachers think they can predict the traditionality of a group, they will find anomaly. Dennis Bowen, an American Indian teacher from the Northeast who teaches in the Southwest, explained that often the degree to which students display cultural difference depends to a large extent on their family's contact with mainstream culture:

◆ Having been raised on a reservation in the East and coming here, [I found that here,] the culture is stronger. And it's stronger because they have had less contact with the Americans. [But] I'd be careful [in generalizing], not wanting to be critical of my brothers and sisters here who may have had the same contact that my people in the East have had. The Southwest has a lot of nations that still have culture intact.

Some teachers also found that, though they were committed to making curriculum relevant to the culture of students, the students themselves would be resistant. Furthermore, some teachers themselves thought they did not know enough. Ingrid, a non-Indian teacher from the Southwest, said:

◆ There's a real [peer] pressure to assimilate, even though that hasn't worked either, because Native Americans, at least in this part of the country, are just not assimilated. [But] whenever I've brought up the idea of a cultural project, everybody's just kind of stared at me. My student teacher wanted to do this kind of Foxfire thing, and I said, "Okay, why don't we see where the kids' interests lie." And only two students in the whole class wrote about culture; the rest of them wrote about teen issues. This summer, I was on a committee that was talking about bringing culture into the classroom, a concern of some native people from the district, and I said, "Well okay, but what does that mean, because I don't know. I don't think it's even appropriate for me to be teaching culture when I couldn't, as long as I live, understand it the way you would understand it."

Other teachers who were trying to be respectful and inclusive of culture found themselves dealing with students critical of more traditional students. LeRoux, from the Southwest, said:

◆ When I first started working on the reservation, I worked at a Bureau of Indian Affairs boarding school. They said: "The students will not look you in the eye, and you should not force them to." Because culturally, at the time, it wasn't something that they did. They won't speak up, but as I've taught more and more, there is a gap between the traditional students and the students who are more modern. And the traditional students are often called "Johns." You would hear students say, "They're just a bunch of Johns," like "They're a bunch of hicks."

Non-Indian teachers also talked of a discomfort they felt in American Indian communities. They had an understandable reluctance to look to the community when something seemed to be going wrong for a student. Northwest American Indian teacher Patty George offered some advice:

◆ I've never been in a tribal school yet that Indian teachers won't tell them [non-Indian teachers], "Well so-and-so's got a bad home life. This's happened to them. You have to be patient with them." Once that [non-Indian] person knows and says to the kid, "Hey, look, I talked to your auntie or to your uncle or to your grandma or whatever, and I know what you're going

through, and I'm sorry. But there are things we need to do at school. And I understand." There's nothing wrong with doing that, but nobody does it. They get in these tribal schools, and they think because they're non-Indian, they can't talk to the community. They're afraid of the community. Instead of just getting out there and calling auntie on the phone and saying, "Look, I'm concerned, what's going on here?"

Kate, an American Indian teacher from the Northeast, was fully able to understand the cultural difference she herself had to deal with as a child, but even so, she had to help her students to accept what they had to accept and help them to determine what they shouldn't have to accept.

◆ There was one place to be on Saturday afternoons as a child: we all went to the theater. Because we were from the reservation, we sat down in the front in the corner, but we would cheer the cowboys. And it's not until you can stand back or something shakes you a little bit that you look at it and say it does not have to be that way. I do it [shake students up] a lot in my U.S. history class. [But] I guess when my husband and I moved away from here, we did what we had to do out there. My husband didn't expect them to accommodate his hunting and fishing unless he had some vacation time coming. It wasn't "This is what I have to do because this is the season." If he was going to maintain that job, then he had to go with what the company demanded. It's like coming here and being a teacher. If you choose to live here, then you have to fit in. I'm not working to change my students to fit in. I'm working to make them see how they have to adapt for the time that they're out there. "If [another] school has a bell ringing every forty-five minutes, and if you really want to be successful there, that's the way it is. And if you need to be successful there so you could come back here to do something useful later, then that's what you do."

And several teachers sincerely thought that the best thing for their students was assimilation. They had deep concern for their students. These teachers' good intentions did not necessarily serve their students' best interests. A teacher from the Northeast said:

◆ The training that I received certainly didn't prepare me for the actual classroom experience because when I went into the school, the first month I spent preparing the kids for how to interact socially with each other and with people with whom they came in contact and spent little time on academics. I guess teachers aren't supposed to say this, but my maternal instincts took over more so than the teaching.

Only three teachers we talked with thought that students would be happier by learning to live in the white world. They didn't seem to fully understand the strength of deep culture. Wayne Newell, a Northeast teacher who became very important to us in our understandings, pointed out that a century of trying to teach children to take on non-Indian ways of being just had not worked. Culture, he pointed out, is just too strong to extinguish. We will end this section with Newell's very important quote, and even though portions of it appear in Chapter 4, what Newell says is worth repeating:

◆ In the 70s, my heart was in the right place, and I was going to make schools just the way the white man wanted me to. "Teachers have to get these kids ready for the outside world." I'm sure you've heard that a thousand times. BIA didn't invent that; it was a missionary philosophy. And it only took one generation, and then what we did was to perpetuate it ourselves. We, the victims, have been the victimizers also. We have been trying to solve our community problems from the white values system that caused them. We never thought that maybe the solution is [solving] them according to the strong values within ourselves, and then the next generation will take over. Right now . . . for me to succeed in today's world, I have to forget who I am? What people didn't understand is that those boarding school terrorists thought that it [culture] could disappear in a generation, and they would have white-thinking children. But they couldn't erase it, and thereby lies the hope. Right there. I might see it in my lifetime. And when that spirit is reawakened, it is more powerful than anything that I have ever met in my whole life. So I am impressed with the strength of culture. Even though the missionaries tried, the boarding schools tried, all the well-intentioned white people tried. And we tried, because we became like the conquerors. But something hasn't died. It's not that dead.

*C*ase Study

I have written the following case so that you can project yourself into a fictionalized situation that is based on a real occurrence. It is similar in many ways to what happened to Tom Ketron when one of his students put a cobra on a pot. Tom's situation ended so that there were positive understandings and learning for all those involved. How should Meg approach this situation so that the same thing can happen?

Meg and the Hurricane

Meg looked out her second-floor classroom window at the relative order in the courtyard below. Fronds still hung at odd angles out of the palm trees, and there were still stacks of plywood on the ground below, purposeless since they had been removed from the windows two weeks ago. Actually the school itself was in remarkable order considering it had withstood the 100-mile-an-hour winds. Many of the other buildings on the reservation were in shambles. Meg turned away from the window. She was deep down tired, and it was playing out in her feelings right now.

She was tired because she had been working hard with her husband to repair the roof on their own house, which had been damaged in the hurricane; she was tired from concern she felt for the scared children whose families had lived in houses that had lost more than their roofs; and today she was most deeply tired because, in trying to help these children cope with nature that had turned cruel, she had miscalculated. And now this. It had been her first hurricane, but this new development held its own angst.

She turned to the wall and started to remove the pictures that the children had drawn to go with the stories they told about the hurricane. She loved these kids and had talked with her husband about how resilient they were. Finding out that she had inadvertently added new worries to her children and their families on top of the hurricane trouble was very distressing to her; it added the edge to her already heavy fatigue.

When school had finally reopened, when temporary housing had been found for those who had sheltered in the school, and when the kids were back at their desks, she had wanted to help them make sense of what had happened. When they sat down to do their illustrations of their hurricane stories, some hadn't wanted to. She realized now the irony of why they were the very ones whose English was not developed well enough to tell her why. She would have listened carefully if they had felt able to tell her. She had learned that it was important to listen hard to her students when she had worked for years at the reservation school in the Southwest. The children here who had not drawn pictures of the storm had drawn pictures of their families, and she had thought it was because they had not fully understood what was wanted of them. She had fallen once again into the misassumption trap. In her own family, you always felt better if you could tell stories or write about things that were frightening to you—or even draw pictures. Other children, and now she realized it was the less traditional children, had drawn remarkable storm pictures.

Meg moved back to her storage closet to retrieve the step stool for the pictures that she had hung higher than the others. She held one up that had stunned her. For a second she shuddered at the power in these pictures. In this one, it was as if the trees were resisting just as much as the wind was blowing, and all the motion and resistance were there in the art of a seven-year-old. When she had them all down and the stack was on the table, she wondered what she should do with them. At least the parents could advise her about that. She still had ten minutes before she had to meet with the parents who had come to complain that she was trying to bring another hurricane to the community by having the children draw pictures of it. What could she possibly say to them to express the regret, awe, and fatigue she felt? And was the expression of this feeling even what they were looking for?

Case Discussion

1. How is Meg caught in the gap between cultures?
2. Based on the knowledge and strategies presented in this chapter, what approaches might she use with the parents in her upcoming conference? Which approach would you choose?
3. What are some behaviors Meg might have displayed or actions that she might have taken to avoid this situation?
4. Meg was trying to make school relevant to her students' lives. List other ways she might have connected the children's curriculum with what was happening around them. What might be some cautionary steps she could take before implementing these relevant lessons?

Things to Remember

Some of you will want some concrete statements to take away with you about the difference between the culture of American Indian children and that of their school and about the effect of that difference on the children.

1. Most American Indian students enter schools that mirror the culture of the dominant society; that culture is often very different from the culture of their homes and communities.
2. There may be visible differences in peoples of different cultures—differences of skin color, dress, habits, and food; and there may be deeper and more subtle differences of values and of ways of being and learning.
3. A continuum exists between traditional and nontraditional students. And within the continuum there are those who show characteristics of American Indian ways of being and belief, and those who know themselves to be Amer-

ican Indian yet do not have what some people might at first see as American Indian behavior or appearance. What is important is that all humans be allowed feelings of integrity and pride connected with who they are, with how they identify.

4. Respecting what others value and do is a way to help them develop both the self-esteem and the feelings of integrity that will enhance their learning.

5. As teachers, we must study the communities in which we teach and ask ourselves: "What things can we do in our classrooms to close the distance between the way students operate in our classrooms and the way they operate at home?"

6. As teachers, we must be flexible enough to give students the room to be who they are while learning skills that will make their lives both purposeful and hopeful.

7. It helps to let American Indian parents know that we are trying to learn about their community. We can ask parents and students to help by letting us know immediately if they are uncomfortable with anything the students are being asked to do.

8. American Indian teachers or teacher's aides in our schools are good people to go to with questions. It is important, however, to ask questions pertinent to work, because excessive questions, for instance about native spirituality, may be seen as intrusive.

9. If we can not begin to see and understand the differences or even to value them, we probably should not do or keep doing work with these children. Children need to be valued for who they are, not for who their teacher wants them to be.

References

Locust, C. (1988). Wounding the spirit: Discrimination and traditional American Indian belief systems. *Harvard Educational Review, 58*(2), 315–330.

American Indian Learner Outcome Team. (1995). *American Indian learner outcomes.* St. Paul: Minnesota Department of Children, Families and Learning.

Moyers, B. (1993). *Healing and the mind.* New York: Doubleday.

Scollon, R. S. (1981). *Narrative, literacy, and face in interethnic communication.* Norwood, NJ: Ablex.

Wax, R., & Thomas, R. K. (1961). American Indians and white people. *Phylon, 22*(4), 305–317.

What Has Gone Wrong

The Remnants of Oppression

Several years ago, I spent the good part of a summer doing research at the National Archives in Washington, D.C. I, Thomas Peacock, have always been a history buff, with a particular interest in the history of my home reservation of Fond du Lac in northern Minnesota and in the continuing impact of that history on the people today. Early into the research, I reviewed the education files of the reservation, looking for information on the old Bureau of Indian Affairs day schools and files indicating where the children of that period were sent to boarding and mission schools. The second file folder I opened contained a letter to the Commissioner of Indian Affairs in Washington. It was written by a mother requesting that she be allowed to keep her eldest son home from Pipestone Boarding School that school year, because she was ill and needed his assistance in the home. It read, in part, "I respectfully request that my eldest son, Harry . . ."

I quickly went to the end of the letter and saw that it was signed by my great grandmother, and that her eldest son was my grandfather. A reply letter was attached from the Commissioner informing my great grandmother that her son must report to the boarding school as directed. Later, in reviewing other files, I was

to find out that my great grandmother died that winter from a flu epidemic that swept the reservation. I remember being overcome by a flood of emotions ranging from anger and disgust to grief. Anger and disgust for a government that believed it was in their right to overlord the personal lives of the people whose nations they had possessed. Grief for a great grandmother I had never known, who was no longer just a tombstone in the old Catholic cemetery up the road from where I live, but a person to whom I suddenly felt a strong emotional connection. I asked myself over and over again if history would have played itself out differently if my grandfather had been allowed to stay home that winter. Would it have made a difference in my great grandmother living through the winter and going on to live a full life or would my grandfather also have become a victim of the epidemic? Who would think that a bureaucratic decision made by some long dead Commissioner of Indian Affairs would have such an impact on me.

Needless to say, it reminded me that we are not abstractly removed from history; we are products of it. The process of colonization, the Christianization and the "civilization" of the indigenous people in this country continue today to affect both the colonizer and the colonized in more ways than we at first discern. Remnants of oppression still affect the daily intercourse of the two peoples.

Questions to Jump-Start Your Reading

1. Is there a relationship between the historical oppression suffered by American Indian tribes and the problems facing contemporary American Indians?
2. How are these elements of oppression made manifest?
3. What are the effects of these problems on American Indian students?

A Chapter Road Map

We begin by describing the nature of oppression, the oppressor, internalized oppression (what we call suboppressor behavior), and the impact of internalized oppression on the American Indian need for harmony and balance. From there we provide more detail on the continuing impact of history on contemporary American Indian people. To illuminate and describe all of the elements of oppression identified by teachers, we profile Odie, a young American Indian. The voices of teachers are used to detail the five elements of oppression identified in our research: institutional racism, overt and covert racism, malfunctioning institutions from the federal down to the local level, communities in trouble, and the devastating impact of oppression on many American Indian students. A case study, "They're Acting Really Squirrelly," illustrates how oppression impacts individual American Indian students and allows readers to bring the concepts of oppression into real-world focus.

An Introduction to Oppression

This chapter has been the most difficult for me to write, but it may have been the most necessary because no existing book and few articles on teaching American Indian students have addressed the complex and troubling issues that characterize contemporary American Indian education within the context of racism and oppression. Although little written material is available on the impact of racism and oppression on contemporary American Indian education, it was a topic about which the teachers, both American Indian and non-Indian, spoke strongly and frequently. To be truly reflective of the collective voices of the teachers we interviewed, we had to deal with this subject. It was of utmost importance, however, that this chapter not be written in such a way as to blame the victims, but to frame the dynamics discussed within the context of oppression. Schools do not purposely fail children, nor do the agencies that fund them, nor do communities and the individuals living in them. Moreover, it is necessary not to view this failure as particular to schools serving American Indians (public, private, federal, or tribal), to the Bureau of Indian Affairs, or to American Indians, or to any group of people. The educational and social problems of children is a growing and troubling characteristic of American society in general.

Oppression and Its Relation to American Indians

The story of humankind is replete with examples of oppression in all of its forms committed by individuals and groups of people on one another, and readers should not assume that all of the problems in American Indian education can be traced to the oppression of the indigenous people of this continent by non-Indians. To lay all of the blame for the ills of American Indian education on European colonialism is simplistic and wrong. To ignore history, however, is equally wrong. The dynamics of conflict in humans may be a universal human problem. The history of Western civilization is filled with acts of genocide, repression, denial of human dignity, and cultural extermination. The Roman army marched over and subjugated many of the people it conquered. Egyptians oppressed the Jews, who in

turn oppressed the Palestinians. Adolf Hitler's Germany nearly conquered and oppressed all of Western Europe. Oppression is not confined to Europe and the Middle East. The Iroquois destroyed the Erie culture, and the Navajo fought the Pueblo. The history of my own tribal group, the Anishinabe, chronicles the extermination of another tribal culture centuries ago. Moreover, numerous atrocities were committed by the Anishinabe and the other tribal groups it encountered during its migration from the East Coast to the Midwest. Oppression does not result solely from conflict between one culture and another. Individuals oppress one another regardless of culture. Some parents oppress their children through abuse. Partners oppress their partners. Individuals commit vicious crimes against each other on America's streets. The list goes on and on.

To frame the dynamics of conflict in humans solely within the context of oppression is also simplistic. Conflict (competition for scarce resources, whether it is money, power, influence, status, etc.) exists without oppression. For example, an ongoing internal struggle exists in some American Indian communities between traditionalists and progressives. Some traditionalists fear that the continued loss of culture and language will result in a continuation of the myriad of ills facing contemporary American Indian communities. These individuals advocate a return to traditional ways as a means of problem solving. Conversely, some progressives believe that the only way to solve community and educational problems is to take what is good from mainstream society and move on. The dynamics of these conflicts do not necessarily result in oppression of one group over another. Only when groups or individuals subject the other to tyranny is there oppression.

Some of you can identify the elements of oppression and of the oppressor. The oppressor enslaves and lords over the oppressed, abuses the oppressed physically and psychologically, and reminds them that they are less. The oppressor ignores that the oppressed have histories, poetry, songs, and literature, as if they never existed. The oppressor relegates the philosophy and religions of the oppressed to primitive myths and legends and silences the oppressed, whose voices go unheard and whose opinions are disregarded or minimized. In their worst acts, oppressors commit both overt and covert acts of genocide against the oppressed.

The recent past of the American Indian people has been told in revisionist history and literature; it is not the aim of this book to retell it. Other books (Gilliland's *Teaching the Native American* or Reyhner's *Teaching American Indian Students*) on educating American Indians offer chapters on the history of American Indian education. Zinn's *People's History of the United States* offers readers riveting descriptions of the oppression that has occurred since the landing of Columbus's ships.

Many years ago, while interviewing elders from the Fond du Lac reservation in northern Minnesota, I heard many horror stories about the boarding and mission school era. Betty Gurno told me of her days at Flandreau Boarding School, where she was punished for speaking Ojibwe. Frank and Bill Martineau told of the indignities committed against them by nuns while attending a mission school in Odana, Wisconsin. While reviewing educational files at the National Archives, I came on box after box of "death files," copies of telegrams and letters written to parents by federal officials about children dying while running away from boarding schools. It is important to recognize the continuing impact of this period on the survivors. Given that we are, in part, products of the people, institutions, and governments that came before us, there is a direct connection between the past and the present.

It is now widely acknowledged that American Indian tribes were decimated by war, disease, and other overt genocidal acts during, and soon after, the period of European colonization. From the initial contact with Europeans to early in the twentieth century, the number of American Indians in North America was reduced from five million (Zinn, 1980) to scarcely 250,000 souls. Whole tribes were exterminated. Whole cultures and languages were forever lost. Many of the survivors were forced to move to marginal reservation lands, which could not support their traditional means of livelihood. Some tribes became dependent on government rations. Assimilationist education policies were implemented to remove any vestiges of tribal cultures in an effort to "Americanize" tribal members. American Indian children were forced to attend mission and government schools, where they were forbidden to speak in their native languages or to live their cultures. In many of these boarding schools, the children were consciously deprived of seeing their parents for extended periods. For the most part, these practices continued well into the mid-1960s, and their impact has been profound and lasting.

Suboppression and Its Effects

Continued oppression eventually turns the oppressed against each other, and in these instances a twisted form of self-hate develops in the oppressed until eventually they internalize their oppression and become the suboppressor. History is replete with blatant examples of this. Some of the best scouts in the U.S. cavalry used against American Indian nations were fellow American Indians. The most feared guards in the Nazi death camps were fellow Jews. The suboppressor is another form of oppression.

There is a need, however, to expand this view of the suboppressor to encompass the more subtle oppression of one's self, because the suboppressor will also try to destroy his or her own self through acts of self-destruction: alcoholism, drug abuse, suicide, and all of the other vestiges of internalized oppression. The problems with alcohol and the abnormally high rates of suicide in some American Indian communities are examples of internalized oppression.

The self-destructive nature of this suboppressor behavior has an impact on the need for harmony and balance (explained in Chapter 2), which is an integral characteristic of the philosophy of many American Indian tribes. The lack of balance in an individual can grow to adversely affect families, communities, and whole tribes. For example, if an individual carries the burden of anger in them, that anger will affect the other parts of their being; their spiritual well-being and their physical health may eventually be impaired. Anger may affect their relationships with others, including family members, and in doing so will adversely affect the harmony and balance of the family. It may eventually affect their relationships with others at school or work, or may cause groups in a tribe to be in friction with one another, and upset the harmony of the community's institutions. Unresolved anger is one of the self-destructive elements of the suboppressor.

The effects of European colonization on the indigenous people of America and the accompanying devastation of many American Indian tribes that resulted have adversely affected the harmony and balance of generations of individuals, communities, and tribes. Only within the past generation has progress been made in dealing with the ongoing effects of both historical and current oppression. Only now are we recognizing the self-destructive impact of suboppressor behavior on us.

Moving beyond Oppression?

There was no question in our minds after reviewing several drafts of this chapter that parts of it were going to make people uncomfortable—uncomfortable because we have laid out all of the issues about the failure of our governments, institutions, and communities in educating American Indian students. As writers, we confront all of the self-destructive garbage that has been holding American Indian people back, and we have done it because we know that to recognize and confront it is the first step toward liberation and freedom.

Oppression theorists say that to be free we must first realize we are enslaved. Paulo Friere, the father of oppression theory, says that we must develop "critical consciousness." Just as an abuser needs to first confront and accept the reality of his abuse before he can cease being an abuser or an alcoholic needs to admit that he is enslaved by alcoholism before he can embrace sobriety, so also must educators confront these remnants of oppression before we can know how to better educate. To make conscious decisions in solving problems, teachers and schools need to understand the roots of overt, covert, and institutional racism and historic oppression. This will help them meet the complex needs of their American Indian students. Agencies such as the Bureau of Indian Affairs and State Departments of Public Instruction need to confront their own limitations. Communities need to confront and recognize the issues that limit their ability to be healthy communities.

Individuals need to confront why they may not be living in harmony and balance. The issues raised in this chapter describe what sometimes happens to individuals and communities that have been subjected to genocide, destructive assimilationist policies, and centuries of racism and neglect. It is a wonder that American Indian people have even survived all of this, and it is a true testament to their cultures that so many American Indian people have emerged from all of this still strong—with their sense of identity and ways of being intact and more powerful than they have been in generations. That is the triumph of all of this.

A Profile of Odie: A Survivor of Oppression

We have talked about the nature of oppression, the oppressor and suboppressor, and their impact on American Indian people. This profile shows how oppression impacts an individual. Of all the persons interviewed for this book, we choose to profile Odie for this chapter because his life story provides vivid examples of many of the elements of oppression. He survived institutional, covert, and overt racism, transcended problems in his community and himself, and emerged from all of it a strong and forceful advocate for American Indian students. A young man in his early twenties when we interviewed him, he was a bus driver, counselor, American Indian culture teacher, and advocate for the students in an American Indian school located in a large Midwest urban area. Odie did not consider himself a victim of anything. He had simply, as the phrase goes, "seen it all, done it all, been there."

Three aspects of Odie's life are relevant here. The first is the way suboppressor behavior played itself out in his life: the drug and alcohol abuse, child neglect, delinquency, and the interference of these things with his schooling. The second is his survival of all this because of some intangible inner strength that led him on the road back to the Ojibwe culture. The third is about fate and all of its characteristics: luck, timing, being at certain places, and meeting certain people who influenced him in ways that helped him turn his life around.

The first chapter of Odie's life is one that could be told about so many young American Indian people. There are many whose lives remain in a sort of self-destructive cycle, which we have termed delayed adolescence. In hearing Odie's story, we had to continually ask ourselves: What is it that separates the dispirited from those who live full, purposeful lives in society, those who are strong in their culture from those who despair, and those who survive from those who perish? It seems to be a thin wall that separates the two. Odie sheds light on those things that make the difference. He began by describing a troubled past in which he became the caregiver of his father, who is an alcoholic:

Mom moved apart when my father became a chronic alcoholic, and he was living in the streets for four years. And, at eleven-years-old, I was having conflicts with my mother, and I thought I could do better for my father, and I thought I'd be able to help him off the street. She never held me back, and she sent me down here [the city] to live with my father. We got on welfare, and I told him we had to find a place further away [from those streets]. We found an apartment over on the east side and things were going all right for the first couple of months.

He got me enrolled in school; he was being sober for awhile. Then when I started going to school, he started disappearing on me, and about every three days he'd return, and in those three days I had to learn how to fend for myself, how to cook and just get myself off to school, wash my clothes and stuff. I was down there for about six months, and by that time he was going for about two weeks to a month. But I always knew where to go to find him. I went and looked in the streets for him, learned how to ask people where he was at because he was pretty well known. I learned how to start paying the rent on my own and how to go buy groceries for myself—eleven years old, fifth grade.

The winter was coming, and it was getting around Christmas time, and I never wanted to tell my Mom that my father was doing this. I was trying to make it sound like everything was going okay and he was getting better. So every time she'd come down, I'd say, "Oh, he went and visited my uncles and I was just coming back from my aunty's house," which wasn't too far away. She always believed it.

Meanwhile, around Christmas time, I had no money to get anybody Christmas presents. So I started collecting aluminum cans and turning those in and shoveling sidewalks and everything else like that. And after Christmas was over, I still kept doing the same thing, collecting aluminum cans and shoveling walks to make $6.25 because that was the bus fare between [the city and Mom's]. My ma never knew when I was coming up. I just started getting smarter then at the time that I had to take care of myself and make sure that everything was looking okay. That's where I started using, doing drugs and alcohol at the same time. I was eleven. One weekend she was gone, and I took off on a Friday to go and see her. She didn't know I was coming up, so she went home, back to the reservation where her parents were living. I showed up on a Friday after she left, and I ended up staying in the stairwell to her house all weekend. And I had enough money where I could go down to the store and come back and wait for her to get home. Then when she showed up, I told her I just got there. She didn't know I was there all weekend.

The pattern of behaviors continued through elementary school and into high school. He moved back in with his mother, and they moved back to their home reservation, where Odie tried out the local public school and then the reservation school. Odie was bright but rebellious, a complicated mixture found in many troubled students.

◆ I started rebelling against the school, I guess. Coming to school drunk or doing drugs at school or trying to tick off the teachers so I could get suspended and go out and have some fun during the day, legally or illegally.

For a short while, he found direction in his Ojibwe culture, with the assistance of the American Indian culture teacher in the school he attended. But it was short lived. He had too many problems and unresolved issues.

◆ He started to ask me if I wanted to learn how to dance and he'd teach me. I said, "Yeah." And he started asking if I wanted to learn how to sing, and he taught me how to sing. Once those two things came about, I started going to pow wows with him. Right around my sixteenth birthday is when I started having a lot of troubles with my friends: should I go out drinking, or should I stay home and just mellow out this weekend, or should I go to this pow wow. . . .

So when that came about, I started asking [that teacher] for a lot of guidance. When January came around, we went down to Pipestone and got a bunch of pipestone. He selected a few students out of the school who would be able to handle a pipe. I was making the pipe. Once we were going to the pipes, and he was telling the stories, what the pipes are meant to be and how they're supposed to be held and all this other stuff, and you can't use while you're making yours . . . . I was straight during the whole two and one-half months I was doing that. I started getting really closer to him and started wanting to learn more and more about my culture. He was doing storytelling and visual things.

Once we got done with that, maple syruping came around, and we got maple syrup. And somebody hit a deer right outside the school. He brought the deer in, skinned it, took the hide off, and threw away the meat, because he showed us how to check if the meat was bad. Then he took the hide off, and he showed us how to tan hides.

That whole time between there, I was having an identity crisis: do I want to be Indian, do I want to know my culture, or do I want to be like everybody else [who] don't give a shit about the culture, [who] can raise hell and talk back to their elders and don't think about a future.

After I got my pipe blessed and got my Indian name, everybody just kind of forgot about who I was. Nobody came to see me anymore. Nobody would talk to me in the school hallways anymore. I don't know if it was because I had gotten all that stuff within that short period of time . . . .

I was talking to [that teacher] and he was teaching me how to use the pipes and be the sweat doorkeeper, door person of the sweat. He was teaching me the ways of the sweat. During a sweat one day, I just asked if I could be let down off this pedestal for a while and take it slowly so I can work my way into it.

After we got done, he said, "Well, why didn't you say this at the beginning?" I said, "Well, you didn't ask." He goes, "Well, you were so in tune on everything; you wanted to do everything." I said, "Yeah. I wanted to do it all, but I didn't know it was going to go this quick, and I would have to give up so much to become the way you are." So he let me off, and he told me to keep my pipe in wraps and keep it in my drawer for a while. And he said, "Whenever you want to use it, just go ahead and use it. You don't have to have people come to you; you don't have to do these masterful spiritual things with it. Just do it when you want to do it, but make sure you're not using or have anything in the house when you're doing it.

For a long time Odie left the culture, something that had given him inner strength. He went back to his troubled ways, abusing drugs and alcohol and going to school in a drunken or drug-induced haze. But he went to school, barely graduated, and ended up as the commencement speaker for his graduation. He was so drunk at the graduation that the superintendent had to lead him from the podium.

Odie sobered up on his own, went into the military, and returned to work with children who had similar pressures to the ones he had, the delayed adolescence that prohibits a smooth entry into adulthood. He had something to say about the difficulties in growing up that so many American Indian students have. Now he is an advice-giver, role model, and American Indian culture teacher. His story is one of moving beyond his self-destructive past to a purposeful, hopeful life.

Present-Day Manifestations of Oppression

The civil rights movement of the 1960s prompted a new policy on American Indians, as self-determination was adopted by the federal government. Efforts were made to strengthen tribal governments, and American Indian tribes were allowed to contract and manage programs for their own benefit, within the restrictions inherent in federal law, rules, and regulations. Some tribes chose to contract and manage former Bureau of Indian Affairs schools. Others opened their own tribal schools. Most of these schools stress the importance of fundamental skills and the teaching and reinforcement of tribal cultures, languages, and history. Much progress has been made as a result of the self-determination policy. School dropout rates in some communities have been dramatically reduced, and achievement has grown substantially. More American Indians are going on to post-secondary education and returning to work with their tribes as teachers, administrators, and in other professional capacities. Still, many problems exist, and the teachers interviewed for this book spoke clearly and eloquently about the vestiges of past governmental policy that may take the efforts of several more generations of American Indians to solve. These manifestations of oppression include institutional racism, overt and covert racism, malfunctioning institutions, unstable communities, and the instability of young people in crisis.

Element One of Oppression: Institutional Racism

One of the attributes of oppression experienced by Odie was institutional racism, a troubling characteristic of some schools serving American Indian students. Institutional oppression results from overt and covert racism and ignorance. An easily observed and tangible characteristic of institutional racism is the conscious and unconscious exclusion from the curriculum of American Indian history, culture, languages, literature, and other instruction relevant to these students' lives. Other less noticeable aspects are the absence or token inclusion of American Indian teachers, administrators, or school board members. Institutional racism is also reflected in school rules and policies that do not respect the culture or lifestyles of American Indian communities. Institutional racism can be embedded in what teachers do not know or do not do: the lack of pictures and displays of past or present American Indians or cultural-specific events in hallways and on bulletin boards and the lack of training and knowledge base of non-Indian teachers about American Indians or teaching American Indians. It is also reflected in the absence of "hard" money (such as local or state revenue that are not subject to cuts in federal program dollars) for American Indian staff or programs and the reliance of American Indian programs on "soft" sources (such as grants from foundations).

The absence of American Indians from the curriculum

Teachers interviewed for this book gave many examples of institutional racism in the schools in which they worked, particularly in the most noticeable area, the lack of culturally relevant curriculum. This was especially noticeable in public schools serving American Indian students. Carrie, a teacher in the Northeast, made the link that the lack of belonging many American Indian students feel in the school comes from the irrelevant curriculum, and this is a reason for lack of success:

◆ From a teacher's perspective, I can understand why they would be reluctant to come here, because even though we have a large population of Native Americans, we don't offer a Native American history course. We offer Russian history, Canadian history, and Maine history. But we don't offer anything for the Native Americans. So I find personally that the curriculum, for the amount of Indian kids here, is sorely lacking. We're basically bussing them into a white school, teaching them all of our history and our language and our culture, and then tossing them back out and expecting them to get a job and conform and be exactly like us.

One common reason given for the lack of American Indian content in schools serving these children is that the demands of American Indians to be included in the curriculum or decision-making processes of schools is perceived as special treatment. Some teachers ask these types of questions: "Why should we teach American Indian history? We don't teach Italian history, or Norwegian or Finnish history. Aren't we all just Americans? Shouldn't we concentrate on just American history?" This mistaken sense that everyone is equal and should have an equal voice is oblivious to the reality that little of what makes up schools is inclusive of its American Indian students. Another Northeast teacher, Pam, eloquently expressed the fear by some non-Indian teachers that catering to American Indians might be seen as special treatment:

◆ Questions come up to me in class, and I don't often know how to fend them off [about how] Native Americans want to maintain their culture, but yet also want other rights too, want to be separate, but yet want to be part. How do you draw the lines, and when do you stop drawing lines and say that everybody is the same? There are no favorites. There are no special privileges. I think that is probably the major crux in this area, and a lot of areas, is what people perceive as special treatment.

Element Two of Oppression:
Overt and Covert Racism

Although the voices of teachers provided many examples of institutional racism, they also told about the impact of overt and covert racism on schools, communities, students, and themselves. Overt racism is up-front, in-your-face racism. Covert racism is often disguised and difficult to measure. Racism can only be attributed to the oppressor because it is associated with power, something that the oppressed have little of. The oppressed, in turn, can become bigots or be prejudiced toward other races, but until they have power they cannot be racists. Overt racism is the blaming of the victims by conferring negative characteristics on a whole race of people. It is the dehumanization of human beings. The voices of teachers clearly and frequently described instances of past and current overt racism.

The American Indian teachers we interviewed all spoke of the racism they experienced as students. As I have, many of them used their own poor school experiences as impetus to change today's schools. They are the survivors in some respects. It must be acknowledged that they are part of a changing humanity in many of our schools. It also must be acknowledged that many schools are becoming more and more learner centered and are attempting to both embrace and deal with the issues of diversity. But change is slow, and it is no wonder that many parents of children attending schools today have negative attitudes toward education. More unfortunately, racism is not a vestige of the past. Although more people are aware of American Indian children's rights, racism is alive today, and it continues to damage both the communities all of us live in and the schools American Indian children attend. It continues to damage the children. One American Indian teacher, Al Zantua, described his feelings when he teaches his students about the struggle for American Indian treaty rights:

◆ It's really hard for me to use those books because they're so discriminatory. A lot of the testimony that's in those books, it tears me up, makes me angry— even the videos on reservation treaties and contemporary issues. You go back and you say, "That was my grandfather there that they were dragging through the mud in that fishing struggle. That was my uncle they were clubbing over the head." Then you think about it. You go out here on the river, and these white guys are still giving [us] a lot of hard times, "Oh, yeah, you think you're under treaty? Come here, chief!" And you're going, "Hey, we already fought this battle. You're wrong here." They don't know. They don't even know.

Overt and covert racism in the community

Racism in the community is not something solely noticed by American Indian teachers. It is also noticed by non-Indian teachers.

◆ Native Americans don't really seem to fit in anywhere. I was just appalled at how Native Americans were considered when I moved out here. I mean, to people outside of the res: "Native Americans are drunks . . . ." On the other hand, the border towns depend very heavily on the economic support of the reservation. If everybody in _____ stopped buying things in _____, _____ would close down, liquor, mall, groceries. Everybody, when they get

71

paid, goes to _____ and spends their money, no matter what color they are. There was an article about that in the paper a few weeks ago; somebody assessed the economic impact of people on the res going down to _____ and buying things. It really would create a tremendous economic depression in _____ if everybody stopped buying things.

—Ingrid

The type of racism described by this Southwest teacher is not confined to the large reservations of the American Southwest, as evidenced by Rachel, a teacher from the Northeast, who also points out that it reaches into the schools through some parents who pass it on to their children.

◆ One thing that impressed me when I first moved here was there's a lot of animosity towards the Indians because a lot of the land around here is owned by either Penobscot or Passamaquoddy through the land-claim settlement. For example, a student in one of my classes, whose father is one of the most blatant racists said, "Well, I'd just as soon shoot an Indian." I guess it doesn't matter where you live, there's always one group that's kept down. There are people whose children go here who feel like that.

If the issues of race were confined to the memories of American Indian teachers and parents and of racists in border towns, schools might do things to prevent them from seeping in. But schools are a microcosm of the community, and the memories of American Indians are something that cannot be forgotten. Moreover, schooling is something that cannot solely occur within the confines of a school building.

Overt and covert racism in schools serving American Indian students

Unfortunately, teachers and other school staff are only human beings and are subject to the same weaknesses as are all humans. People who work in schools can also be racist. When this is the case in schools serving American Indians or other people of color, everyone loses. In some schools, racism reaches epidemic proportions. In these instances, American Indian students, parents, and the whole race are blamed and condemned for most anything wrong in the school.

◆ A lot of the staff, and this does not just include the teachers—I'm talking custodians, maintenance men, receptionists, secretaries—they truly and sincerely believe that the destruction of this school, both building-wise and temperament-wise, is because of the Indian kids. They're resentful of them here. You get comments about how they're getting these big paychecks, and all they want is a free ride, and da da da da. "The government checks are in. They have no respect. They're the trouble makers." So there's a lot of negative attitudes toward the Indian kids. But it's not everywhere in the building. It's from the certain individuals that have made clear what their attitude is. For the most part, they encourage a lot of the negative things that happened because they're not willing to put aside their stereotypical beliefs, their prejudice. If they meet these kids with any sort of animosity, these kids react in the same manner.

—Carrie

On rare occasions, teachers will admit their racism without ever directly naming it. What was covert becomes overt. It will well up in the anger and frustration they feel toward the students and the community in which they work. One Midwest teacher described how her negative feelings toward American Indians had grown as a result of her teaching experience. She had come to teaching American Indian students with a good heart. Like most teachers, she loves children and wanted to be a good teacher. But she encountered student anger and mistrust of non-Indians and of schools. She was called a "white bitch" too many times to count. She experienced failure because her students sometimes did not come to school, did not participate in school when they were there, and seemingly did not care. Her anger grew out of frustration and mutual mistrust and because she believed she was a failure as their teacher.

◆ These people can get anything. They can get money for school just because they're Native American. And they can take advantage of so much. They could go to any school they wanted to, free ride. We give them everything that we've got as teachers, and all they've got to do is take it. And they don't. I don't understand it. But they kind of take it all for granted, and they don't spend the money on what they should spend it on. They spend it on booze. 90 percent of them do. They're wasting themselves. Then they complain that it's our fault. It's all my fault because I'm a white woman. I have to work my buns off to make $15,000 dollars working in [this] cruddy school. That's not enough to live on. Then you go out there and get yourself a education, and you could make more money than I do because they need Native American people everywhere. I can't get an even break, and they're constantly crying, "Oh, I just have it so rough, and people are so prejudiced against me." Bull shit. I know that what happened to the Native Americans shouldn't happen to dogs. But in another sense, what conquered nation has been given so much? It's kind of a sick thing to say, but when the Romans invaded all over

the Mediterranean, were the Jews given a reservation? No. When the Galls or the Jesuits or the Anglos or the Saxons invaded Britain, what happened to the Britons? They were turned into slaves, and they were not given nearly so much as the Native Americans have been given. Do they want us to educate them and help them become members of the world society? Or do they want to be enclosed and trapped on their reservations? If you really want to live your culture, then let's go back and take the houses off and help you reinstate yourselves into tepees and wigwams. If that is what you really believe is your culture, let us help you do that then instead of us building ramshackle houses on your properties that are going to get [wasted].

The only thing we can agree with regarding the above teacher's comments is that oppression may be a universal attribute of the human condition. The history of oppression, however, should not be used as ammunition to continue to oppress.

Element Three of Oppression:
Malfunctioning Institutions

Institutional, overt, and covert racism are not the only major issues facing American Indian students and the schools serving them. Other unresolved issues abound in the institutions serving American Indian children. The federal government's Bureau of Indian Affairs (BIA), which funds tribal schools or directly operates 180-plus schools throughout the country, is often blamed for many of the ills of American Indian education. If there is something wrong with American Indian education, the BIA is sure to take the brunt of the blame from tribes, Congress, and other sectors of the federal bureaucracy itself. The relationship between American Indian tribes and the BIA is complicated at best. Although the BIA is seen by many American Indians as an obstacle to any progress in American Indian education, efforts by Congress to significantly alter or eliminate its educational functions are often met with cries throughout American Indian country to allow it to continue its role as federal overlord of American Indian education. Yet the problems continue. The lack of adequate funding to operate these schools and the bureaucracy managing the money flow to schools, combined with decrepit school facilities in many communities, contribute to a long-neglected educational infrastructure. These problems contribute to a destructive cycle of upheaval and change of administrative policy at both the federal and local levels, making any long-term improvement plan difficult, if not impossible, to implement. All of this is not to say that the individuals within the agency are bad. Far from it. The Bureau of Indian Affairs Office of Indian Education Programs has some of the most talented, articulate spokespersons for American Indian children. But the system itself stifles and kills good effort. It is a mass of rules, regulations, policies, proclamations, declarations, and decrees, all of which are subject to change by Congress and the Executive Branch. It makes highly effective and motivated people seem ineffective and bureaucratic.

Inadequate BIA school facilities

Facilities at many of the BIA-funded schools are in an advanced state of deterioration and need replacement. Unfortunately, there is a large backlog of buildings in need of minor and major repair or replacement. Most tribes do not have their own resources to build new facilities or to keep existing facilities in even a minimal state of repair. Unlike most public schools, which can rely on a tax base to support capital projects through referendum or normal budgeting processes, most tribes have no tax resources to back the issuing of bonds to construct facilities. Congress has been reluctant to allocate sufficient funds for facilities because of the BIA's poor educational track record. The end result is that many American Indian children attend schools that meet few fire or safety codes. This is not to say that tribes have not committed a great deal of their own funds to building schools for their children. Some tribes that have gone into casino gaming have invested these resources into schools, including the Mille Lacs Band of Ojibwe and the Oneida of Wisconsin.

One Northeast teacher expressed her frustration with both the school facility and the policies by which it was run:

◆ I wasn't used to having to work on snow blizzard days when everyone else was off work. I was plowing my way through snow drifts to sit in a barren classroom that had no electricity in it because, as a BIA employee, I was expected to be there.

As we traveled throughout American Indian country to interview teachers, we came on nearly third-world conditions in some of the schools. High school students on my own reservation are being educated in dilapidated mobile homes. Students in another school (since replaced with a new facility) were using outhouses. In yet another school, I could see through a large crack in the gymnasium wall.

The overburden of paperwork

Wearing down every administrator we talked to was the burden of paperwork required by the BIA. One school principal considered returning to teaching because of this demand on his time:

◆ We're not instructional leaders; we're business managers. We run a school from the standpoint of regulations, policies, procedures, and then paperwork. If 90 percent of the paperwork that we do was done at a district level, then you could be instructional leaders. But the way the BIA is set up, and the way that the policies and regulations are set up, the money goes directly from central office to the school, so we have to do all the paperwork. I tell you, for the last four years, it's just gotten worse, and I want a change. I'm leaving; I'm tired. I'm going back into the classroom. I'm going to go back and teach. I want to get into teaching kids and not have to worry about all the policies and procedures.

—*Shobothteau*

The lack of continuity in leadership and policies on all levels

Continual shifts in policy and direction often hamper change. The BIA is not considered a change agent for innovative educational practices; it is more often accused of mandating changes from above without implementing change within itself:

◆ The government is pushing site-based management. And the Department of Education (Office of Indian Education within BIA) is saying, "Site-based management, site-based management." This [my school] is as far away from site-based managed as you can possibly get. BIA, it's all silly putty. If everyone up there that sends me a memo would come down and read a story to my kids, maybe my kids would learn how to read! So what are we wasting our time sending memos for? Fifty percent of the principals turn over in the Indian schools every year because of all the silly putty that goes on with papers. And I'll defy anybody to tell me what it means. So why do we do it?

—*Joseph*

Most teachers we interviewed had experienced frustration brought on by constant upheaval and change in leadership. Many questioned why they had entered the teaching profession and wondered if they had made the right decision. They felt alone in making important decisions about curriculum and what children need.

◆ There are too many other really annoying, infuriating things that happen; the place is always in a state of turmoil. It's been that way ever since I've been here. And I guess, considering the original reason why I went into teaching, when I look at this, I think that there are probably better ways that I could help people and feel that I was actually helping, [but] to help here I have to swim upstream all the time. The faculty changes so much, and maybe not as much as some other schools around, but it does change quite a bit. And there really isn't a curriculum. When I first came here and asked, "Would you give me a curriculum, so I can look at it?" The department chair laughed. It became very clear to me that I was kind of on my own, so I just tried to figure out what I felt the kids needed and did it. And that's really always what I've done.

—*Ingrid*

Lack of adequate funding of schools

The lack of funds for basic things, such as books, pencils, and paper, becomes a real issue in many of the BIA-funded schools because they are notoriously underfunded. A teacher in a small Northeast public school commented on how class size increases impact her getting to know the students:

◆ What's going to end up happening with those budget cuts is that student ratios are going to increase. They're already approximately thirty-two to one in a classroom. And if that happens I won't be able to talk to any of those kids. If you start talking to them on a one-to-one basis you get to know a little about their personal life. It turns them around. It shows to them that you're interested in them.

—*Carrie*

Friction between American Indian and non-Indian staff

Contributing to the problems in some of the institutions serving American Indian children is friction between American Indian and non-Indian staff. In most BIA-funded schools, non-Indians constitute the majority of the teaching positions because few American Indian teachers are available. Local American Indian people fill the noncertified positions, such as teacher aides, cooks, maintenance workers, and bus drivers. There is, however, a growing cohort of American Indian teachers and administrators.

Non-Indian Terri gave her perspective on the general mistrust she thought that the American Indian staff harbored toward the primarily non-Indian teachers

in one school. Her feeling was that it happened because the non-Indian staff did not live in the community and because of their high turnover.

◆ The Indians' distrust of the white man is legitimate. [The Indians] say, "Well they come and they go. We stay. We're always here. They drive in from [the city]. They leave. They're not one of us." So why should they trust us?

In some cases, it is not the fault of the non-Indian teachers that they are viewed as carpetbaggers. Some tribes have ordinances that do not allow non-Indians to own land on the reservation. Some non-Indian teachers feel the same uneasiness of being a minority when they attend community functions, such as sporting and cultural events. They feel excluded because they are non-Indian. They experience firsthand what people of color must experience all their lives—prejudice and bigotry and other aspects of oppression.

Element Four of Oppression:
Communities in Trouble

Up to now we have described the impact of racism (institutional, covert, and overt) and malfunctioning institutions on the education of American Indian children. To add to these problems, many of the communities these children live in are also in trouble. It would be simplistic to say that if all children came from healthy communities, they would all be healthy. In many cases, however, we know it would make a difference. It is acknowledged historical fact that European colonization wrecked havoc on the communities in which American Indian people lived. Today, the memories of this time are forever etched in the minds of many American Indian people. Many say that the losses suffered as a result of colonization were so great that people continue to grieve; that communities suffer from the effects of historic grief; that this grief is one of the self-destructive characteristics of the sub-oppressor.

The problems (alcoholism, drug abuse, poverty, crime, racism, class conflict, etc.) that trouble many American communities of all classes and colors also trouble American Indian communities. The teachers whose voices are heard in this book, however, identified several issues unique to the people and communities served by schools that American Indian students attend. Teachers felt a general mistrust of educational institutions on the part of many American Indian community people, including parents, and they acknowledged that the historic mistreatment of American Indians in schools gave good reason for such mistrust. Some non-Indian teachers felt the general mistrust of education was made manifest in negative attitudes toward non-Indians by some American Indian staff, parents, students, and community people. Many teachers also believed school-community politics, including nepotism, had an undue and troubling influence on the operation of primarily American Indian schools, contributed significantly to the frequent upheavals of administrators, teachers, and support staff, and caused constant changes in policy and direction.

The role of families in the education of children

The need for harmony and balance in the family was made clear by one American Indian teacher, who acknowledged what teachers all over this country have known for generations—that schools cannot solve all the social ills of society; that schools are simply a part of the communities in which they exist and manifest all characteristics of those communities; that families must play a critical role in the education of children.

◆ We think academics and the schools can solve everything. Actually education is only about 10 percent of a student's life. A lot has to do with the stability of the family. If you don't have that, you don't have anything. It's a lot like building a house. If you don't have the foundation, there is no way of putting the top together that it's going to be stable. An earthquake's going to come, and that building is going to come tumbling down. A strong wind comes, and that building is going to come down. The family is the one that is supposed to teach the responsibility, the discipline, the philosophy, the focus of that child. And if it is not there, we as educators cannot do anything. Unfortunately, our society here is on unstable ground as far as families are concerned. We have a lot of cases where the mothers and the fathers don't know what life is all about, and the kids start growing, not knowing what life is all about. The education cannot do a thing for them.

—Lena Mann

Mistrust of teachers and schools

To make the hard work of understanding cultural difference and acting on it even harder for both sides is a history of mistrust and misassumptions. As Therese Sullivan said of American Indians, "Their lack of trust has been beaten into them through circumstances, through their history, through their experience with the white man."

Because of understandable mistrust, the two groups view education differently. Ketron talked about the serious consequences for learning if historical mistrust is prolonged:

◆ For Indian kids, there's not an instant respect there for teachers. They'll test you to make sure that they know how much you know. Where non-Native kids are more trusting; they come in with this whole attitude that school is somewhere where you're going to go to, and it's part of the whole game that you play. Indian kids see it as a chore, somewhere where I have to go. It's kind of like the old reservation [boarding school] syndrome, it's somewhere where they're putting me. If the room feels like a jail cell or a hospital room or they feel uncomfortable in the room for any reason, they're not going to learn.

Many non-Indian teachers either observed or felt mistrustful attitudes in students. American Indian teachers saw the mistrust of both the schools and non-Indian teachers in the students they teach. They recognized the suboppressor, the oppressor within the oppressed, and saw it played out in anger. More important, they knew it was misguided and counter to traditional teachings.

◆ In a sense, we the victims have been the victimizers also, sometimes. We have had to react to the prejudice by being prejudiced. Some people have tried to justify the prejudice. Prejudice is prejudice.

—*Wayne Newell*

School and community politics

Because schools are a microcosm of the communities of which they are a part and because politics are so much a part our contemporary American life, politics are also manifested in schools. Sometimes outside politics influence what goes on in schools, and at other times internal politics plague schools, tearing them apart, contributing to low staff morale, or acting as the primary ingredient of the upheaval so common in some schools. In some instances, conflict is necessary for change; however, too much conflict can tear things apart. In schools serving American Indians, all of the manifestations of politics are present, with several notable differences. In some primarily American Indian schools, there is contra-preference against American Indian teachers and administrators, in which American Indians will not hire their own because of politics. It is a complicated characteristic of the suboppressor, in which the word of non-Indians can be deemed more worthy than that of their fellow American Indians and in which American Indians may be politically at risk with their job because of internal tribal politics. Sometimes, however, school-community politics result because the community is viewed as more important than an individual, and when an individual makes what non-Indian people would see as a success in life, the American Indian person is seen as separating from the community.

◆ I was told the Indian crab story. The crab theory applies very well because my Indian friend who's a teacher up in Cherokee had heard it, and I didn't understand it. If you normally catch a whole box of crabs, they will struggle to get out. That's how crabs function. Most of them will eventually all get out of the bucket. Well, with Indian crabs, the first crab starts to get out, and all the others grab its legs and pull it back down in so [that first crab] can't escape.

—Terri

In interviewing, we heard variations on this crab bucket analogy again and again, in fact so frequently that even the research assistant who was transcribing tapes told us, "One more crab bucket story, and I may be out of here!" A Northeast American Indian teacher said:

◆ But as far as the crab bucket, that has nothing to do with education. It's more in the politics of the tribe. If somebody happens to be doing something that someone else doesn't think is in the best interest of the tribe, that it's more of an individual gain, then they start pulling them back down. Sometimes that's tribal survival, too. Your first move should be in the best interest of the tribe as opposed to individuals. When people come home, they bring home those talents and gifts. Everybody in a way, it might take a while, but everybody benefits. I've been pulled down. I mean, everybody at some point has been pulled down.

There may be a link between the politics described above and the cultural issue of leveling described in Chapter 2, "Ways of Being." Sometimes it is difficult to determine the influence of culture on community politics.

◆ In other instances, it is simply raw politics at its worst—personal, vindictive, and mean. Today I am exhausted with what seems to be an unending clan battle. Double clan battle at one of the reservations. I just—it's like a forest fire. You think you've got it out and it springs up over here. And you get that one out and now it's over here. It plays out in the school system.

—Brian

There is no way this book can address all the issues of tribal politics, and perhaps the only thing that we can do is to make teachers aware of its reality. The sometimes vicious nature of tribal politics is another characteristic of oppression, an attribute of the suboppressor when the oppressed turn on their own. Further complicating these issues is that tribal scandals and internal conflicts often get extensive media coverage from the non-Indian press.

Nepotism

Nepotism in some schools is one of the reasons for the high turnover of administrators in communities. It is an area of culture conflict between many non-Indian and American Indian people in primarily American Indian schools because in small American Indian communities, nepotism is impossible to avoid; everyone is related. The rules on nepotism are necessarily different in some communities because it would be impossible to employ tribal people in any of the programs serving the community without it. But many non-Indians do not understand that, and it inevitably leads to conflict. Many non-Indians also do not understand the nature of tribal politics, which in many communities uses a spoils system. When a new tribal council comes into power, it is not unusual, and often expected, that a housecleaning of the most prized positions in the various programs occurs. These purgings are a regular but often troubling part of any community undergoing rapid social change because it is common for such communities to be sharply divided into various factions all jockeying for power. One Midwest teacher observed:

◆ People who were in power on the tribal council also put into place the principal, the administrator, and several of the other people at the school—some of the important people at the school. So there was a big change in the spring, and the person who was the administrator was on the wrong side, and the person who was the principal was the administrator's brother. We're talking nepotism in a big major way. Because of the fact that the administrator was not in good graces, they got rid of him right away, and that meant the principal was probably gonna go.

All of these issues of malfunctioning institutions have a negative impact on the effectiveness of schools to meet the educational needs of American Indian students. Moreover, their effects are cumulative and debilitating on the adults who serve these students.

Element Five of Oppression: Effects on American Indian Students

Finally we need to ask, what is all of this doing to a significant number of American Indian students? What becomes of students when history spills into the classroom? What happens to students when they are the targets of overt, covert, and institutional racism and all the vestiges of racism? What happens to students who are the products of malfunctioning institutions, from the federal level (BIA) down to local schools? What happens to the children who are the least conscious of why they are humiliated, who see and feel the remnants of oppression without understanding them? What happens when the communities in which these students live are out of balance? It should all be obvious. Painfully obvious.

We know that many American Indian students do just fine in any school setting, be it tribal, BIA, or public schools. Many of them are perfectly well adjusted. We know this because many of them (55 percent) graduate from high school. Many of them become working and contributing members of the community, but some do not because of all of the obstacles put in front of them. The Indian Nations at Risk Study (1991) suggested that the national dropout rates of American Indian students hovers near 45 percent and is even higher in many communities. American Indians rank far behind their non-Indian peers in standardized achievement scores (Quality Education for Minorities, 1991). Irregular attendance is an issue in many schools, particularly at the secondary level. But all of that is simply a meaningless collection of numbers, and it is not the intent of this book to cite table after table of statistics. For those who are interested, these data are readily available from the Office of Indian Education Programs, Bureau of Indian Affairs, and in quantitative studies and reports of American Indian students. We believe that numbers alone do not tell the human story that needs to be told, of the ones who do not make it or the ones who make it but leave school with a bitter taste in their mouths and with hidden injuries that travel with them for years. The voices of teachers describe what they see as anger, delayed adolescence, reactive-passive behavior, resistant behavior, a sense of hopelessness, an abnormally high number of students referred into special education programs, disturbing behavior, lack of essential skills, fear of success, poor attitudes toward education, low self-esteem, and perceived higher levels of fetal alcohol syndrome and fetal alcohol effects. In urban areas, there were additional teacher concerns about gangs and issues of identity.

Delayed adolescence

Although we have identified delayed adolescence, in which the internal struggle for identity continues well into middle age, as an issue with some, it was not readily identified by the teachers interviewed. It is, however, an issue in many American Indian communities. The pattern is for some American Indians to drop out of school as soon as they can legally do so and to accomplish little in terms of finishing their schooling or finding a career until their mid to late thirties. At that point, they become responsible, contributing citizens of the community. Some of the formerly young men I grew up with fit the characteristics of delayed adolescence. Some of them quit school at the legal age of sixteen, had problems with alcohol and drugs, moved a lot, and worked a variety of odd jobs. Many could not hold jobs be-

cause of alcohol abuse; nor could they maintain stable relationships. Some of them wandered in and out of treatment centers, training programs, and relocation centers (programs set up in large urban areas to serve people who moved from reservation areas). This self-destructive cycle continued for them until they were middle-aged, when those who survived the period settled down, maintained stable relationships, completed schooling or training programs, and became contributing members of the community.

Attendance issues

Poor attendance and declining attendance, a precursor to dropping out of school, are difficulties that upset teachers the most. It requires teachers to be innovative and flexible in their teaching.

◆ The only problem about teaching here is the students' rate of being here. Some students will miss fifteen periods in a quarter; they'll be gone quite a bit. So what we've had to do here is we've had to individualize their program. It's taken away me getting up in front of the class explaining how to do a certain type of concept because half the class will be gone and half the class will be here. And then a week later, the people that were gone would've missed last week's lessons. So we've had to individualize, which means the students have to do the work at a pace, and I kind of set a pace for them. [I] say, "Okay, you have three weeks to get this chapter done and complete this test." That way, I won't hold some students back if this student's missed. And I won't have to push some students faster because they miss so much time. I think it works out pretty well to individualize their program.

—*Bart Brewer*

Attendance issues become dropout issues, as attested to by the high (45 percent) dropout rate. It is an issue that needs to be viewed as part of the whole, to recognize it as something in which the individual, community, and school all bear some responsibility.

◆ But we all know that there are problems on the reservation. You can talk to any of the students here, and they'll tell you. I think that our society is changing, and we're losing kids so fast, dropping out of school and just tuning out the world. But especially you can see it with American Indians, just because I'm so close to it. I hear about it. I think they lost fourteen kids from the dorm this year. Some of them left for alcohol problems or substance abuse, and a couple of them transferred closer to home. Others have legal problems,

problems with the law. One student was in jail. He left before that happened. He dropped out from school. So I don't know what we can do.

—*Rachel*

Anger

What is happening to some of these students to cause such high rates of failure? Some of them are angry, full of frustration from all the bad that has happened to them. Anger is a reaching out for help. Anger comes from not having anywhere to turn when they need help. Sometimes the anger is something that needs to be named, so students can move on, so it does not delay them and weigh them down for their whole lives.

◆ She worked on her composure because she was really an outspoken, ready-to-knock-you-down kind of person. She always had a defense up, always had a wall. She was sexually abused when she was younger, and I got her to open up and talk about all that stuff. I said, "Now that's all in the past; what can you do now?" She goes, "Well, whatever tomorrow brings." And I said, "Yeah, tomorrow. Yesterday's yesterday. Tomorrow's always a new day." I said, "You can wake up and turn your underwear inside out and start walking tomorrow." She says, "Yeah." I said, "You can't go back to yesterday and turn them back inside out and walk the other direction." She says, "No."

—*Odie*

Sometimes it is just generalized anger; historic anger; centuries of anger that is passed down from grandparents to parents to children.

◆ I went to the meeting and just encountered incredible hostility. I mean, anger. Unbelievable anger. Not toward me. Just generalized anger. I mean, 200 years of anger built up. Here was a forum for Indians to speak out. More or less preaching to the choir, but there were a few non-Indians that went to it, I suppose with similar motivation as myself.

—*Brian*

Special education issues

People who work in the education profession know that students who become discipline problems are often referred to special education for services. Unfortunately, some special education departments have become dumping grounds for behavior problems. More unfortunate is the fact that American Indians and other students of color are most often those referred for special education. One of the reasons for

such high placement of American Indian students in special education has to do with culturally biased testing, a possible genetic hearing problem in some American Indian students, and an assorted collection of other educational and social issues.

◆ I've seen perversions of that [which] still amaze me, how kids are mislabeled, misdiagnosed, and I don't know if that's done through agenda or just through ignorance, but it still happens all over the place. When I was doing more psychological testing, that would be one of the first things I'd make sure. If a standard IQ is a measure of anything, it's a measure of verbal skills as featured by the white middle class community in this country. When it comes right down to it, that's what your verbal IQ is all about. The greatest single predictor of general IQ is the vocabulary sub-test. So if you're using that, you're mislabeling kids all over the place as mentally retarded.

—Norm Dorpat

Many educators assume that a higher proportion of American Indian students than non-Indians have either fetal alcohol syndrome (FAS), a combination of physiological, emotional, and learning problems caused by the mother's use of alcohol during pregnancy, or fetal alcohol effects (FAE), in which the physical effects may not show but learning or behavioral problems exist. The numbers have not been calculated in most instances, but it can be assumed that communities with more general social and economic problems (poverty, unemployment, alcohol and drug abuse) might have more instances of cases of FAS or FAE. We have to assume that FAS/FAE are issues in some communities and not in others. One reservation community (Fond du Lac Reservation in northern Minnesota) has eliminated FAS births entirely for four years by establishing an aggressive prevention program, but lingering problems abound in other communities and in the schools serving them. Nonetheless, to assume that many of the students have FAS/FAE would be to contribute to another negative stereotyping of American Indians. In addition, it is disowning the problem, as if all learning (emotional and behavioral) problems could be blamed on FAS or FAE. Educators might believe they can do little about the fact that their students cannot read because these children are FAS/FAE. All of these assumptions only serve to simplify a complicated situation. What needs to be accepted is that it exists, in unknown numbers of students, in many communities regardless of class or race, and that teachers need to be trained on educating students in their classrooms who have been diagnosed with FAS/FAE. Unlike the efforts of the Fond du Lac Reservation in preventing FAS/FAE, some perceive these problems as getting worse in their communities.

◆ The environment here is getting worse. It may look like it's getting better, but as far as the drugs and alcohol, it's getting worse. You can tell it by the kids, because of their behavior. I guess it started [with] the kids I got from first grade; they were terrible. Now they are in third grade. Alcoholism has always been here, but it is the younger generation now that are having babies at fifteen, sixteen years old. There is bound to be something wrong with your baby having babies that young, whether it's emotional behavior or whatever. But I'm not the only one that has noticed the change. Drugs came in about that time, in the last six years, cocaine and crack.

—Jenny

Passive-aggressive behavior

We found that many non-Indian teachers were frustrated by what they described as passive-aggressive behavior, an attribute we also described in Chapter 2.

◆ They're different as far as confrontations go. The kids here will seem to back away from it. They'll shut down or get away from the problem as fast as they can. If you confront them with work missing, you won't see them in school for a couple of days. It's as if they avoid the problem, thinking it will go away. Where in other places, the kids will become very defensive and get right back in your face, try to displace whatever it happens to be. Where here, they'll back down; they won't even deal with it; they'll try to avoid it if they can. That's the main difference that I've seen. Another school I worked at, I'd show them what they had, and they'd say, "Well, I turned that in," or, "Okay, I'll do that," and then they'll try to figure out a way to deal with it. Where here they'll try to avoid it and go on.

—Matt

Low self-esteem

Teachers described low self-esteem among many of their American Indian students and believed that it occurred for a variety of reasons. They also stated a need to be cognizant of it and address it as part of instruction. A Northeast teacher, Carrie, described how low self-esteem might manifest itself in the classroom:

◆ They know how to do the work, but if you give them an individual task, every five minutes their hand will go up. And it's not that they don't know how to do it; they just want reassurance. Because if you stand right there by the corner of their desk, they'll [go] right down through it and they'll get every single answer right. But it's just the uncertainty. You have to be constantly walking around the room, and giving them that verbal praise.

Powerlessness and hopelessness

For some students, there is both an overwhelming sense of powerlessness and a hopelessness in the future. There are just too many unresolved problems. Teacher Brad Hibbard poignantly described some of the issues that led to these feelings of powerlessness and hopelessness in some of the students in his school:

◆ In the last year and a half, five of my students have gotten killed by the gang violence. Not because they were even in the gang, but just because they lived where the gangs were. One of them was sitting in his house playing Nintendo with his brother, and in a shooting he got it, and his brother was okay, didn't get hit. When you get to know them over that period of time, it's a bigger loss than if you just had them in one class. When they have family tragedies, you have to be a little more for them, too. Because you see it weighing on them at school. And have to make adjustments to get them over it. I've never seen any group of people that had more tragedy to face than the Native population. It just seems to haunt them from one end to the other. Whether it's the system or alcohol or drugs or whatever; it's always something. I never really realized that life could be so rough. I was pretty well insulated when I grew up, I guess. I wouldn't want to be a teenager now.

Fear of success

In such a world, there is sometimes a fear of success. If there is little on the horizon to hope for, young people dare not think of being too successful because they fear the world will let them down again. So there is a need to work on small successes first.

◆ You really have to be careful. Because once they open up and they've had success, then if they reach a point where they can't have success, they shut down again. If they come to a point where they can't go beyond that. . . . You have to be careful about how you approach it with some of them, or they'll shut down on you. Small successes, small steps, and small successes over a long period of time. Give them something they can be successful at.

—Jane

Low school achievement

It is widely recognized in the academic community that American Indian students generally do not perform well in standardized achievement tests, and the reasons for this are attributed to the cultural bias of the test or the lack of student skills in basics, such as reading and mathematics. In some cases, teachers think that students have been pushed from grade to grade. One teacher articulated his belief and echoed what other teachers said:

◆ What bothers me is, if I give my students a rectangle that's two by three feet and they're supposed to find out what the square footage of the windows are in their house, they can't do it. None of them can do it. I know [teachers and schools] channel a lot of the low-level students in terms of motivation, kids who have been neglected up through the years and then passed when they couldn't read, [or] passed onto the next grade when they should've been retained.

—Thomas Smith

Issues of urban American Indian students

Inner-city American Indian students face different issues than most reservation students, and it deserves more space than can be treated in this book. Generally speaking, teachers believed that urban students had more difficult access to their traditional culture and were more prone to become involved in gang activity as a way to have an identity and self-esteem. Schools must deal directly with the gang issue, as described by one teacher:

◆ We have some kids that live right in the midst of all the gang violence. We've got some students who are involved in the gang situation, who are actually really bright students. I don't know if it's a reputation that they want to up-hold of being more of a gang member than a student. What the school says is, "This is a safe place to be." We have some Bloods that go to school here; we have some Crips that go to school here. For the most part they get along to-gether in the school setting. If somebody wears blue on a daily basis, we'll put them on a contract, and we'll say, "You're wearing too much blue. This is a safe place. You're going have to limit the number of days you can wear blue." Likewise if someone wears red on a daily basis, because those are the two ma-jority colors, we'll put them on a contract. We'll eliminate the intimidation factor. We've got some clothing that's banned at school, where students can't wear San Francisco 49ers stuff or L.A. Raiders or L.A. Kings. Because two years back, those were worn by a lot of gang members. We've basically out-lawed colors and articles of clothing.

—Al Zantua

Many thought that, because inner-city American Indians had less access to their culture, schools needed to provide those connections to bring them pride and identity in the power and beauty of their traditions.

89

◆ The inner-city Indian is not like the reservation Indian. They have to go through more struggles down here than they do up there. They see the iron walls instead of the beautiful, whereas you can just go up [on the reservation] and live your culture every day. Down here they can't do that.

—*Odie*

Case Study

The case "They're Acting Really Squirrelly" provides some insight into both the complex issues plaguing schools serving American Indian students and the multiple issues that contribute to the failure of schools, homes, and communities to deal effectively with students in trouble. It shows the real impact of racism and malfunctioning schools and also the self-destructive characteristics of suboppressor behavior on two individual students.

They're Acting Really Squirrelly

Dale had been a science teacher at the Big Lake secondary school for just over three years. Depending on the situation, time of day, day of the week, or time of the year, it felt like he'd been there for a century. It was a decent enough school, Big Lake High, located in the lakes and woods country of northern Wisconsin. The district of Big Lake served just over 800 students, 335 of them attending the grades seven to twelve secondary school. Big Lake was a decent enough community of 1,006 souls, a community that survived, when other communities had failed, because it had a thriving lumber mill and a good summer tourist trade. It survived also because of the growing economic influence and government jobs brought in by the Forest County Ojibwe Reservation bordering the primarily non-Indian community of Big Lake.

The school's student body was a reflection of the community. The students were nearly an even mix of Ojibwe and non-Indians, with the Ojibwe student population growing every year and the number of non-Indian students declining, as families moved south to Madison and Milwaukee for better jobs. Each school year, Dale noted an increase in Ojibwe students, as the Forest County Tribal Council (FCTC) added housing complexes and business enterprises, such as a casino, restaurant, gas station, and a bowling alley. Recently, the tribe had one of its members named to the Board of Directors of the Big Lake Citizens Bank—a first—and a local Ojibwe (and Big Lake High graduate) became the town's Indian police officer—another first. These and other signs indicated to Dale the growing influence of the tribe, accompanied by the growing uneasiness of the town's aging non-Indian power structure, one of whom had been overheard at a local cafe complaining that it ". . . won't be too long now before them Indians take over everything."

For the most part, the Ojibwe students seemed to be very much like the non-Indian students he encountered on a daily basis. They seemed like typical secondary students. There were Ojibwe and non-Indian jocks and cheerleaders, Ojibwe and non-Indian druggies, and Ojibwe and non-Indian nerds. Some of them were heavily involved in school activities, with one student in particular, Rich Bender, recently elected president of the student council. Others were the shadow side of the Rich Benders of the world, particularly a group of Ojibwe girls, led by Jessica and Marila, who kept Dale and other teachers on edge by continually skipping classes, being disruptive when in classes, and conducting a reign of terror on other students.

The principal, Bill Stevens, usually had to call Jessica and Marila into his office three or four times a week. He made a point of doing it every morning during Jessica and Marila's first period science class, after reviewing the teachers' disciplinary referrals and drawing up a list of names for Milly, the hall monitor, to retrieve for conferences. Because Jessica and Marila were in the same section of eighth grade science, they always went to the office in tandem. It seemed they rarely ever spent a full period in Dale's class.

"I need your little darlings," Milly bellowed as she shooed the pair from the classroom. "You ain't going to be seeing these two again today because they're going to end up with a day in ISS (in-school suspension)."

Dale knew what this was all about. He had reported the pair skipping school the afternoon before, when he had seen them while he walked across the street from school to do some business during his preparation period. Milly told the pair what her visit was all about.

"It seems Mr. Bird saw you two hiding in the Laundromat on his way to the bank yesterday during fifth period. Aren't you two supposed to be in phys ed, or was phys ed held at the Laundromat?"

Marila laughed. She always laughed. Jessica looked at Dale with her patented sneer, one she must have practiced every day in the mirror because it combined elements of surprise, disdain, and humor.

"Geez Dale, why did you have to narc on us?"

Then she looked at Milly. "We ain't going to that Miss Krupp's class because she's a b - - - -," said Marila. "And we ain't wearing them gym clothes she tries to get us to wear. She's a queer too. Always looking at us in the locker room. She just stares at us."

Milly shot a look at Marila and said, "You watch your mouth and be more respectful. I should take you in the bathroom and wash out your mouth with soap."

Milly always said that to Marila or Jessica. She had never followed through with it, and she never would.

In his three years at Big Lake, Dale had heard everything at least twice, and few things shocked him. He finished chewing on a pen and looked over toward the pair, saying, "You two don't have any business in the Laundromat during the school day. Whether you like it or not, phys ed is a required class. If you don't like the gym clothes Miss Krupps has to offer you, bring your own."

He turned to Milly, "Take these two to the office. I have a science class to teach."

Jessica mumbled something under her breath, as she was being led out of the room, about not "sitting in that f - - - - - - ISS room all day." Marila laughed and offered her wrists to Milly as a gesture that indicated it was time for her to be cuffed and escorted to serve her time. Dale looked out the window at the approach of winter. It was only October.

He spent the rest of first period working with his eighth graders on a frog unit. He used cooperative groups in his classes as much as he could, and the students seemed to really enjoy it. Even Jessica and Marila seemed to enjoy working in groups when they were in class.

At about 1:00 PM, Bob Moyority, the school's ISS supervisor, sent a note down to Dale, which was delivered by Milly. It read, "Those two lovelies you saw hanging out in the Laundromat yesterday ended up here with me, and they aren't going to last up here the rest of the day unless I get some work for them to do. They'll either walk or I'll make them walk. They're acting really squirrelly."

It was Dale's preparation period, so he gathered up some science worksheets and took the slow climb up the stairs to the ISS room, which was a room of windowless cubicles located off the old band room. At one time they were a series of three practice rooms, but they had been converted to a single ISS room after a decline in the number of students joining band or chorus and an increase in the number of discipline problems. He opened the door and approached Moyority, who was helping a student with an assignment. Moyority motioned him outside the door, warning the five students in the room to "keep your flippers to yourselves," and "don't leave your seats." They knew that if they were sent from ISS, it was an automatic three-day suspension from school, and most of them didn't want that.

"I think Jessica and Marila are on something. They've been giggling constantly since they came up here. I keep warning them to be quiet, but they just won't quit. I think they should be sent home. It's like they are high on something. They sure as hell aren't going to last in here."

"We ain't high," shouted Marila, who had been poking her head out of the ISS door. "You're full of s - - -, Molar Teeth," referring to Moyority with the name students only called him behind his back. "Let's get out of here Jessica," Marila motioned to Jessica, and they both walked out the door, down the stairs, and out of the building.

Dale sighed and walked back down the stairs to his classroom. He knew he wouldn't be seeing either of the girls in his class for another three days because now they were suspended from school. It was like a Catch 22, he thought. These students should be in class. It was the only way they were going to learn from their schooling. Half the time they were either skipping school or sitting in ISS, which was more like a holding pen than anything else. Now they were suspended. Jessica especially seemed so bright, and Marila needed to be consistently in class to really benefit from it. It just seemed like such a waste of potential, time, and effort on everyone's part.

Just before the end of his preparation period, Dale took his customary walk through the halls to the soda machine, which was located up near the ISS room. He came on Milly, the hall monitor, who chided him on the afternoon being "too quiet without those two lovelies." He poked his head into the ISS room to drop off some work for the other students there. Moyority was reading *Sport's Illustrated*. The three remaining students, who had long ago finished their other schoolwork, were asleep with heads on their desks. Numerous graduate summer session lectures about "time on task" and "teachable moments" ran through his head. He sighed, shook his head slightly in disgust, and closed the door.

He returned to his classroom and looked out the window toward downtown Big Lake and the town Laundromat. There on the street corner in front of the Laundromat, smoking cigarettes, were Jessica and Marila. They each smiled and waved at him, and he waved back. With that formality completed, they put their cigarettes out on the sidewalk and walked into the Laundromat. Later he saw them get on the school bus with the rest of the students. A part of him wanted to intercept them, to tell them that he wanted them in his class, that their success in school was important to him, that their success as students was important to his success as a teacher. But it had been a long day.

The next day he came to work as usual and went into the office to check his mailbox. In the pile of junk mail was a phone message from the school secretary, which read: "Mrs. Whitehorse called and she was quite angry. She said the school suspended Marila because Bill Moyority and you said she was high on drugs. She said she took her daughter to the public health clinic after Marila had come home and complained about being falsely accused of being on drugs. She says the doctor found *no* trace of drugs in her and that she was going to see Indian legal assistance about this."

Dale looked out the window of the office. It was one of those gray October mornings in northern Wisconsin, and the cold wind was pushing leaves against the corners of curbs and old brick buildings that collectively called itself downtown Big Lake. Overhead, a flock of geese were making their way south.

"Take me with you," he whispered. "Take me with you."

Case Discussion

1. What are the issues facing Jessica and Marila? What is the school doing about these issues? What could the school do?
2. What can individual teachers do to make school more successful for students such as Jessica and Marila?
3. Do you see any overt, or covert, institutional racism or suboppressor behavior in this story?

Full Circle

There is a need to return full circle to where we began this journey—with the elements of oppression. What happens to these young people? Many become victims of oppression, exhibiting suboppressor behavior or suffering from the oppression of others. They drop out of school; they graduate with few skills; they become angry; and they lose hope. They simply survive.

But many, in fact, move beyond all the wrong they have endured. They move beyond surviving and live purposeful, hopeful lives. They become, as said by one American Indian school administrator, "livers":

◆ You can never forget who you were. You cannot ever forget where you came from. The past is there, and you learn from the past; it should influence everything you do. I think, if you're a survivor from your past, that means that many things have controlled this. You are going to carry on that resentment from that. I think one of the hardest things to do is to forgive. The opportunity [is] there to forgive.

—Mike Rabideaux

Moving beyond surviving is something many of the American Indian teachers in this book have done. They moved beyond the oppression they experienced and did not let it burden and destroy their spirit. They moved beyond the suboppressor and did not become an oppressor of their own people but became models for their students, not solely as survivors but as American Indian people who live hopeful, purposeful lives. To be a "liver" is to not let the suboppressor destroy the inner self, not to be consumed by anger or alcoholism or drug abuse or all of the other self-destructive attributes of the suboppressor. To become "livers" is a triumph of the human spirit. It is the triumph for a growing number of success stories throughout American Indian country.

How can teachers lessen the effects of oppression on students? Teachers should build trust in their students by demonstrating in their actions and behavior that they are worthy of trust. They should be fair and consistent in their treatment of students. They should become knowledgeable of the people and issues in the American Indian community, as well as get to know their students on a personal level by assessing where students are on Maslow's hierarchy of needs. Teachers need to refer students to the school counselor and work with them to help students become "livers." They shouldn't be afraid to go to the homes of their American Indian students to meet and confer with caregivers. Teachers should seek the advice of others in effective ways of dealing with passive-aggressive and resistant behavior in students. Teachers need to encourage parental support and involvement by having a written parental involvement plan. Teachers should be able to recognize the attributes of institutional and overt racism in their schools and become active participants in eliminating racism. Teachers should be mindful of the tendency to refer a disproportionate number of American Indian students for special education services.

Finally, how can teachers protect their own well-being and dignity so they can effectively deal with all of the remnants of oppression they might encounter in schools? Teachers, especially first-year teachers, should focus on students. They should find ways of achieving harmony and balance in their own lives.

Things to Remember

1. There is a direct relationship between historic oppression and many of the troubling issues facing contemporary American Indian people.
2. There were five elements of oppression identified by teachers:
   - Institutional racism, or the lack of significant American Indian representation in the staffing, curriculum, or decision-making processes of schools
   - Overt racism, the ongoing discrimination, name-calling, blaming, and stereotyping of American Indian people

◆ Malfunctioning institutions, from agencies of the federal government and state departments of public instruction down to some local schools. This may include American Indian/non-Indian friction, upheaval, and constant change in policies, direction, mission, and staff, the lack of money, and poor school facilities.

◆ Communities in trouble, including the usual array of issues common in many communities (crime, drug and alcohol abuse, poverty, etc.) and some issues that may be unique to American Indian communities. This self-destructive behavior is characteristic of internalized oppression, or what we call suboppressor behavior.

◆ All of the above elements are having a serious detrimental effect on some American Indian students, who have some of the nation's highest school dropout and lowest attendance rates, and generally have poor school achievement compared with the majority culture.

References

Indian Nations at Risk Task Force. (1991). *Indian nation at risk.* Washington, DC: Office of Education.

Quality Education for Minorities. (1991). *Education that works: Quality education for minorities.* Washington, DC: Quality Education for Minorities.

Zinn, H. (1980). *A people's history of the United States.* New York: Harper and Row.

Creating a
Two-Way Bridge

Being Indian in a
Non-Indian World

I, Thomas Peacock, often have difficulty finding a relationship between my home life on the reservation and the workday world of the university. The need to be shifting back and forth between my reservation persona and my professional academic persona can be difficult and tiring. The university demands that I be the American Indian expert. I am expected to interpret and translate all that is American Indian; I am expected to know everything there is about tribal life, from our religions to casino gambling and treaty rights. I find myself answering questions ranging from which season is appropriate to tell Waynabozho (the Anishinabe teacher and trickster) stories to which slot machines at the reservation's Black Bear Casino are hot. Considering academia's demands of me, it is easy to understand why I often relish the evening drive back home to the reservation, where all my professional degrees are meaningless, and where others believe that who I am as a person is more important than what I do for a living. Yet every weekday morning I make the drive back to the university, and I do so because that part of me is also

important to who I am as a person. I enjoy the intellectual stimulation provided in academia. The French Impressionists inspire me, and I must admit to playing Ravel's *Bolero* while driving to work on an occasional autumn morning. So these things from the majority culture are also an important part of my soul. But it is home on the reservation and with my own people that I feel the most comfortable. It is at the summer pow-wows that my spirit is renewed. It is in my ancestor's sacred places that I pray.

From my own personal experience, I know that finding comfort levels in both worlds is critical to my own sense of well-being. I do not, however, buy the assertion of some that it is possible to feel completely comfortable in both worlds. The bigotry and racism I experience as an American Indian in majority society—and my own mistrust of many non-Indians and the society they represent—will always negatively influence my comfort level while in majority culture. Conversely, it is sometimes difficult to live in my own reservation community. Although I am completely comfortable with my reservation persona, I cannot share the academic part of my persona with many reservation peers for whom the academic world is foreign. So when I unsuccessfully try to communicate the academic part of my persona, I suffer from an accompanying sense of loss.

I was not surprised when both American Indian and non-Indian teachers interviewed for this book thought that the most important attribute contributing to American Indian student success in majority society schools was the ability to manage in both American Indian and non-Indian worlds. These teachers recognized that students need to feel comfortable with both worlds and need to possess the necessary skills and attitudes to move in and out of these worlds without sacrificing their American Indian ways. Examples of this are provided by the American Indian teachers in the book, whose lives exemplify both their ability to be successful in the dominant culture's academic and work environment and their ability to retain their American Indian cultures, values, and languages.

Questions to Jump-Start Your Reading

To enter into reading this chapter with a strong sense of your own experience connected with the chapter's content, think about a time when you found yourself in a place that was not comfortable.

1. What made you uncomfortable in that place?
2. Did you feel like escaping?

3. Did it become comfortable?
4. If so, how did it become comfortable?

These are the types of issues facing many American Indian students as they move between their culture and that of majority society.

A Chapter Road Map

We begin this chapter by reminding readers of the historical basis for the metaphor, "bridging two worlds" and link it with discontinuity (Chapter 2) and the elements of oppression (Chapter 3). A profile of Wayne Newell, a Passamaquoddy teacher, provides context for some of these issues. Next, we consider the challenges students face in finding a comfort level in both worlds, and the resultant challenges for teachers, schools, and policy makers, offering American Indian teachers as successful examples of the bridging of two worlds. We then argue for the need to move beyond metaphor and to be proactive about these issues. A case study, *The Storyteller,* highlights the struggle of a young man to retain his American Indian ways in a predominately majority culture school.

Making Connections with Other Sections of the Book

There are obvious links between the ability to feel comfortable in both worlds and the other issues raised in this book. In Chapter 2, we described both the obvious and the more subtle differences between mainstream schools and the homes of many American Indian students, and we also discussed the students' attempts to negotiate between the differences. This requires that American Indian students find a comfort level with the obvious sorts of differences and also with the more subtle cultural differences, such as perceptions of time, values, worldviews, and ways of expression, learning, and being. To help students negotiate these differences, teachers must seek ways to make their classrooms feel more relevant to American Indian students. Moreover, the teacher needs to become the learner and find a comfort level of knowledge with the students' cultures.

There is a traditional basis for being able to live successfully in both worlds, because being able to do so is part of the harmony and balance traditional American Indian people seek in their lives, something we described in "Ways of Being"

(Chapter 2). To feel alienated or not a part of one world, or both worlds (as in the case of anomie), is to be emotionally and psychologically out of balance.

There is an obvious historical connection between these cultural issues and the history of Indian–white contact. The history of American Indian education is replete with examples of the attempts by the federal government, missionaries, and later public school systems to strip tribal people of their cultures, values, and languages. Sun Chief, a Hopi, described the effects of this in his autobiography (Deloria, 1982):

♦ As I lay on the blanket I thought about my school days and all I had learned. I could talk like a gentleman, read, write, and cipher. I could name all the States of the Union, with the capitols, repeat the names of all the books of the Bible, 100 verses of Scripture, sing more than two dozen hymns, debate, shout football yells, swing my partner, and tell dirty stories by the hour.

It was important that I had learned how to get along with the White Man. But my experience has taught me that I had a Hopi Spirit Guide, whom I must follow if I wish to live, and I want to become a real Hopi again, to sing the old songs and to feel free to make love without fear of sin or rawhide.

 A Profile

Wayne Newell reminded us in Chapter 2 about the tenacity of culture, that despite the all-out efforts of the federal government and churches, American Indian cultures have survived. We chose to profile him in this chapter because he is a successful individual who has found balance between his Passamaquoddy culture and the school in which he is a teacher. Newell struck us as inherently complicated and wise, a person who is not just a respected Passamaquoddy language and culture teacher at Indian Township School in northern Maine, but who is also a respected and acknowledged traditional person in his community and throughout American Indian country. He has also lived successfully in the non-Indian work and academic environment, possessing a master's degree from Harvard University and being in a doctoral program at Boston University at the time of our interviews. Fate has led him to accept his own physical limitations. He is legally blind; nevertheless, his vision for Passamaquoddy people, indeed for all people, was eloquently clear. While he described his journey in the American educational system, he acknowledged the utmost importance of also knowing who he was as a Passamaquoddy and continuing his struggle to ensure the Passamaquoddy culture is given due attention in schools.

◆ One of the things I've always believed in is there's a place within the [educational] process for continuing affirmation and enhancing of the culture and the language and the belief systems and the spirit of our people. There has been no place in the journey thus far that has affirmed any of that aspect of it. We have to tug and fight to get any attention. There's been little semblances of what I call tolerant activities here and there. But there's never been a full embracing of it. I just happen to think that there is a real place for it. Because on the one hand, while I'm describing all of this to you, this is my journey in the white man's educational system. On the other hand, there's been a parallel journey in terms of the passing of the culture that my grandmother gave me. And there are elders. I like to hang out with elders. And one of the reasons that happened has something to do with that I love stories. So I'll remember all the stories they told me about our mythology and about our creation.

The key to producing successful American Indian students in our modern educational system, he believed, is to first ground these students in their American Indian belief and value systems. Only when this is done will these students and the communities from which they come find success in the schools. Newell recognized that the problems within the community were in part because American Indian people have been trying to solve their problems within the context of the majority culture's ways.

◆ The pressure is [that] they have to get these kids ready for the outside world, and I'm sure you've heard that a thousand times. That's the predominant BIA philosophy. BIA didn't invent it; it was a missionary philosophy. And it only took one generation, and then what we did was to perpetuate it ourselves. That's right. You raise a generation that think predominantly [majority society] ways, and they will educate the next generation. It works the other way around, and that's the thing that we have been missing. We have been trying to solve our community problems from the white value system. It's so simple that we never thought that maybe the solution is doing them according to the strong values within ourselves, and that if we do a good job in this generation, then the next generation will take over. Then and only then—and this is a real strong belief—can we actively say, alright, now we're supposed to be joining the society. This is our criteria. Right now we have no criteria.

Newell told of the impact of historic oppression on the Passamaquoddy culture, language, and value systems and of how many believed the Passamaquoddy

spirit had died. In describing this era, he told of the indomitable strength of culture, of culture being something so deeply imbedded in the people that it was not destroyed. He talked of a powerful personal experience, a personal awakening of sorts, in which he realized the importance of finding balance and living his culture.

◆ What people didn't understand is that those boarding school terrorists thought that it [culture] could disappear in a generation, and they would have white-thinking children. They couldn't erase it, and therein lies the hope. Right there. And when that spirit is reawakened it is more powerful than anything that I have ever met in my whole life. I am impressed with the strength of culture. Even though the missionaries tried, the boarding schools tried, all the well-intentioned little white people tried. . . . And we tried, because we became like the conquerors. But something hasn't died. My first response is it's not dead. Yes, lots of people had the culture dead and buried a long time ago. Even us. Even us. I mean, we were the biggest helpers of that. Our own stories, for example, our beautiful mythology, we took it and conformed it to the church. All of a sudden when somebody has a supernatural experience, they go to the priest and chase away all the evil spirits. Most of those spirits aren't evil. They have a purpose.

Lutskaf is a good example. Lutskaf is our helper. Today when we ask people to translate him: "Who's Lutskaf?" Well, the liar. When you look at the language structure, Lutskaf is the bearer of the great truth. And when that spirit is reawakened, and it's within our own language, you've become a whole new person; you're alive again. And I remember one time, and I'll share a real personal experience with you, and I don't care if you write it because it was so powerful. I was in a sweat lodge. It wasn't the first time. I mean, I've been in sweat lodges, but it was the first time I had a profound experience. And I don't know what it was. I was in the right place and whatever, and the person that was leading the prayer—because a sweat lodge is a purification ceremony—and the first time, and I'd heard these words before. At least, I'd heard them physically, but I didn't hear them totally. [The person was] talking about being in our mothers' womb, because that's what a sweat lodge represents. This is the womb and the mother earth; we're in it. All of a sudden, there was a connection between that and something. I didn't know what it must have felt like in our forming stages, because you know we are entities by then. We just don't remember it. But we are living creatures, and all of a sudden, there was a big void. All of a sudden, I just . . . the words came out in my own mind, you know, it was a real comfortable thing. And I knew then that for the rest of my life that would be the basis for whenever I am feeling destroyed or unbalanced. I would go back to that moment and use that to energize my life.

Challenges Facing Students as They Seek a Comfort Level in Both Worlds

There are difficult challenges facing students as they seek a comfort level in both their tribal world and that of majority culture. This was illustrated in a canoe/boat metaphor told to us by several of the people interviewed for the book. It had different versions, but the message was essentially the same. Here is Dennis Bowen's version:

◆ I think that saying "living in two different worlds" comes from an age where people thought that we were the vanishing race, that we were going to be no more. That saying came from the time around the 1800s—1880s or 1890s, and that saying was introduced to say, "Condone the destruction of our people." Our own people now hold that up as a motivational speech, and they always quote Sitting Bull: "Take the best from both worlds and make a good life for your people so they can live." A lot of the Native American teachers [that I talk to] say that, and they don't see beyond that; they don't see that the teaching was once used to confuse our people. And the teaching that was shared to me that we hold onto is that you can learn another culture, but instill yours first. That's similar to language; you can learn two languages, but you need to start with your home language first. So that's very crucial. Because when you live in two worlds, the first time you have a problem at your home, at your job with your co-workers, with your teammates on the sports team, with your classmates in the classroom, you're straddling that way. It's the analogy that the white man has their boat. We have our canoe, and we're traveling on this river and we can be neighbors, but if you are a person that has a foot in each boat you're going to come to a rapids, and you are the one we're going to lose. We are going to bury you and have a sad funeral. It's going to be painful for all of us. So stay in your canoe; it's okay to understand how that other boat was made and what they do, but you have your place here. It's almost like you have to keep your one foot—the weight—in one [boat]. I would like to see us outgrow that thinking, that two-world psychology that we're laying on our kids. And yet it has no meaning to them.

Non-Indian Brian Smith used a sailing metaphor and soon found out he shouldn't be stealing American Indian metaphors.

◆ The Indians call it feet in two canoes. Matter of fact, I used the canoe analogy a couple of times, and one of my board members came to me and said,

103

"Brian, you should not be using Indian metaphors. You should come up with your own. That makes you look suspicious."

Of course they can do it [bridge both worlds]. Question is, do they want to do it? I think that's the bigger question. Native Americans, they had it all. What was going on here in this real estate 250, 300 years ago, in terms of complex social interactions; there were some wonderful things happening. And it's been bastardized by the superimposition of somebody else's value system, and language, and economic ideology. Well, we raft sailboats [tie them together] all the time in sailing. I was a sailing instructor. You have nice cleats and you have good lines. You have bridges [ropes] that hold those two boats together, but your feet are still in two boats.

American Indian and non-Indian teachers are trying to find new metaphors to give them direction. In most all of them is a concern for the retention of culture.

The Loss and Strength of Culture

The fear that American Indian cultures were in danger of extinction was a common thread of the teachers who were interviewed. Priscilla Day, an Anishinabe and an assistant professor of social work at the University of Minnesota-Duluth, commented that up until now educators have been telling American Indian students to bridge both worlds without first assuring that the students were grounded in their own cultures. This kind of bridging, she thought, was just another way of telling them to learn the non-Indian's ways because all the while they were learning to survive in the world of non-Indians, there was no parallel educational journey into learning about and surviving in their own world. The consequence of this was a continuing loss of American Indian culture in these students. Moreover, she believed it is American Indian people who must learn the other world. But what about non-Indians learning the cultures of indigenous people? What about the teachers of American Indian students learning about the histories, cultures, values, and languages of their students? "About this bridging two worlds metaphor," Day said, "Why does the bridge always have to be one way?"

Priscilla Day's concern over the loss of culture is not solely an issue of the American Indian people; it is an issue of colonized people all over the world. In every indigenous culture of the world colonized by western Europeans, the pattern of cultural loss has been the same:

◆ We should add that he [the colonized] draws less and less from the past. The colonizer never even recognized that he had one; everyone knows that the commoner whose origins are unknown has no history. Let us ask the colonized himself: Who are his folk heroes? His great popular leaders? His sages? At most, he may be able to give us a few names, in complete disorder, and fewer and fewer as one goes down the generations. The colonized seems condemned to lose his memory. (Memmi, 1965, p. 102)

In some schools, it is American Indian parents who are the biggest obstacles to the teaching of culture in schools. Some of them came from the boarding school era and were programmed to believe American Indian people must forget their American Indian ways and become assimilated into majority society. Other parents remember their own pain of trying to live in both cultures without being totally accepted in either; they do not want their own children to experience the same rejection. Others believe culture is better taught at home, and that schools should emphasize traditional academic subjects. Teachers need to be cognizant that the issue of teaching American Indian cultures or languages in schools is not just an issue debated by those who work in schools, but is an issue in American Indian communities as well. Barry Dana, a Penobscot culture teacher in the Northeast, described how parents sometimes do not see the importance of culture or recognize its intrinsic strength:

◆ The parent might say, "Well, they don't need to know that anyway." It might be nice, but it's not important. Because when you go to the shoe factory, when you work down in Bangor Mall, you work in the real world; your culture is not critical to your survival. But to me, it's critical to our self-preservation as a people.

Anne, an American Indian teacher in the Midwest, made a link between the anger and accompanying aggressive behavior found in some American Indian students and the lack of knowledge in their traditional ways. She believed that anger and aggressive behavior are symptoms of a lack of harmony, and that sometimes students confused being angry and being American Indian.

◆ Students with attitudes, students who are very aggressive because they've learned to be aggressive, are aggressive to the teachers but also to each other. If many teachers are reading these books and learning that the Indian student is a bashful, quiet student who sits behind in the classroom and doesn't say anything, that isn't quite the case. They're very verbal; many are very verbal, very aggressive, and some don't have the values that traditional people do have because of the changes in our lifestyle.

Cultural Loss and Its Link to Tribal Prophecy

The fate of tribal cultures was sometimes foreseen in prophecies by the spiritual people in American Indian communities. For Arlene, an American Indian teacher from the Southwest, learning to live in both worlds and teaching her students to be successful in both worlds is something that is as important for her own being as it is for her students. It is a part of what she was taught by her father, a traditional person of her nation.

◆ I come from a very traditional background. Both of my parents do not speak English. My father always told us that we are moving forward, and you have to get the education in order to survive. You have to get the educational skills. That was pounded into us, and I went from boarding school to boarding school, hardly ever seeing my parents. But my dad was always coming around whenever he could. I used to go to a dormitory school up in Richmond, Utah, and my father would hitchhike all the way up there just to see us and to say hello, to see how we were doing. He was very concerned. My father is a medicine man and they prophesied, just like they do in an ordinary religion, and he told me things he foresees, that he was told would happen. He knows what will happen, that we will eventually lose our religion and our language, and he tells us these things. He says the only way we will survive is to get us that education. His belief is that eventually we will not herd sheep, that it is in the prophecy that we have to merge. And for that reason he pushed all of us to education. He said there is no turning back on this. That's the way it is. The way the Bible says we will keep going until the world ends. Kind of the same theory that you will keep going until we are a conglomerate of people, until there is nothing pure; we are all going to mix in. We might as well start by getting our education, so we can all survive, all of us. The biggest message he was sending to all of us was that his way of survival was different from ours, but if you have the basis for survival, you can [survive], and education was survival.

Bernita Humeyestewa, the Southwest teacher who was taught by her grandmother about ceremonials and strength, also knew the importance of her students knowing the non-Indian world. It was important so the young could return to take care of the elders. She spoke of her grandmother:

◆ But she had this belief in her that some of the older Hopis did, that some day the future generation should come back and take care of them. And the only way we're gonna succeed in the future is to learn what the Anglo society is. Their language, their values, their way of life, so that we can help our people adapt to that when changes start coming.

106

The Effects of Peer Pressure on Tribal Cultures

There was consensus on the part of many of the teachers, American Indian and non-Indian, that the outside influences on American Indian students might be overwhelming. The pressure to conform and be like everyone else, to be like the people they see on television and in the movies, the pressure to not accept the American Indian part of their being, has been leading to the further loss of culture.

◆ It's going to be interesting to see whether this generation, the kids we're teaching now in high school, whether those kids are going to have any culture left at all, whether their grandchildren will have any at all. Because television is everywhere, even in places where there is no wired-in electricity. People have generators, or they hook up to the car battery, and they run televisions. Or they have satellite dishes. You can drive outside of town here and see hogans and satellite dishes. So television is everywhere, and everybody wants to live the MTV life. The kids don't want to live in a hogan when they see what a condo looks like or a house in whatever they perceive L.A. to be. Well, I think it's really true, things that I've read about. That if you don't have any language or any kind of cultural roots at all, you suffer for it. And the more the Native American kids leave here and go, the more they get distanced from it, too. If it doesn't get stopped in this generation, I think it's going to be a memory by the time these kids have grandchildren. Unless there's a really strong aboriginal movement among people all over the world to try and keep these things alive.

—Ingrid

It is not like some schools are not trying to integrate American Indian culture into the curriculum. In some cases, high school students just aren't interested in learning it. There is intense peer pressure, for all students, to conform to the group. Moreover, some students lack the maturity to see any relationship between their American Indian cultures and their lives. Teachers should not be surprised if this is an issue in their American Indian students. One teacher, Kay Lasagna, described her school's futile efforts:

◆ I gave a pretest on Sioux culture to my students, and 94 percent of them failed it; they knew little or nothing about their culture. I was given some federal money to start a culture center, and I couldn't get any of them interested in a cultural center or participating in it. They were interested in the same things other kids were interested in; they were interested in cars, in dating, in the school dance that was coming up, in the basketball game on Friday night. And their background just wasn't that important to them.

107

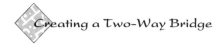

The Importance of Students First Being Grounded in Their American Indian Culture

Other researchers confirm the need for American Indian students to be grounded in their tribal cultures and the schools' responsibility for assuring that students are grounded. Van Hamme (1996) cited several recent studies (Estrada and Vasquez, 1991; U.S. Department of Education, 1991) that indicate how schools that acknowledge, accept, and teach a child's cultural heritage have significantly better success in educating these students. James et al. (1995) found tribal cultural identity highest among successful American Indian students. One of the outside reviewers of a draft of this book noted, "More and more research shows that the Indian student who is 'grounded' in his/her Indian culture has lower absenteeism; dropout rates; higher test scores; and is more likely to advance to higher education and return to their own tribe valuable knowledge and skills both needed and wanted by tribal elders and leaders."

An American Indian teacher, Lena Mann, agreed that American Indian students who were grounded in their culture did better in schools because they had a basis for school content before they even entered school. Knowing who they were as an American Indian person made it easier for them to feel comfortable with the non-Indian world. They knew the purpose of things, the whole of things.

◆ If a child comes from a parent who is knowledgeable in the old traditional ways, the kids will be more successful. Probably because they have a basis for things. For instance, when I took philosophy at college, it was not hard for me because I already knew the things. The same thing with lasers in physics. In our philosophy, our elders talk about lasers. They talk about plants as medicine. I knew all that; the only thing was that I had to make that name with it, so things kind of fell into place with things that my father told me.

Traditional children do better because they have a mother language, something that they can hang onto. But the child in-between, he doesn't really have anything. For instance, a laser might be foreign to him because he never heard the legend. I was told about our ancestors fighting with lasers. Our legends involve the moon, how the moon moves certain things. We know about the different qualities of the stars and how it relates to the months. So when you know all of that and you go into science and they start talking about all that, all you need is to translate the English name to what your father called it.

Our younger generation was never taught that, so they're groping around, like learning something brand new, nothing to hang on to. So that makes it hard for them. That's why some other tribes are completely lost, because they have lost the basis; they have nothing to live for, nothing traditional, no education. But somehow they need to pull together. We have something to live for.

The Need for Early Instruction in Tribal Cultures

Teachers believed that helping American Indian students become grounded in the tribal cultures needed to be done in schools and communities early on. Patty Houghton, an American Indian secretary/aide in a Northeast school, summed up the feelings of many American Indians in her community:

◆ If you start young, which they are doing now, and give them a strong sense of their culture, and their identity, and their history, I think they can take some of that in the outside world and use it. It would help them; it would be to their advantage. To me, you have to know where you come from. It's always interested me, who my relatives are, the struggles they had to get where they are, and how they dealt with the environment and got along with other tribes.

Challenges to Teachers, Schools, and Policymakers

Teachers, schools, and policymakers that accept the responsibility of helping their American Indian students become grounded in their tribal cultures must often decide how this can best be done. How can they balance the teaching of "culture" with the teaching of traditional academics? Furthermore, can they teach American Indian students to live in both worlds in segregated American Indian school settings?

Culture and Academics

Teachers in our research believed there was an ongoing struggle between recognizing the need to have schools teach American Indian culture while also teaching what most educators perceive to be academics—mathematics, science, reading, and writing. Although all teachers realized the importance of teaching American Indian cultures, most American Indian teachers saw it as an imperative, essential part of the school. Non-Indian teachers were concerned with both their ability to teach American Indian cultures and the appropriateness of tribal cultures being taught by non-Indian teachers. There was also concern that culture belongs in the

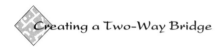

home, that schools cannot be held solely responsible for the survival of cultures, that parents and communities needed to accept their share of the responsibility, and that partnerships needed to be made between the community and schools to ensure a proper job is done in the teaching of culture. A real concern of some of the teachers in tribal and BIA schools was that they possess little knowledge of a tribe's culture, but are required to teach it. Their training was in strict academic disciplines, and it was comfortable to teach what was familiar to them.

◆ I would like for the community to buy into our own part of what we as educators in the school are supposedly trying to do, and that is bringing the culture back to the children. As a non–native American, I respect what is trying to be done, but I think it just can't be done solely within the classroom, school environment. We have to have the involvement of the community in order to pull that one off.

—Jane

The struggle between academics and culture was not an issue spoken of only by non-Indian teachers. Some of the American Indian people also acknowledged it. Mike Rabideaux, a school administrator in the Midwest, thought it was a real issue at the tribal school in which he worked.

◆ Culture is a very hot topic, not only in our school but other Indian schools. We have a responsibility to educate our children, our Native children, in academics. If we don't arm them with academics, then we're cutting out one very important component of their overall education. That's the way we have to look at it. Now with the culture, the culture is as important. It is.

Can We Bridge Both Worlds with Segregated Schools?

There was some concern by a few teachers that primarily American Indian schools may be more harmful for American Indian students in the long run because they would not successfully teach the students to live in both worlds. In these schools, they said, students were sheltered from the "real" world. It may be comfortable for students, these teachers thought, but in the end these schools were causing more harm than good. Patrick Pytte, from the Midwest, summed up the feelings of this small segment of the teaching profession:

◆ I think it's a real mistake, in my opinion, to have separate schools. I think that's something that we should get away from. That's just isolating them in their own particular group, and I don't know if that's good because they're only doing it in school, but then you got to go out into the world and you got to face all the other good things. I don't think it's a real world for them there, and sooner or later they're going to have to come out into this world and how they adapt then I don't know.

It wasn't solely non-Indian teachers from the public school sector that saw danger in segregated American Indian schools; Mary, a teacher in a primarily American Indian school, had similar thoughts:

◆ I think that's one of the problems that we have working at the reservation is that it's total starvation. I mean 97 percent are Native American. I just feel like we have to expose our students to other people because the real world is not just Indian people; it's only 1 percent of the U.S. population. So I really tried to instill that in my students, that the school that they're going to at the time is not indicative of what it's going to be like the rest of their lives. Even if they stay on the reservation, they still have to be a part of the white dominant society and also be exposed to other races.

American Indian Teachers as Models of Being Grounded in Their Tribal Culture

Many of the American Indian teachers we interviewed are successful examples of individuals who are grounded in their tribal cultures and able to function successfully in majority society. Bernita Humeyestewa believed American Indian culture could be valuable in the lives of her students for its own sake. She also acknowledged the strength of culture in her own life, of how it gave her purpose and meaning. This is the example she herself was setting as a role model for her students.

◆ When my grandma was alive, she used to give me a lot of advice and things. And I never went back on anything she advised. If it was a ceremonial and she said "do this," I did it. Like going to the altar and praying for strength; I did it. When I was younger, I really didn't understand what it meant. But as I started to grow older, I found out that there's a certain kind of strength that comes from those kinds of moments. And right now in my life, especially during ceremonials where there's prayer involved and where there's the offering of cornmeal involved, that's like a cleansing for me, and at the same time it's a gaining of strength for me. And then during summertime, in the summertime we do a lot of farming. And when we go to our fields, we will pray

111

every day that we are working in the fields. I sing to my corn. It's just little things like that. They have my culture in with it, and that is renewing and also strength-providing at the same time.

American Indian Teachers Who Find the American Indian Part of Their Being

The American Indian teachers raised in traditional environments provided the best examples of those successfully finding balance between the two worlds. Wayne Newell is an example of this, as are teachers such as Lena Mann, Arlene Masayesva, and Bernita Humeyestewa. But there are also American Indian teachers who were raised in dominant society environments. Somewhere along their educational journey, they discovered they could not have balance in their lives without learning the American Indian part of their being. These teachers are a true testament to the need to find harmony and balance to be whole.

Mike, a Midwest American Indian teacher, learned about his Indianness as a result of racism directed against him in a predominantly majority school. He did not truly discover the other part of himself until well into adulthood.

♦ I started visiting the rez because I heard that it was kind of a wild community. Maybe I started listening to the kids. Maybe some of the teachers had said, "You know, you're acting like an Indian. You know, you're acting like some of those wild people from the rez." I heard that. I thought, well, I've got to go see. Wouldn't you know it, I couldn't even get along with people out here. All of that awareness is only very recent. It's when I was twenty-eight or twenty-seven, and started taking classes at _____ that changed me. Because they had an Indian program. That's the first time I became aware. I didn't know anything about reservations. I didn't know any of that. But that program at _____ changed all that. That college experience was the first time that I became aware of being Indian, other than all the negatives.

For the mixed-blood American Indian, acceptance in either world can be difficult. They must know who they are from both perspectives and be able to deal with rejection from both worlds. They must deal with the inevitable conflicts because they are part of two worlds.

♦ It's always been important to me to know where I come from. It's just useful. All knowledge is useful, and the more you know about yourself and your culture and your society, the better you're going to be. I'm not a traditional full-blooded Indian. It's hard on the reservation. Then [again] I'm also Indian in the white world. It's kind of hard from both perspectives. But I have a strong family, and I know where I'm coming from, and I feel good about myself. So I've always felt comfortable about myself no matter which situation I'm in. There's conflicts in both worlds, but I'd rather just take it in stride. But it is hard. Because I'm really not a full-blooded Indian according to the reserve Indians. And I'm not a full-blooded white according to the whites.

—Bart Brewer

Moving beyond Metaphor

Bridging both worlds has been used as a metaphor to describe the need of American Indian students to find a comfort level in both their own and the majority culture, to be able to move in and out of both worlds, to shift gears, so to speak. It also could be seen as a metaphor for the true self-determination of American Indian people. For those who have been both participants and witnesses to the regeneration of tribal cultures, to be a part of the cultural and spiritual awakening throughout American Indian country in the past quarter century has been inspiring. There has always been a recognition in many tribes of the deep strength of culture, of its ability to heal the emotional, psychological, spiritual, and physical parts of people. There has also been a recognition of its ability to foster harmony and balance by giving purpose and direction to life. That is the spirit Wayne Newell spoke of, and it is worth repeating.

◆ And when that spirit is awakened, it is more powerful than anything that I have ever met in my whole life. I am impressed with the strength of culture.

That American Indian culture could not be killed in boarding schools is something noticeable to non-Indians as well.

◆ It's kind of like watching the Phoenix rise from the ashes, the whole drama of the Native situation—everywhere, actually. I kind of like to think in terms of the death and dying, the seven stages of dying, only in this case at some point, they realized they weren't going to die. And so instead of going through the last few stages, they're picking themselves up, and they're using the system for their benefit.

—Brad Hibbard

The second metaphor used in this section of the book has been the canoe/boat metaphor, the need for American Indian students to have a foot in two canoes at the same time, but to have their full weight grounded in the tribal culture so they can successfully have an unweighted foot in the majority culture. **Metaphors are meaningless** unless their visions are fulfilled by action. The key to bridging both worlds and riding in two canoes without ending up in the drink is to move beyond metaphors and to ensure they are realized. This can only be done by making conscious decisions, by ensuring that schooling gives these students the tools to bridge two worlds and the balance to ride in two canoes at the same time. It can only be done by collectively deciding what needs to be done to ensure the success of American Indian students in contemporary society. It can only be done by making conscious decisions now that will affect these students' future.

Gary Zukav's book, *The Seat of the Soul* (1989, p. 29), offers one way to view this issue by suggesting that making conscious decisions today will impact and determine our individual and collective future:

◆ The decisions that you make and the actions that you take upon the earth are the means by which you evolve. At each moment you choose the intentions that will shape your experiences and those things upon which you will focus your attention. These choices affect your evolutionary process. This is so for each person. If you choose unconsciously, you evolve unconsciously. If you choose consciously, you evolve consciously.

Like individuals, cultures have a collective consciousness, shared perspectives, shared outlooks, shared sets of values, ways of doing things, and ways of being. Collectively, as tribal communities, if they choose to enter the future consciously, they will determine what that future will be. The same is true for teachers and schools.

In practice, teachers can help ensure a two-way bridge between the cultures by becoming a part of the American Indian community, by attending community social functions such as pow-wows, feasts, and other community events. Teachers may need to initiate their own involvement in this regard. Moreover, teachers need to have knowledge of the American Indian community, the people, situations, relationships, and community issues. In the classroom, teachers can integrate culture into their classes and help their American Indian students to find a place in their tribal cultures. Amy, an American Indian teacher in the Midwest, helped her students identify their clans. Teacher inservice on American Indian cultures can add to teachers' knowledge base about American Indians. Inviting elders and American Indian role models into schools and encouraging American Indian students to become involved in extracurricular activities or sports are other ways teachers can help students bridge both worlds. Non-Indian children must learn about and respect American Indian cultures before a true two-way bridge can be opened. Finally, teachers should recognize when cultural loss is a real issue and acknowledge the issues of some American Indians in trying to live in both worlds.

Case Study

"The Storyteller" is about an American Indian high school student, Ron, who helps organize an American Indian Week at the primarily majority society school he attends. The case provides insight into the minimal attempts of many schools to integrate American Indian content into their curriculum and of American Indian students' struggle to negotiate between and live in both worlds.

The Storyteller

I.

The Wakefield High School Native American Club had met during lunch recess and decided to plan an "Indian Week" at Wakefield High School in early February. Some of the club members scoffed at the idea, proclaiming that because Wakefield High had a majority American Indian population, **every** week should be American Indian week. But for the most part, the club members thought it would be a good way to put some "Indian-ness" in the school. The week would consist of a series of events, and members were given specific organizational tasks. Jenny Shaugobay would ask Mrs. Columbe, the home economics teacher, if they could use the kitchen area to hold an Indian taco sale. Indian tacos were made with taco filling on fry bread and constituted a serious meal. The taco sale was a good idea for two reasons: It would raise money for the club's spring trip to Valley Fair (a suburban Minnesota amusement park) and would also introduce the staff and students of the school to a favorite Red Cliff meal. Julie Loons would ask her older brothers, members of the Makoonce Bay Singers, to perform a song and dance demonstration for the entire student body. Ron Andrew's job would be to find a traditional storyteller to speak in several literature classes. Jenny, Julie, and Ron would meet with the principal to secure his approval to hold the events.

Ron knew it would be approved by Mr. Angell because the principal had in the past shown genuine concern for the well-being of the Indian students and had openly acknowledged the growing economic and political influence of the Red Cliff community in the area.

"If he says no, we'll have a walkout." Everyone laughed. Everyone was serious. It was a classic example of Indian humor.

That day after school, Ron walked down to the LaPointe Store, the only store in Red Cliff, and bought a small pouch of Prince Albert tobacco. The clerk, the daughter of the owner, was a classmate of his at school.

"You ain't old enough to be buying tobacco products, Ronnie." She winked as she handed him the tobacco and change. He just smiled and walked out the door. He wondered about that wink all the way to his Uncle Eddie's house.

Uncle Eddie lived in the hills above Red Cliff in an old house that had been built during the Great Depression. Like Ron's yard, it was decorated in modern reservation art—a refrigerator that had been converted into a fish smoker, an old wood stove, several old pickup trucks, and long-abandoned rabbit pens. Eddie's old dog "Chief" (named after Robert Parish, formerly of the Boston Celtics) flopped a nervous tail as he greeted Ron's entry into the yard. Ron approached the house and knocked on the door.

"Bin di gaan (come in). Nu bi da bin (sit down)."

"Hi uncle. How are you doing?"

He always talked to his uncle in a soft and gentle way, a respectful way.

Eddie motioned Ron with his lips to have a chair. Ron smiled and accepted it, taking off his coat and hat and laying them next to the chair beside him. Before he sat down he handed Eddie the pouch of tobacco, saying:

"Uncle, we're having an Indian week at the school in three weeks. We were wondering if you could come in and speak to a couple of classes and tell Indian stories and stuff like that?"

Eddie sat back in his big old chair and eyed Ron with bemusement.

"What kind of stuff? You want me to tell stories about all my old girlfriends?" He was laughing. "They'd probably kick me the hell out of there if I did."

"You know, Indian stories. Some of the stories you've told me about what it was like a long time ago and stuff like that."

Uncle Eddie was fingering the tobacco. He was so proud of his nephew but could not let himself show it. He remembered all the times he had reminded Ron that when he wanted something from elders and traditional people, be it advice or assistance, to offer them tobacco. He also knew that the request could not be turned down.

"Sure, why not." Eddie got up and poured Ron some tea into a former jelly jar. "You want a commod (U.S. Department of Agriculture food commodities) peanut butter and honey sandwich?"

"Uh huh."

II.

Ron was able to schedule Uncle Eddie into his American literature class. The other class, English literature, was too consumed with Shakespeare, according to the teacher, Mrs. Enger. It was decided to publicize the storytelling period in the weekly bulletin and open it up to any high school student interested. They would need to get passes from their regular period teachers.

Every time he saw his uncle for the next three weeks he reminded him of the day, room, and time his uncle was to come to the school. On storytelling day, Uncle Eddie showed up at the school a half an hour early. Ron was called down to the office to meet his uncle.

"I don't believe in Indian time," Eddie laughed. There was that familiar twinkle in his eye.

Eddie was dressed the part of a storyteller, with a beaded vest and tobacco pouch hanging from his belt. His hair was slicked back and he smelled like English Leather. He had on his Sunday go-to-church shoes.

When the time came, Ron walked with his uncle down to Mrs. Enger's sixth period American literature class. With the ringing of the bell, they waited until the classroom was empty and then entered. Ron introduced Eddie to Mrs. Enger, and she proclaimed how wonderful it was for him to come in and share his stories with the students. After the introductions, she excused herself to go into the classroom next door to borrow some chairs for the extra Indian students she knew would be attending the class that day.

"She ain't bad," winked Uncle Eddie.

Ron just rolled his eyes.

Soon the classroom was filled with over forty students. Mrs. Enger introduced their guest.

"Today, students, we have Edward Bainbridge from Red Cliff. Mr. Bainbridge is going to tell us some traditional Ojibwe legends as part of our celebration of American Indian Week here at Wakefield High School. We are extremely grateful he volunteered to do this for us today. Mr. Bainbridge is one of the few remaining Ojibwe storytellers in the area. He deserves your respect and your complete attention."

She emphasized the last sentence and looked toward several noteworthy class troublemakers.

Uncle Eddie stepped forward. From his front shirt pocket he pulled out the pouch of tobacco his nephew had given him. He looked at the tobacco the whole time, never once looking directly at the class. He explained how his nephew had approached him to come into the school and tell stories, and how he had offered the tobacco and how important that was. He went on to explain that after he had told the stories and left the school he would offer some of the tobacco to the animals and spirits that live in the stories. The class was pin-drop quiet when he said that.

"Now I am going to tell you about the plant-beings," he said, and the story began:

"Plants were here on this earth before our elder brothers, the animals, and before humans. They can exist without either animals or humans. All the plants, like all the animals and humans, have their own unique soul-spirits. It gives them their form. It allows them to grow. When they get ill or injured, it allows them

117

to heal. One of the most wonderful things about plants is that they can join with other plants and animals to form a larger spirit. When we say a place has spirit, that is what we mean. When we say a place is sacred, that is what we mean. It is the spirit of a place. Each one of the Apostle Islands out there on Gitchi Gummi, what you call Lake Superior, possesses a spirit that reflects the state of being of that place. If the soul-spirit is peaceful, the island is peaceful. It **feels** peaceful. If it is angry, the mood of the place is angry."

Uncle Eddie was fingering the tobacco. Never once did he look directly at the class.

"I can prove this to you. If you destroy a part of a sacred place, a special place, the mood and spirit of that place will not be the same as it was before. If you cut down the trees or pick all the flowers, the mood and spirit of the place will change forever. All of us, you know, we have special places where we go when we want to think and to be with Gitchi Manito, God. They are sacred places. Even you white people have these places, even though you might not think about it the same as we Indians do. Think about that. That is why the plants are so important to the Ojibwe people."

He then told the students about some of the different plants and how the Ojibwe used them as food, medicine, and in ceremonies. He told them the story of when rabbit ate all the roses, and how that affected the balance of things and how all the animals that depended on roses were harmed. And in telling the story he explained how the rabbit and the rose came to be as they are today.

With the exception of Matt Girard, Ron noticed that most of the students listened intently to his uncle. Matt was one of the students Mrs. Enger had specifically looked at when she told the class about expecting respect and attention. Matt would occasionally make faces and smile over to his friends, and Ron couldn't help thinking about what he'd like to do to him after school.

When Uncle Eddie was done telling the stories, he was given a polite round of applause. Because it was only five minutes to the bell, Mrs. Enger let the class visit, "quietly," she emphasized, and thanked Eddie for such a thoughtful and fascinating presentation. Ron saw his uncle talking to Mrs. Enger and felt so proud of him. But he also noticed Matt Girard was laughing with his friends and he overheard him saying, "That was stupid. Why did we have to listen to that old Injun dude anyway?"

With the ringing of the bell, Ron walked his uncle to the door of the school and thanked him for coming into his class and sharing the stories. As he walked down the hall with his uncle, he noticed how many students stared at them and he wondered what they were thinking. It just wasn't too often that an elderly Indian man came in to the school, especially one dressed in traditional attire. Ron was also thinking about what he was going to say to Matt Girard as soon as he saw an opening. What he wanted to **do** to Matt could wait until the weekend, when Ron was in town and would settle with Matt off school grounds. He knew his parents would kill him if he got suspended from school for fighting.

With the ringing of the dismissal bell, Ron bounded from the school to await the exit of Matt Girard from the school building. He'd mention something to Matt before he got onto the bus. Because Ron had a reputation amongst his peers for "taking no prisoners," when Matt saw him he immediately sensed he was in deep trouble.

"You're getting your a- - kicked, Matt," Ron said matter of factly as he strode past him.

"What you going to do that for? I didn't do nothing," stammered Matt.

Ron stopped and pointed to his intended victim. His face was twisted in rage, and it felt like all the blood in his body had risen to his head. He was so angry he could hardly talk.

"You . . . are going . . . to get . . . your f- - - - - - - . . . a- - kicked."

Matt turned to several of his friends, pleading that he didn't do anything. He jumped onto his bus.

Friday passed and the weekend came.

On Saturday night Ron made a point of going into town with several of his friends in search of Matt Girard. He knew he would find him because Matt wasn't too bright and wouldn't know well enough to lay low. He caught up to him outside the Pier Restaurant and satisfied the ego of his shadow side. Matt was left with a fat lip, bloody nose, and wounded pride. Ron felt pretty cocky.

III.

On Sunday mornings in Wakefield there is a custom for many community people to go to the Pier Restaurant for breakfast after church. That particular Sunday was no exception. Although Eddie wasn't a churchgoer, breakfast at the Pier was his Sunday ritual. There he would gather with his old friends and they would talk about the old times, of fishing and of the latest gossip. On this particular day, one of the waitresses told him about his nephew.

"Your nephew Ronnie Andrews was down here last night, and I heard he beat the hell out of some other kid."

Eddie was disappointed, and it showed on his face. It showed in the way he ate his meal because much of it was left in the plate. And when he got up to leave, he couldn't help but think about what, if anything, he was going to say to his nephew.

At first he thought he wouldn't say anything. Ron didn't have a reputation as a bully, and there must have been a good reason for what happened. Then again, he knew that this wasn't the first time he had heard about his nephew's fighting. He wondered if he should say something to his brother or to his sister-in-law. He wondered these things all the way home, and when he got home he wondered it some more.

On Sunday evening, Uncle Eddie showed up at Ron's house like he did every Sunday night. On Sunday nights, Ron's mom, dad, and his uncle would sit around the kitchen table and visit. His mom always served some kind of dessert, usually chocolate cake and red jello with whipped cream. It was an old family tradition. This Sunday was no different.

On these evenings, Ron liked to listen to the adults as they told stories about their adventures as young people growing up in Red Cliff. Always there would be teasing about their "wilder days," especially between the two brothers.

When it was becoming late, Uncle Eddie stood and yawned like he always did, picking up his pack of cigarettes from the table and putting them in his shirt pocket. As he put his coat on and got ready to leave, he turned to his nephew and spoke to him. All evening he hadn't said much to Ron, and that had made the boy wonder what was going on.

"I have something for you to read," Uncle Eddie said, digging in his jacket pocket. He took out a book.

"I've been reading this Momaday book and I think you might like it, Ron. It's filled with all kinds of Indian stuff."

Eddie laughed softly. His eyes were serious.

Ron took the book and thanked his uncle for letting him borrow it. After Eddie left, he took it into his room and set it on the lamp table.

His first intention was to go immediately to sleep because it was getting late, but he decided to page through the book to see if it might interest him. It wasn't all that unusual for Uncle Eddie to offer books to people to read after he was done with them. It was unusual for him to offer one to his nephew.

As Ron was paging through the book, he noticed one of the pages was folded over. It was the only page in the book where an ear had been folded over as a marker. Page fourteen. And he opened it and saw a sketch of an Indian man, and written above it Momaday told of "The Fear of Bo-talee:"

◆ Bo-talee rode easily among his enemies, once, twice, three—and four times. And all who saw him were amazed, for he was utterly without fear; so it seemed. But afterwards he said: Certainly I was afraid. I was afraid of the fear in the eyes of my enemies.

Case Discussion

1. What impact might the ability to live in both worlds have on Ron's success in school?

2. What conditions and issues in the case affect Ron's ability to live in both worlds?
3. What role do tribes, communities, parents, schools, and teachers have in helping Ron be successful in both worlds?
4. What role does the school have in teaching Ron his American Indian culture and language?

Full Circle

Unfortunately, many American Indian students struggle like Ron with issues of being successful both in school and in their tribal communities. Likewise, I sometimes face the same dilemmas. One of my younger brothers came to my house to borrow some money while I was writing this chapter. I knew that loaning him the money was one way I could help him bridge his life on the reservation with the reality of modern-day living. He noticed me feverishly pounding away on the computer and asked, "What [are] you doing?"

"Writing a book."

"Oh."

That word "oh" said it all, because, although I was able to understand his reality, he could not do likewise to the academic part of my persona. Although I have begun reporting my research findings in articles and at lectures in front of various academic and educational audiences, I need to tell the same story to my brother in ways he can relate to—someone who sees the reality of reservation life in front of him and lives every chapter from this book on a daily basis. This bridging both worlds thing is difficult and something I will never feel completely comfortable doing. And sometimes the bridge only goes one way.

Things to Remember

1. A primary ingredient of American Indian student success is the ability to live successfully in both the American Indian culture and the majority culture.
2. The examples of this ability are provided in American Indian teachers, who have lived successfully in the majority work and academic environment while retaining their American Indian cultures, values, and languages.

3. The key for American Indian students to live successfully in both worlds is to first be grounded in their American Indian culture. This grounding is best when it begins at an early age.

4. American Indian students who are first grounded in their American Indian culture exhibit fewer at-risk behaviors, such as academic difficulty and social, emotional, and psychological problems.

5. American Indian students, particularly at the secondary level, are under the same intense peer pressure to conform as all adolescents. Their American Indian culture may not be a priority during this time.

6. There is internal debate within some American Indian communities about both the need for schools to teach American Indian culture or languages and the schools' ability to effectively do so.

7. There is ongoing debate about whether schools can or should teach American Indian cultures, whether schools should emphasize academics over culture, and whether the existence of primarily American Indian schools may run counter to the need for students to bridge both worlds.

8. Tribes, communities, parents, schools, teachers, and the students themselves all share responsibility in helping students to be successful in both worlds. This responsibility must be consciously acted on to enable students to live hopeful and purposeful lives.

References

Deloria, V. (1982). Education and imperialism. *Integrateducation,* Special edition, 58–63.

James, K., Chaoez, E., Beauvais, F., Edwards, R., & Oetting, G. (1995). School achievement and dropouts among anglo and Indian females and males: A comparative examination. *American Indian Culture and Research Journal, 19* (3), 181–206.

Memmi, A. (1965). *The colonizer and the colonized.* New York: The Orion Press.

Van Hamme, L. (1996). American Indian cultures and the classroom. *Journal of American Indian Education, 35,* 21.

Zukav, G. (1989). *The seat of the soul.* New York: Simon and Schuster.

Issues of Native Language

In some respects, the tribal language loss evident over several generations in my own family reflects that in many American Indian homes. My Ojibwe grandparents were the products of federal boarding and missionary schools in which speaking the language was strictly forbidden. One of the methods of indoctrination in these schools was to tell of the evils of speaking Ojibwe and practicing the culture. This led my grandparents not to teach these things to their own children—my parents. In terms of Ojibwe language use, my parents were part of a lost generation and were not fluent in their tribal language, even though they retained many aspects of culture. With the spiritual and cultural regeneration beginning in the 1960s, my brothers, sisters, cousins and myself sought ways to relearn and reestablish the language. In a frantic attempt to make up for the loss, many of us from my generation sat in Ojibwe language classes in droves, learning to say all the basic animals, counting to ten and beyond, saying hello, and memorizing frequently used phrases like, "Daga sagaswayzhun?" (Do you have a cigarette?). One of my fondest childhood memories is of listening to our Ojibwe grandmothers sing Christmas songs in our language during Christmas Eve mass at the old reservation church. Their voices were more a wailing, so characteristic of more traditional times, and their songs are buried deep into my soul.

My children have also taken Ojibwe language classes. The oldest (Brady) has taken courses in the language in college up to level six (whatever that is). The youngest (Beau) has practiced his budding language skills at the dinner table, asking me to pass him the butter (dodoshabo bimiday), milk (dodoshabo), or bread (bakwayzhegun). But it always leaves me wondering what will remain of a language that was spoken by our ancestors for countless thousands of years. Like Latin, will it be relegated to academia, to be taught and spoken only in area tribal schools and universities? Will it only survive in sparsely distributed Ojibwe coloring books? Will it survive in our ceremonials only until the last elder has passed on? Will it survive only in church hymns or in fractured sentences around dinner tables? These are troubling questions in need of serious discussions and decisions.

These language issues affect not only my own sense of being; the loss of tribal languages during the boarding school era continues to have a tremendous impact on American Indian people all over the northern continent. Of the over 300 pre-contact tribal languages, slightly more than 200 remain, and only 11 percent (20) of those are still being learned by children the old way, from parents and others (Krauss, 1996). This chapter takes a look at the desperate state of American Indian languages and the disparate ways in which schools are dealing with it. Complete loss of hundreds of languages may be imminent.

Questions to Jump-Start Your Reading

1. What aspects of the culture of your ancestors have your grandparents retained?
2. What have you retained?
3. Do you know the language of your ancestors?
4. Why or why not?
5. Are you concerned about it?

A Chapter Road Map

We begin the chapter by presenting two schools of thought about language preservation, one that language is critical to cultural survival and the other that certain aspects of culture can survive despite language loss. A profile of Guy, a Navajo language teacher, provides context for many of the issues we present. What other researchers have to say about the ways people learn second languages, the motivation to learn another language, and language loss theory are provided. We then move on to reminding readers of the recent history of language extinction efforts. The bulk of the chapter, however, is spent presenting issues posed by the teachers: cultural and religious issues of language maintenance, the extent of language loss, orthography (accepted ways of spelling the language) wars, dialectic differences in communities and varying levels of proficiency amongst students, unique situations facing urban American Indian students, relationships between English and tribal language use, and American Indian language strategies. A case study puts some of these issues into context. Finally, we pose both a question and possible answers by asking who is responsible for maintaining these languages if they are deemed important.

Schools of Thought about Language Maintenance

The preservation and maintenance of tribal languages is a paramount concern of many American Indian people, and a quick scan of the multiplicity of efforts by tribes to ensure language survival attests to the extent of that concern. One common strand of belief is that if a language dies, the culture also dies because the language contains and perpetuates the depth, subtleties, and nuances of culture. This school of thought would say that without language, the songs, ceremonies, and oral tradition are lost. Certain concepts fundamental to specific cultures can only be expressed in a tribal language. Certain words carry the meaning of a whole story. The other belief is that some aspects of culture are distinct from language (Harvey-Morgan, 1994), and that there are many communities in this country that speak English but maintain distinct cultural practices. Contemporary examples of this might include the modern-day pow-wow, the concept of the extended family, and culture-specific value systems. There is discussion about these schools of thought in American Indian country, but the discussion is part of a larger debate about whether cultural evolution is dynamic, about what is "American Indian" and what is not, and about what must be maintained and brought into the future. Examples of the fact that tribal cultures are dynamic (evolve or change with time) rather than static (not evolving) can be seen in my tribe. Before the coming of the Europeans and their trade goods, Ojibwe people relied on porcupine quill work to decorate items such as moccasins. As a result of trading, much of the quill work was replaced with colored beads received from non-Indian traders. Jingle dresses (women's dance outfits decorated with snuff can lids) often worn by Ojibwe women traditional dancers are a relatively new addition to dance regalia.

Language maintenance is by far the largest and most desperate of these issues, as tribes wrestle with how to maintain it and seek to maintain natural uses for

it in the communities. Understanding these and the other language issues that face tribes means first gaining a historical context of efforts by the federal government to exterminate tribal languages.

# A Profile

Many of the language issues facing American Indian people were experienced by Guy, a language teacher on the Navajo Reservation. We would like to think the attempts by the boarding schools to eradicate American Indian languages were something from the distant past, but they weren't. These attempts ended only a few decades ago. Guy began by describing the federal government's attempt to eradicate American Indian languages by forcing American Indian youngsters into Bureau of Indian Affairs and mission schools, where American Indian languages were forbidden:

◆ A few years ago there were only Navajo speakers. Navajo speakers came to school, and they tried to learn English, and the teachers used to say, "Don't speak Navajo." They'd put soap in my mouth, and they told me not [to] speak Navajo and to speak English. I had soap in my mouth in grade school. We weren't allowed to speak Navajo. [You did and got soap]. Yes. Even from our own people. You see that was in, then. That was big. They were trying to do good things the wrong way. I think [that] is what happened. They didn't see the consequences that would happen today.

The traditional upbringing of teachers such as Guy and the teacher preparation (or lack of it) to teach the languages is another common issue in American Indian language programs. Many language teachers come into schools with rich cultural backgrounds to share with students, but they may not possess the necessary teaching credentials (degrees and licenses) to be considered "regular" teachers by their peers. Many of them lack formal training in the theoretical foundations of language and the teaching–learning process; they also may lack training in methodology and assessment and have little background in developmental psychology. Guy's background typifies these characteristics. He comes from a traditional Navajo home and does not possess formal teacher training. This does not mean, however, that he does not possess the knowledge necessary to be a good teacher.

◆ The reason I can teach language is because when I was very young, eight or nine, my mother was blind. She was Christian so she liked to listen to the Bible. So I read the Bible to her in Navajo. At first it was hard for me, but then

I started to pick it up. I [already] read in English first. I knew how to pro-
nounce the English letters of the alphabet, so I read Navajo like I thought that
it was written there. Gradually I would read it the way it was supposed to
be. Eventually I started to read really well. It was life training for me too.
Thought training.

If the languages are to survive, the responsibility may rest with teachers such as
Guy, who because of life circumstances possess fluency in both English and tribal
languages.

Like most tribal language teachers, the obstacles in front of Guy are tremendous. The topic of language loss encompasses other issues as well: the dynamic
nature of language evolution; dialectic differences and developing a common orthography of the language; differing levels of tribal language use among students in
schools; the intense peer pressure to either speak English, the tribe's language, or
both.

◆ Around here they look down on students who speak Navajo. If children's first
language is Navajo, it gives you an accent, and that is what people look down
on. People laugh at the accent. They use the term "Johnny," and you are lower
because of that. "Johnny" is a put down. They are "real Johnny;" they are
backwards; they lack education. Students around here want to be cool and
not be classified as Johnny. It depends on the context of what you say whether it is disrespectful or not.

Eighty percent of my students don't know how to speak. I think they
[the students] really want to know the Navajo language. The problem is the
peer pressure. And I think that causes them to kind of like [ask], "Should
I learn it? I wanna learn it, but should I really learn it, and be Johnny?" And
I've seen kids snicker at other kids because they try to sound out the Navajo
words. It's real hard to get that out of the way for them. They're divided in
themselves, and they feel pressure to be English speakers. And that's cool, that
they can talk English real well. They're at that point where I think they're trying to reason it out. And they're at the point where they're trying to figure out
where they should go—to be Navajo speakers or English speakers.

I think some of them go home to an English-speaking environment so
their parents want them to speak Navajo here; learn it here. Some of their
parents don't know how to speak Navajo. We have a mixture of it in here,
from non-speakers to writers in Navajo. So it's hard for me to just cover all of
them. So I just aim for the middle, and to some of them that's too easy. But
there are a lot of our students that need to learn this. Right now it's a lot of
work. Nobody has done anything for high school students that has been successful that I know of. And those that have, are teaching it now, do not want
to share their curriculum for some reason. Because maybe they're also trying

127

to develop it. So I'm doing the same thing here. I'm just going along, testing different things out, see what works. It's hard to develop something like this.

Navajo language expresses primarily verbs; 80 percent is verbs. There is no such word as computer, but they describe it in different ways. Everything that is used in Navajo are words that can't change. It is resistant to change. Like stove is described as fire in metal. So the new things that come into our language are just described. The new words are borrowed from parts of words. People also talk back and forth between English and Navajo. People talk some English, then some language. Grandma wouldn't understand the dynamic nature of language. She would only object if she was having trouble being a part of the conversation. If Navajo goes, it is going to be because parents aren't teaching their children.

Guy believes that neither he alone, nor schools in general, can be responsible for the survival of the language, but that communities and homes are also responsible. He is doing his part, though, developing language curriculum where none has existed before, integrating high-interest material such as historical information on the famous Navajo code talkers, and suggesting that immersion may be the real key to language survival.

◆ I'm not sure how I learned how to teach. I listened to my teachers, learned from different teachers, looked at my professors and at the paper work they give me, and I picked it up from different people. I'm expected to get certified. I have so many things going on, so I won't do it right now. I would like to teach Navajo and computers. I'm very familiar with computers, and it connects with language. I'm also developing programs for the computer that will work on HyperCard on a Macintosh computer. It begins at their level and then they go at their own pace.

I attempted in the early part of the year to talk about the Navajo code talkers, what they did in World War II, and how they defeated Japanese by their language. Maybe that would be something that would instill pride in the language. In their mind they really like [the] Navajo language. That's really neat to know that.

If they really want to know Navajo, they should go back to grandma for a month at a time, or stay a week at a time, start it out and then do that all the time. They need to hear Navajo around them all the time so that their mind can get into gear in speaking Navajo.

Some other tribal communities have only a handful of tribal language speakers left, elders, many of whom are far advanced in age and unable to transmit the language to younger generations.

What Others Have to Say about Second Language Acquisition, Motivation for Learning a Language, and Language Loss Theory

Miller Cleary (1991) presented Stephan Krashen's (1982) description of how people learn second language processes: acquisition and learning. People acquire a language inductively and unconsciously if they are brought up or immersed in the language. For example, young American Indians who are fluent in both English and their tribal language generally have been brought up in homes or communities in which both English and the tribal language are used in daily communications. Second, people can also learn a language by being explicitly taught the rules of language use. People can learn another language by taking courses in which they learn the rules of the language and its vocabulary, but this method can be difficult for many people who have become accustomed to the rules of their first language. Fluency is harder to acquire using this method of second language acquisition.

Miller Cleary also cites Gardner's (1986) reasons on what motivates people to want to learn another language: the integrative motive and the instrumental motive. A desire to become a member of the new language group is the integrative motive. For example, people are motivated to learn their tribal language when they wish to be identified with that language group. Second, people learn another language for instrumental reasons. Students may be interested in learning their tribal language when knowing the language will enable them to get through daily community life and participate in tribal celebrations. Unfortunately, it is easier to lose a language than it is to acquire it.

Crawford (1996) presented seven hypotheses for language loss and provided telltale signs of when languages were in trouble:

◆ How do we know when a language is threatened? One obvious sign is that the number of its speakers is declining, as exemplified by most Native American and "old immigrant" (i.e. European) languages in the U.S.A. Other symptoms include: fluency in the language increases with age, as younger generations prefer to speak another (usually the dominant societal) tongue; usage declines in "domains" where the language was once secure—i.e., in churches, cultural observances, schools, and most important, the home; growing numbers of parents fail to teach the language to their children.

Crawford's description of these telltale signs fits what teachers in every community in which we interviewed said about the state of the local tribal languages.

According to Crawford, a critical element of these signs is the decline of tribal language in places where it was once the dominant language. Many tribal languages have declined in use as a daily purposeful language. They no longer are spoken in the course of daily interaction. At local cultural events, fewer and fewer tribal people understand the prayers of the traditional people. The language becomes the language of elders and those few who have been raised by elders who speak the language. This absence of authentic language use is why and how languages disappear.

Crawford goes on to say that the shift from indigenous languages to the language of mainstream culture (in this case, English) occurs for a variety of reasons. External forces, such as past federal Bureau of Indian Affairs school policies that prohibited tribal language use, contributed to language decline. Moreover, many tribal speakers became assimilated into mainstream culture. Second, internal forces such as changing demographics (in and out migration), economics (jobs and commerce requiring English language usage), mass media (television, radios, etc.), and social identifiers (the attraction to mainstream culture) contributed to tribal language loss. Third, language shift was effected by changes in values in some tribal communities. Values such as individualism (putting self ahead of community), pragmatism (what is "useful"), and materialism (e.g., "Teaching tribal languages doesn't lead to a job") lead to language loss. Fourth, he believed efforts to reverse language loss also must reflect a shift in values. An example of this is Hebrew (discussed later in this chapter), which became the official language of Israel by governmental action. Fifth, language loss cannot be reversed by those outside tribal communities. These must be internal tribal decisions. Sixth, language restoration efforts that work in one community might not work in others because communities are at different stages of language loss. Finally, Crawford believed that broad-based community efforts were needed to establish tribal language survival as a social policy issue. Crawford's hypotheses not only give a clear description of the issues, but offer a pathway to schools and communities truly interested in saving their tribal languages. Some of these strategies are discussed later.

An Overview of Language Extinction Efforts

Like Guy, the education of other American Indian teachers is replete with examples of the federal government's efforts to exterminate tribal languages. Given the deplorable state of the surviving languages in many communities, the government's efforts have to be considered successful. What must be remembered is that language extinction efforts are quite recent, within the memories of some of the teachers interviewed for this book. The federal government, acting through the Bureau of Indian Affairs, maintained these policies well into the 1960s. The policy shift by the federal government promoting language maintenance and preservation is recent, and unlike the eradication efforts of a few decades ago, is not backed by any significant infusion of federal effort or money. It is no wonder that American Indian people remain skeptical of the constantly shifting federal education policies toward American Indians.

Several American Indian teachers described language extinction efforts in their early schooling. One of them used the memory of this painful period as impetus for wanting to become a teacher.

◆ I think I always wanted to be a teacher ever since my elementary school. I used to play school with my Indian dolls. I was the teacher and they were my students. I mimicked my teachers trying to speak English. Making English sounds, but not words, and including the few words I knew, like "No!" At the school, they refused to let us speak English, spanked us, used the ruler. They had a paddle in the office, and I liked to speak. I was crying at first during recess. I had to wear a sign in English saying that I had spoken my language. It was humiliating; the other students laughed at you. I'd get angry; "How else am I supposed to talk," I'd yell. Those are hurtful memories. I didn't treat my dolls that way. I used to ask the dolls to help me learn, and I'd tell them what to do.

Lena Mann also described the language extinction efforts at the boarding school she attended. It included the use of other children as spies.

◆ Boarding schools were the only schools we could go to. I went to boarding school when I was five years old. I was quiet and I did what you were supposed to do. The only thing that you couldn't do was to talk Navajo. That's about it. Not even when you were alone together because they sort of had spies all over, girls that participated in that, and if you got caught talking Navajo, they would report you.

Cultural and Religious Issues in Language Maintenance

If one believes that "when a language is gone, a culture is gone," one lives with a powerful imperative. It is connected with the use of American Indian languages in ceremonies. For example, traditional Ojibwe people believe that Gitchi Manito (The Great Mystery) will only speak to the Ojibwe people in their tribal language.

When an Ojibwe person dies, they believe Gitchi Manito will present them with two paths, a path where they will go to live forever with their ancestors or a path for non-Indians. The Great Mystery will ask them their Ojibwe name. If they cannot understand or have no Ojibwe name, they will follow the path of the non-Indians. In addition, ceremonies and songs that have been practiced for centuries would be forever lost without the Ojibwe language. Much of the knowledge of the use of plants as medicine would be lost forever without the language because many of the healing and prayer ceremonies are accompanied by song and prayer in the Ojibwe language. I have asked myself the question posed by Rosemary Ackley Christensen, an eminent Ojibwe language advocate. When speaking of the real danger of forever losing our languages, she asks: "Will Indian people become just brown white people?"

Sometimes languages are prevented from being taught to others because of religious or cultural reasons, and these reasons need to be respected. This is for internal discussion within the tribe, and until they decide, if they decide, the language will not be taught in their schools. It is more than a disagreement over a common orthography. This is the case with the Hopi, according to Arlene, a Southwest American Indian teacher:

◆ My sister is doing it [orthography], and people objected because if we have it in writing, then other tribes will pick it up, other people who are not supposed to speak the language will speak the language. What they say is—what do they call that—a prophesy, that if that should happen, then we're losing our identity as Hopis. For that reason, it is not to be written. Stories are not to be told in writing. It's only supposed to be oral, from Hopi to Hopi. And there's that constant battling between some of us who feel like it should be written. Others say no. And I'm also caught in the middle because I think it's appropriate for our children to know, but I do object to someone else learning my language and speaking my language. There's a saying that when we're in the next world (this eventually will end), we're supposed to tell the Creator that we are Hopi and speak to him in that tongue. For that reason, we're supposed to keep it to ourselves. This is why it's important for us to continue, and we're not teaching our children that. It's almost like I'm saying, "Well, once the world we're living in is over, then my daughter goes this way, and I go that way."

When it was brought up at the [school] board that we teach [Hopi language], the Hopi parents did not want Hopi taught to anyone else other than our own children. And another set of parents said, "We don't want Hopi taught in the school. It should be taught at home." So we have two schools of thought here. I was on the other side; I was hoping that we could teach it here at school to only our Hopi children. But, from what I understand, if we do that, we will have a discrimination suit brought against us because we are discriminating. It's a public school, and we're offering a class, but yet we're saying, "only the Hopi." So there was just really no way around it, so then it just sort of totally dropped. And so now we're not doing anything.

I think we could also differentiate between the use of the language. For example, we could use just conversational skills, and teach that here. Like, when you first approach someone, what do you say? And stay away from the, of course it's kind of hard, but stay away from the religious part of it.

So in a case such as this, there is a real dilemma because, although the home has been given the sole responsibility to ensure that the language is taught, in some cases no one in the home can speak the language. In other homes, the tribal language is the first language. For example, it was critical for Bernita Humeyestewa's son to learn to speak Hopi to participate in religious ceremonies.

◆ My son is sixteen, and he doesn't speak Hopi. He understands Hopi and he's beginning to speak more. He's the one being initiated, so my husband keeps telling him, "After you're initiated, you'll have the privileges of going into the kiva, participating in what the men participate in for your age level." And he said, "I'm telling you now, the kachina don't sing in English. The men don't talk in English. You can't say your Hopi prayers in English. So it's very important if you're gonna participate in the kiva that you start speaking the language."

The Extent of Language Loss

Some years ago, a group of Ojibwe people went to an elder and posed the question (Christensen, Ruhnke & Shannon, 1995): "How can we make our children successful in education?" After some time and careful thought, the direction given to them by Jimmy Jackson, Sr., Ojibwe medicine man, was that if the children were to succeed, their parents must learn and speak the Ojibwe language. He believed that if parents learned the language they would also practice the culture, and they in turn would teach this knowledge to their children. He also thought that young people grounded in their language and culture would experience fewer problems in the educational system. But Jimmy Jackson's advice has not yet been followed. Few fluent language speakers remain, and the extinction of the language is looming on the horizon as each year passes, as each fluent speaker passes on, and as each effort at language maintenance fails. A preliminary survey done by Ojibwe Mekana/American Indian Associates (Christensen, Ruhnke, & Shannon, 1995) indicates that there may be no more than 500 Ojibwe fluent speakers in the three-state area of Minnesota, Wisconsin, and Michigan. The results of the survey show that all of the fluent speakers are older than forty-five years of age, with most over sixty and some in their nineties. No children were found in the survey who were fluent speakers.

The Fond du Lac Reservation in northern Minnesota is an example of a community that is down to a small handful of fluent speakers. Although language enrichment programs are taught in several public schools on the reservation, and although the tribal school has set a goal that future graduates of the school will be fluent in the Ojibwe language, the Fond du Lac dialect of Ojibwe is in grave danger of being forever lost. One teacher at the school, Mary, summed up the situation:

◆ On the whole reservation there are probably only four or five who speak Ojibwe fluently, and those are the elders. They're not long to this world. And that's sad, that's really sad. But that's another problem, the cultural awareness. How much culture? How much do you teach them? Because if they haven't been brought up in a cultural family, it's foreign to them. It's like teaching German to a Japanese person and thinking that they're going to be able to speak German in Japan. Well, with who?

It is not just the Ojibwe people who are in danger of losing their language. American Indian and non-Indian teachers from all over the country spoke of the danger of language loss. It needs to be pointed out that although a number of American Indian language programs were described throughout the interviews, most were enrichment programs, offering an introduction to the language for non-speakers and some maintenance for the few fluent speakers in the programs. Moreover, language loss is not solely an issue with tribes who have had more or longer contact with majority culture. One fallacy of language loss is that East Coast tribes lost their languages long ago, and that is simply not true. The Passamaquoddy (Maine) are one example of a tribe that still has many fluent speakers, but language loss is still an issue in their community. Language loss was an issue in every corner, in every community, reservation, and urban area of the country.

◆ At our school you had a bigger percentage of the kids not knowing how to speak, a bigger percentage knowing how to understand. They couldn't speak it, but at least they could understand it. Here, for example, last year I had twenty-one kids, and out of twenty-one, only two of them could respond to anything that I said to them in Hopi. And it was only on an understanding level. It wasn't on a real communication level where they could answer me back in Hopi. Two of them out of twenty-one understood what I said. There's more English in the home now.

—Bernita Humeyestewa

An American Indian teacher, Kate, affirmed the reality of language loss among her tribe in the Northeast and cautioned that tribal language will survive only if it is taught to children and if there is a natural use for it.

◆ Well, unfortunately, our language is almost completely lost. We've been trying [to maintain the language]. We have a language program in this school. Our culture teacher teaches language. And it's such an uphill battle because no one speaks it fluently except for a very few elders, maybe two or three. So it's very difficult for someone to go and learn from them, and then come back and teach it to everyone else. Because you just can't learn it that way.

In one Southeast tribe, the language is also in trouble. This situation can be followed with each age-group of people, and it is frustrating to see little being done about it.

◆ But again, getting back to some of the things that you see will disappear very quickly in a generation. Because, I bet if you looked right now, say 100 percent of the people fifty years old, probably 90 percent of the forty-year-olds, and then 70 percent of them, oh, probably 50 percent of the thirty-year-olds, probably 20 percent of the twenty-year-olds. So you can see how quickly this thing's gonna go. Probably thirty years. That's kind of frightening. See, I've gotta really look at this whole thing from a different, a whole different angle.

—*Joseph*

Tribal languages are still strong in the Southwest as compared with the language situations of most other tribes. But language loss is an issue in the Southwest and is becoming more of an issue as students are exposed to the outside world and lose reasons to use their language, practice their culture, or live like their parents and grandparents. This was pointed out by Tom Ketron:

◆ A lot of kids, they don't speak the language. I got a kid who's dressed like a heavy metal, and a serious 'do. And he goes to Phoenix to go to rock concerts, and he's doing some drugs. And mom comes in dressed traditional, and I've got to get an interpreter because she can't speak English. We're talking a big gap. Something really changed. But when I dealt with them, I had no idea they could speak some Native American language, because, see, they decided to go the dominant society and culture. And you'd say, hey, this kid's just some kid from Phoenix. But when mom comes in, you realize, wow . . . what happened between the parent and the kid?

The most frightening story came from a teacher who told about a tribe that attempted to buy the language of another. There is no proof the story is true, but that is beside the fact. The fact is that languages are in trouble. That is clear.

◆ I had a student in my Native American class today who said, "Did you know that the _____ wanted to buy the _____ language? They paid the government to send them down a language because they'd lost their own, and it's Algonquian." And he said, "I don't think that's right. I don't think they should sell our language."

Orthography Wars

One impediment to developing a language maintenance program is argument over orthography, a spelling system of the language that is acceptable to everyone. This is assuming that there is internal agreement within the tribe that the language should be written, an issue presented earlier by Arlene with the Hopi people.

One insight into written language issues was provided by Patricia Kwachka, a linguist, who indicated that having the written language is no guarantee of language maintenance (Harvey-Morgan, 1994). The example she provided was the Choctaw of Mississippi, where the language has been written, and approximately 85 percent of the children still speak Choctaw. She pointed out, however, that in Oklahoma only 20 percent of the Choctaw people (none of them children) are fluent in the language. Kwachka also pointed out that there need to be natural uses in the community for the language for it to be maintained and that communities need to avoid "the twin treacheries of the orthography wars and wars over what constitutes sacred versus secular texts." These wars, she believes, impede the development of an acceptable orthography and a body of written material.

In other communities there are no orthography wars, and having an accepted written language has become one of the key strategies being used to maintain the language. Herein lies hope, because one community is using the written language to maintain its language. Wayne Newell (Passamaquoddy) described the system he was using:

◆ In Harvard, I worked with this linguist to develop or to enhance a system which was already developed. I asked him permission if I could modify that [his system] so that we could write books in it [the language], and he said fine. So I really worked from his work. One of the things I thought of was to build a model of developed curriculum pretty much based on the school model, the standard curriculum approach to get children to be literate in Passamaquoddy, to teach a writing system. And we did that really effectively. At the time I thought that was the best approach because my thinking was that the language was dying and if we didn't write it down it was going to be forgotten. There were a whole bunch of pressures that I personally felt, and I saw time fleeting.

Dialect Differences and Varying Levels of Proficiency

Within languages there are different dialects, and these can become issues in language instruction. Schools that have brought in language teachers who are from other communities and who speak another dialect can face criticism from parents and community members because the dialect their children are learning is not of their community. In situations in which a community has few speakers of the language, the schools may have no choice. Related to this are varying levels of language knowledge by students in language programs. Some students know little if anything about their tribal language, and others might be proficient oral users, presenting the obvious need to individualize instruction or let them learn from each other. Differences over dialects, meanings, contexts, and personal differences were pointed out by Bruce, a teacher in the Southeast:

◆ I had elders come in to teach the children, but other elders refused to come in. They said that the first elders had taught the children wrong. There are jealousies. And [students] get lazy with language. They need words for new things in their world or they will just revert to the English language to be able to talk, and then they will lose their own language.

Varying degrees of oral proficiency also may be an issue with teachers of the language, just as it is often an issue with teachers of other world languages. All speakers grow in the language.

◆ I just learned everyday language in my tribe's language. I just don't know the hard words. For a long time I couldn't converse with the elders because I didn't know enough, so it was hard for me to make them understand. They didn't understand what I was talking about. And they would say, "What did she say?" And they'd have to translate for me. That was hard, but not anymore. I can talk to the elders and find that I'm a translator.

—June

So the goal is to get everyone better in the language—the teachers and the students. As teachers feel more language proficient, they will pass their newfound knowledge on to their students.

Urban American Indian Language Issues

Urban American Indian students encounter a different set of issues in maintaining or acquiring their tribal languages. Many urban communities are far removed from their tribal homelands, where the language is used in ceremonials, pow-wows, spoken in homes and used in daily intercourse, or even taught in the local school. Urban communities often are represented by a variety of tribes, and although most large urban communities have both formal and informal means of bringing American Indian people together (organizations, programs, American Indian magnet schools, etc.), it is often difficult to meet the language maintenance needs of all of the tribes represented. At both urban sites represented in this book, this was an issue. Bart, an American Indian from the Northwest, spoke of the issue:

◆ By having over fifty tribes here, it makes it kind of tough to isolate one language. It wouldn't be beneficial for someone who's a Seneca from New York to learn Puyallup.

In addition, some students are part one tribe and part another, or a teacher may have knowledge of one or more tribal languages, and students get a mix of several languages. This issue was pointed out by Odie, an American Indian teacher's aide in the Midwest.

◆ Most of the kids have two kinds of Indian blood: Lakota and Dakota or Lakota and Winnebago or Winnebago and Ojibwe or Ojibwe and Sioux. But it's hard to pick out what to teach them and what language to teach them. If we start out with one, students go home and tell their parents what they learned that day, and they call up and say, "I don't want my student learning about the Ojibwe language or the Winnebago language. I want them to learn about . . ." If she's a Sioux or Lakota, she wants them to learn her ways. So I get them from the kindergarten teacher who's teaching strictly Ojibwe, who says, "I know Ojibwe, and I feel it's in their best interest to learn the Ojibwe." When they go into first and second grade, they get _____, who's half Lakota and half Ojibwe. He knows a little bit of both, so his kids have the best of two worlds, because he can teach them two different languages. Then they get their third and fourth grade level, and they get two of these white European teachers who learn the night before from me, and then teach them the next day. And if they have any problems with it, then I go down into her classroom, and I teach them the Ojibwe, because I'm Ojibwe. Then they get into the fifth and sixth grade, they get _____, he's northern Michigan, so I think he's Winnebago. And now all of a sudden, they start learning some Ojibwe and Winnebago. So in between kindergarten and sixth grade, they're learning three different languages.

Relationships between English and Tribal Language Use

There are obvious relationships between proficiency in English and tribal languages, issues that are not often clear to people who can speak only one language. Persons with limited English proficiency often are thinking and translating from their tribal language to English as they speak. June, a teacher's aide in a Southeast school, described this:

◆ When you say it in English you have to translate, you have to flip it around. I think I have a hard time because it's like that. I think I always talk broken English. I try to say it in my mind the right way, and I feel handicapped, trying to think in English. But some words . . . Maybe I just don't know enough English words to say it right. I just haven't learned enough words.

This becomes an issue for students when they do not have full command of the standard English required in schools. Al, an American Indian art and culture teacher in the Northwest, pointed out the situation:

◆ If they're bilingual, to go in the classroom and expect them to get into *War and Peace* or something like that is just insane. It's just crazy. It's just a lot of the words they don't understand. If you look at a lot of the test scores, I think where we're really lacking is high language arts skills. That's not to say they're not articulate. They are in their own language.

If students learn both English and their tribal language from pure speakers at an early age, they usually do not have these problems. In these instances, children are able to be bilingual.

There are many myths about bilingual programs that deserve more discussion than can be provided here. For example, elementary students in language immersion and magnet schools who are taught core subjects in a language other than English do not suffer from lower achievement test scores than students who are taught in English-only speaking environments. I, Thomas Peacock, recently witnessed a presentation by elementary students in a St. Paul Spanish magnet school (Mounds Park) where students representing a variety of racial and cultural backgrounds all exhibited Spanish fluency while also performing at or above average on standardized achievement measures. These students received all of their basic skills instruction in their second language (Spanish). The performance by these students and their achievement also disproves a common myth that bilingual programs are too cognitively demanding and may overload students.

American Indian Language Strategies and Related Issues

Because American Indian languages are a relatively recent addition to the curriculum in some schools, a variety of different strategies are used to teach them. Although a few programs are modeled after existing world language programs, most are not, because many language teachers do not have the formal training in linguistics or in teaching and learning theory and methodology. They may not possess teaching degrees from postsecondary institutions, but they can make up for it in their traditional knowledge and life experiences. Moreover, there are few commercially sold or widely distributed materials on many of the languages, so teachers must develop their own materials from scratch, which means much curriculum development time. There is also the need for early exposure to the language. Several American Indian teachers told of these issues and ways they have accommodated for them.

◆ The best way to teach is to grow up with a language. Everybody around you is speaking the same language. You learn it by the time you're three years old. I don't know how many words you know by the time you're three, but . . . [complete grammar by six, 9,000 words] by the time they're three years old. . . . We do a lot of pictures. With younger ones, I draw the picture and they color it. Older kids draw their own pictures, making their own books, developing . . . Taking a story that may be in English, like Jack and Jill, and putting it in Penobscot. Songs in Penobscot. And the songs they learn really quick. They don't always know what they're singing, but they get the words really quick. So it's a lot of song, a lot of cue cards. Sentences given to them.

And they get a test every Friday with the answers on the bottom. Not in order, but it's my belief that as soon as you hear the right answer, you know that's the right answer.

We make up our own stories to teach language so that the kids can use everyday language. Instead of recreating a legend, they'll just recreate a scenario that might happen in school or outside of school, at home or whatever.

—Barry Dana

In some communities, tribal languages are being put on computer for drill and practice exercises.

◆ It's fascinating to see how they're inventing a writing system. We're putting it on computer. Just had a computer donated. It's going to be able to print out the Penobscot language. So it will be really fascinating to watch it and see it progress.

—Jane

We have purposely chosen not to highlight the effectiveness of specific language restoration or maintenance programs because we concur with Crawford (1996) that what works in one community may not work in others because communities are at different stages of language loss. Equally relevant is that the person teaching the language has as much to do with the success of the program as the model itself. This is true for many exemplary educational models. There are a variety of tribal language programs in various stages of implementation. The education department in Minnesota funds nearly twenty language and culture programs in public and tribal schools. Some of these programs focus more on language appreciation, including counting, basic animals, and rudimentary sentences, rather than on teaching toward fluency. Other programs have developed interactive Ojibwe culture and language software using computers. Fond du Lac Tribal and Community College has put its Ojibwe language program on the World Wide Web (WWW). The University of Arizona holds a summer institute to help tribal language teachers develop curriculum materials. The Navajo Nation has a number of exemplary language programs that are worthy of replication by other tribes looking for models to implement. Tribal language programs exist in many colleges and universities with high American Indian enrollment. Most tribal and Bureau of Indian Affairs schools we visited had tribal language programs. Each of these programs is tailored to the tribe's needs. Whether an individual program is achieving the job of successfully maintaining or restoring the language can best be answered by the communities in which the program exists, and possibly by comparing results with Crawford's telltale signs of language loss.

We concur with Krauss (1996) that the only way to bring a language back into use by children who do not now speak the language is to **immerse** them in it. They need to live the language, to speak it in play, and to converse with it to parents and elders and siblings. They need to come to know it so well that they think in their tribal language and dream in it. What a specific immersion program might look like will depend on a school's resources, the extent of language loss of the tribal group, and the seriousness with which they face the issue.

◆ Children learn to swim in the water, not in the classroom. One could even get a Pd.D. in swimming and write a book about it, then jump in the water and drown. Anybody who has had four years of high school French and then gone to Paris has probably had a similar experience. The academic approach has its own value, but it does not, by itself, produce a vital living language.

Crawford's (1996) hypotheses of language loss (described earlier) may provide some clues on strategies to develop successful language maintenance or restoration programs. External forces, including the Bureau of Indian Affairs, can make tribal language a priority by advocating for its inclusion in its funding formula for BIA and tribal schools. The key word—funding—is important here, because advocating without backing it up with funds will not suffice. Second, many reservations are experiencing in-migration as tribal members return from living in urban areas to be closer to family and to work in tribal enterprises. A few tribes are having economic success because of casino gaming. Some of these tribes need to consider using some of their new-found resources for tribal language programs.

If the Language Is Deemed Important, Who Is Responsible for Maintaining It?

If a community believes that it is important to maintain its tribal language (and most American Indian communities do), who is responsible for seeing that it is maintained? For tribal languages in the throes of extinction, there are few successful examples of successful revitalization. Hebrew is the only language that has been fully revernacularized (Fishman, 1996) and revived from its written form. The Israeli government established Hebrew as the required language of government, assuring it would be learned and used. A few people learned Hebrew and taught it to teachers, who in turn taught it to young children. Tribes serious about reversing language loss might have to consider following Israel's successful effort. In some communities, tribal or primarily American Indian schools have been given this responsibility, one I strongly believe they cannot bear alone. Some primarily American Indian schools have made substantial investments in language maintenance programs with limited success. But if tribal languages are to survive, they need to be supported in homes, in the communities, and in schools. In the schools, the language and the importance of knowing it needs to be reinforced by both American Indian and non-Indian teachers. Most important, the community must have a **natural** use for the language (Harvey-Morgan, 1994). It must serve a purpose. It must be spoken in the course of daily intercourse, such as tribal council meetings, at cultural events, and during normal day-to-day interactions. It needs to be more than just the language of ceremonials. Students must know there are immediate purposes for knowing the language other than solely its importance in maintaining the culture. They look to adults as examples. If they see significant adults learning it, practicing it, and using it, they see it has both immediate and long-term purpose. Simply stated, if tribal languages are to survive, communities and schools need to move beyond merely saying languages are important to actually demonstrating it. Particularly with our American Indian languages, we seem to have real and pretend theories. As tribal people, we purport that maintaining the languages is important, when in actuality our efforts to maintain the languages are not enough to ensure their survival. We pretend we are making serious efforts with language maintenance, but our actions belie the reality of our efforts. It almost appears we are in denial. **Now or never, we need to decide if tribal languages will survive. Most young American Indian people are not using their tribal languages in natural settings. Loss will happen if it is not a priority.** A Southeast teacher described what happens when significant adults cannot agree on the importance of maintaining their tribal language:

◆ The head of education in the tribe is college educated, with a master's degree from a prestigious university. She wants to improve the standard of living, wants children trained to get jobs in the mainstream community. She also appears to want children to only learn English, afraid that there isn't room "inside" students to learn two languages. On the other hand, the tribal leader wants to retain the native language and acts as though he wants no school.

Bernita Humeyestewa noted that language must also be valued and reinforced at home to remain viable.

◆ It's got to be valued also in the home. And that's why we have so many conflicting opinions about where it should be taught. It's a subject that gets tossed back and forth continually. I knew I was getting into a delicate situation this year by teaching it, but I was really surprised that no one really complained. One parent said that they thought that it was useless. But I don't grade them on it. It's just something that's enrichment for themselves. I really

feel that if it's valued in the home, it's going be valued in the school when the teacher does it. I think the entire community needs to come together if they really feel strongly about the language because everyone needs to reinforce the other person.

Several teachers indicated that even non-Indian teachers need to model tribal language to students because they serve as models to all students, including American Indian students. Several examples were provided, including this one from Barry Dana:

◆ I think you'd find a higher rate of success in a school system whose complete staff is behind the program, as opposed to one or two people here and there. I always take the outlook that it's my job to make those teachers get up, as far as learning Penobscot. But I don't do it necessarily. I sort of wait for them to come forth, and if they want to, good. I've grabbed 'em in the hallway in the morning, and say, "Come on, you're doing the intercom." And they say, "I can't do it." And I say, "I'll teach you." So it's one word at a time, and they say it. It's usually a big moment for them. So it puts them on the spot. You hear the kids say, "Hey, did you hear Mr. _____ this morning on the intercom?" So I think when kids see that all the adults buy into it, then they're going to want to learn it that much quicker.

When non-Indian teachers model the language, they do more than set an example of the importance of American Indian languages. They learn about the American Indian students they are teaching, about their cultural backgrounds and the deeper meaning of culture.

◆ The language itself—what little I've learned—is such a difficult language. But the language itself and the way it expresses things shows a different way of thinking about things. For example, there are no nouns for rain or snow. Those are verbs. Those are active, alive things. And that thinking gives you more of an idea of the culture, just by knowing that. And, from my understanding, although I haven't mastered it yet, there are different ways of speaking of a tree. If a tree is away from you or if a tree is near you; or if you're talking to somebody you know, you might say tree differently than if you're talking to somebody you don't know. I mean, there are whole different ways of thinking that are involved in the language that help you more deeply understand the culture. I think once the Native learns the language, there are probably kind of cultural, collective unconsciousness awareness or whatever that will make more sense, in many ways, just by living in the culture. But I think there's even more than that. So I think it's real important for the Natives to learn the language. And I learn the language because I'm fascinated by it, because I have fun with it, and I tease the kids when I know something they don't think I know. But also because I really do think it helps me see the world differently. And it's such an important fact of life for those people who still know the language. They're saying, we need to save the language because the language is in our culture. And if they feel that strongly and they want to pass that on, then it just adds more weight.

—Kendra Richie

Putting pressure on all the school staff to learn a tribe's language is also a difficult burden. Even worse is giving them the responsibility of teaching it to their American Indian students when they themselves don't feel competent using it. Teachers need to find a comfort level themselves or learn the language from students who know it.

◆ We have incorporated this year the first fifteen minutes as language time. And by that we are completely emerged in _____. Now, again, a lot of the kids, especially the junior high kids, are reluctant to do this. "Why do we have to speak this? I don't know this." So it's something that we as teachers have to buy into too. And I feel very uncomfortable teaching _____ to my kids because it's a difficult language to learn, and I don't think that I am prepared, that I am capable of doing this. The philosophy is wonderful, but in actuality, we need to have the bilingual staff doing that, or somebody from the community coming in. We have a bilingual staff here in our school. But, again, it's a limited number, and of course they can't hit every classroom. So we have done flash cards, and we have students that really know the language take over, too. And I have to get the kids psyched out, that this is something that they want, sort of use reverse psychology. When I sit down with the kids, I'll get them to repeat it very slowly, because they're teaching me, rather than my teaching them. Again, it's something that took me a week or two to figure out, how are we going to do this? And when the kids thought that they were showing me a whole new language, then it's something they enjoyed doing. [But] that's still a problem for me.

—Jane

What was the consensus of teachers of American Indian students on the place of American Indian language maintenance in schools? It was nearly unanimous: Languages should be maintained because they are the key to deeper understandings of the cultures. Language needs to be taught in context with plenty of practice in real-life situations and not as isolated content subjects. Schools need to bring elders who are fluent in the languages into classrooms so students can hear

and engage in language. Schools have a responsibility for maintaining tribal languages, a responsibility they share with homes and communities. Communities and parents need to be committed to language maintenance and provide natural uses for the languages in day-to-day life, and adults fluent in their tribal language must demonstrate its importance by speaking it to young people. Parents need to be educated about language loss, and communities need to find ways of providing language instruction for adults desiring it. Orthography wars need to end. Urban American Indian communities need to consider a systematic approach to language instruction that might include regularly returning to reservation communities to be immersed in their tribal languages. In primarily American Indian schools where the community has determined the tribal language must be maintained, language programs must be moved front and center in the curriculum. In other schools, American Indian language programs need to be elevated to the same degree of importance as other academic subjects. Without this commitment from everyone— parents, communities, and schools—many of the languages are forever doomed. That would be a tragedy no one from this generation should be a party to. We need to move beyond saying it is important to actively demonstrating its importance, taking seriously the lesson provided by Wayne Newell:

> The new dawn in Indian education is a real affirmation and recognition of the place of the language and culture within the system. Not tolerating it, but making it a vital part of the learning process. I think that's just been totally ignored. And what you have is, the bottom line is, you have languages disappearing. You have tribal customs disappearing. And most of the models that we're familiar with are assimilation models. You know, we're at the very, very threshold of it, but I really see an exciting time for the next thirty years, because if we don't, then you can kiss off the majority of the languages in the next thirty to fifty years. That's sad. It happens real fast.

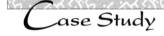

Case Study

Ruth and the Videotapes

With a sinking feeling, Ruth jammed the videotapes in the well-worn L. L. Bean bag that she took back and forth with her to work. That would at least buy her the night to think about what she should do. She walked out of the school much earlier than she usually did; she was usually the last one to leave the reservation school. Sometimes the janitor was even grumpy because he had to wait for her departure so that he could lock up and get on with whatever it was he did there in the evenings.

Ruth wished she could feel anger, wished she could simply slam the door and walk out. She would like to feel that way, but she knew too much about the situation to be able to feel real anger. Anger was too simple an emotion; instead she was simply frustrated and sad.

She left her office and sought out Betsy, who had been the school secretary for fifteen years now. Sometimes she thought Betsy was the most continuity the school would ever have. Betsy would still be sitting at this desk when her contract was up. She bent over Betsy's desk to take care of a few details about the upcoming business meeting and then, using the tribal word for farewell in response to Betsy's evident surprise at her early departure, Ruth walked out the office door. Betsy's eyes followed her, searching for clues to what was wrong, but Ruth couldn't afford to explain.

On her way out, she passed the school's new circular library. It didn't have enough books to fill the space, but the murals were on the walls, finally, and the computers were hooked up. There were students there now, even after school hours, working on one of those projects that Dave always had going. She loved seeing his students so engaged in what they were doing. Today they were on the Internet, connecting with an Aboriginal school in Northern Australia about their respective weather conditions. She half wished she could clone Dave, who had also initiated the controversial videotaping project. His kids were excited about learning.

The twenty-minute drive to her apartment was normally one of the nicest parts of her day. She passed the basket shack, drove past the other reservation buildings, down past the lake, and then finally over the short bridge that separated the main part of the reservation from the paper company land. She usually had twenty minutes of pines and peace until she entered the closest small city to the reservation, but there was no serenity to be found in those surroundings today. Near the wetlands, she did her daily check to see if the eagles were still nesting on the stand at that border of the state park. One was there, bold and white-headed, with who knew what underneath.

She had gotten word through the school's culture and language teacher today. The new tribal chair was trying to decide whether to appropriate and destroy the language tapes that Dave's students had been making. At least some elders were concerned—and a few were mad—about how the recorded stories and historical memories would be used. Oral histories and stories were supposed to be just that—oral, spoken. So some elders had not been responsive to the students' invitations to be recorded. Word had it that the tribal chair was seeking advice from some elders who had been recorded and others who had been unwilling to participate in the

147

project. There weren't very many elders to consult, so Ruth didn't have much time to act if she were going to act. She was glad that she at least knew about the chair's seeking advice, but this language thing was frustrating. Was she perhaps damned if she did act and damned if she didn't? Certainly the language was lost if she didn't.

Finally at home, she hauled the L. L. Bean bag upstairs and slumped into the easy chair near the window. She normally saved this part of day for thinking, but today she went beyond thinking, even getting out a pen to try to list some things that she might still have time to do. A linguist at the local university had offered his expertise if she might find a way to use his help. She'd call in that offer of assistance, but she probably couldn't call on him to intercede in any way. Ruth's life would be much simpler if she didn't do anything at all, if she just let what would happen, happen. But this might be just the opportunity to push hard on the language issue that everyone was avoiding. From what little she knew, she figured that there were about ten years left for the tribe to either ensure that the language survived or to lose it. Maybe the videotapes weren't the answer at all; maybe the answer was still to come forth from this response from the community. Ruth began to scribble fast onto her list of things that needed to be done immediately and those that needed to be done in the next year, or two years, or five years.

Case Discussion

1. As an American Indian educator, how might you get information about how to proceed in such a situation? As a non-Indian educator?
2. How might you proceed when action might be perceived as interference?
3. What are the risks if you don't do something?
4. What should the school's role be in saving a language?
5. How might you get the process started? Who could be called on to help in the process?

Full Circle

There is a need to come full circle to where this chapter began. I mentioned that both of my children are learning their Ojibwe language and that I possess rudimentary Ojibwe language ability. When a colleague recently offered to share Ojibwe language tapes, I jumped at the chance. The writing of this book has served to remind me that sometimes I have been too consumed with being a professional

American Indian educator and have not taken the time to model all that I write and speak, that maybe I have spent too much time in meetings discussing American Indian educational issues or sitting in airports going to and from Indian education conferences or speaking at educational gatherings in St. Paul about the need for our schools to put American Indian educational issues on the front burner. It reminded me that true advocates for American Indian children model what they advocate. So all of this has caused me to assess some things. And there was another reminder.

Several months ago one of my former foster children called me, now twenty years older and a singer in a traditional drum group, to ask about the history of a drum used at one of the reservation schools that I know the whole story about. And he reminded me of the time he lost some of my pow-wow tapes and how I had been so disappointed because the tapes contained old songs we rarely hear at today's intertribal gatherings. "I've made you a tape," he said, "And it has some of those old songs."

Recently, while organizing my music collection, I came upon an audiotape I hadn't bought myself or even knew of until that day, a recording studio's release of some traditional Ojibwe songs. There on the cover, among the names listing the singers, was the name of my foster son. The incident was a reminder of the tenacity of culture, and of the important role adults play as cultural role models for young people. Mi-i-iw! (That is all).

Things to Remember

1. Historical attempts to eliminate American Indian languages are having a profound effect on American Indian education today, with the possible loss of hundreds of tribal languages. Only a concerted effort by schools, homes, and communities will ensure their survival.
2. Language maintenance is a paramount concern in American Indian country, as attested by the multitude of efforts in many communities.
3. There are two schools of thought about the relationship between American Indian languages and culture. One would say that the demise of languages will mean the demise of culture. The other says that aspects of culture can exist without language.
4. American Indian language teachers possess rich cultural backgrounds but may not have been trained as teachers. Teachers must develop much of their own curriculum materials where little or none had existed before.
5. Some American Indian students are under intense peer pressure not to learn or use their tribal language.

6. Cultural and religious issues sometimes clash with language maintenance efforts.

7. Developing an orthography (spelling of the language) that is acceptable to the community is an impediment to language maintenance in some communities.

8. Dialectic differences and varying levels of proficiency complicate language efforts.

9. Urban American Indian students may find access to American Indian language instruction hindered by the number of tribes and languages represented in their schools and their communities.

10. There are obvious relationships between tribal language use, literacy, and English.

11. Teachers can encourage the preservation and maintenance of American Indian languages by modeling and encouraging its use in schools. Communities must seek or retain natural uses for the language in the community. Students need to understand the purposes for knowing the language.

12. Immersion programs are strongly recommended for teaching tribal languages that are not now being spoken by young people.

References

Christensen, R. A., Ruhnke, W., & Shannon, T. (1995). *Ojibwe language institute: Elders speak.* Unpublished proposal.

Crawford, J. (1996). Seven hypotheses on language loss causes and cures. In G. Cantoni (Ed.), *Stabilizing indigenous languages* (pp. 51–68). Flagstaff: Northern Arizona University.

Fishman, J. (1996). Maintaining languages. What works? What doesn't? In G. Cantoni (Ed.), *Stabilizing indigenous languages* (pp. 186–198). Flagstaff: Northern Arizona University.

Harvey-Morgan, J. (Ed.). (1994). *Native literacy and language roundtable proceedings.* Unpublished manuscript.

Krauss, M. (1996). Status of native American language endangerment. In G. Cantoni (Ed.), *Stabilizing indigenous languages* (pp. 16–21). Flagstaff: Northern Arizona University.

Miller Cleary, L. (1991). *From the other side of the desk.* Portsmouth, NH: Heinemann.

Ways of Learning

*U*nlike most of the other American Indian students who made the trip to school on the reservation bus each day, I, Thomas Peacock, had some success in school. In the predominantly non-Indian elementary schools we attended, I displayed good penmanship, and, unlike many of my reservation peers, I did not have any red correction marks on my papers. In classrooms that always contained three or four of my reservation neighbors, I was the only American Indian student in the first reading group. For some reason, mathematics was fun for me. When the class chose sides for any kind of academic competition, I was always one of the first chosen. I had lots of gold and silver and blue stars after my name. On the playground, I also led a charmed life. Many of the reservation kids spent that time alone, but I got to play with the town kids. "You're an honest Injun," some of the town kids would say, and in my charmed and innocent way I would not realize until later in life that I had been adopted by them as some kind of pet. It was like that all the way through my schooling. As I moved into junior high school, I noticed that there were fewer and fewer reservation students on the bus with me going to and from school each day. One by one they became dropout statistics, and of over twenty reservation students at my grade level, only two of us made it through and graduated from high

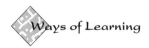

school. Later, I was to find out that there were actually three of us because one student was able to survive in school by denying his Anishinabe heritage

Toward the end of my senior year, I went into the guidance counselor's office to find out about financial aid and colleges I was considering attending. Since the seventh grade I had dreamed of college, and I told the counselor of my dreams and intentions. I remember him sitting back in his chair, putting his hand on his chin, and looking me directly in the eye, pretending to be deep in thought. "You know," he said, "you people are good with your hands." I remember wanting to use those good hands to strangle him. And I have channeled the anger and degradation of that moment to try to change all of that for the sake of my own children and all of the other American Indian children who have had to take that lonely bus ride to school each day, who have had to endure being told the only good in them was in their hands.

The memories of that day in the counselor's office served to remind me that in the writing of this chapter about American Indian learning styles there is an inherent danger of adding to the stereotyping of American Indian people. Stereotyping has been such a destructive force in the historic relationship between American Indian and non-Indian people. And stereotyping is destructive even if we perceive the labels as positive rather than negative. Being labeled noble savages has been just as destructive as being pegged as drunken, lazy alcoholics. Labeling whole tribes of individuals as creative, holistic learners is equally as destructive as being stereotyped as a people who are good with their hands.

In the gathering of data for this book, obvious relationships appeared between the literature on American Indian learning styles and the perceptions of the teachers we interviewed, and these relationships raised several questions: Might there be some ways of learning that are unique to many American Indian students, or will this book simply contribute to the growing body of research that may be creating new stereotypes about how American Indian students learn? How much of what teachers say is learned from workshops on American Indian learning styles (or multicultural education workshops or courses), and how much is based on unbiased observation and experience? Moreover, if some American Indian students do not learn in ways prescribed by existing research or the findings of this book, does that make them anomalies or unique in any way? Does that make them more acculturated or less traditional in a tribal sense? We think not. Any attempt to categorize the ways humans learn is fundamentally flawed because humans are inherently complicated beings. The tendency of researchers to put ways of learning into category boxes is an attempt to make sense of it. So what is presented here is our attempt to make sense of the complexity in human learning and all about it that is unknown. This chapter is our view of the forest of reality, our fraction of the truth.

Questions to Jump-Start Your Reading

1. What do you think of when you think of American Indians and learning?
2. Do you know how you have come to know what you know about the learning of American Indians?
3. How much have you learned from what others have said? How much from observation?

A Chapter Road Map

In this chapter, we begin by melding a review of relevant literature on learning styles of American Indian students with the voices of teachers we interviewed. The literature review is not in any way exhaustive, but is merely an effort to show how the research findings from other studies echo or conflict with what the teachers we interviewed said. Both existing research (particularly that done by American Indian researchers) and our own findings caution readers of the dangers of overgeneralizing learning styles, of applying the results of studies to all American Indian students or tribal groups. We also review the common strands of belief about the impact of culture on learning and about how cultural differences between the home and schools (described in "Ways of Being") play out in the education of American Indian children. Based on the literature review and our own findings, we offer suggestions of how these findings might be incorporated into classroom practice. We then present a case study, "The Great Circle of These Things," as an example of how culture may impact learning styles and of ways in which congruency may be found between teaching and learning. Finally, we return full circle to the personal story in the beginning of the chapter and close with a chapter summary.

American Indian Learning Styles

There is a growing body of research on American Indian learning styles, and it seems an Indian education conference would not be considered complete if it did not have at least one presentation on the latest research findings. It is impressive to see the dramatic increase in the numbers of American Indian people conducting research. Furthermore, it is heartening to see that as tribal people we are exploring issues of learning in the search for solutions to the educational problems besetting

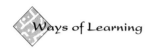
many American Indian students. We recognize that knowing and teaching all the diverse learning styles is one part of improving the education of our children.

American Indian tribes are among the most studied of all groups. Many museums are filled to overflowing with tribal artifacts, and until recently some museum basements contained tens of thousands of American Indian remains, our great-grandfathers and great-grandmothers. Their sacred medicine bundles adorn the walls of museums and the homes of American Indian art collectors. Dominant society anthropologists and archaeologists have had the brain sizes of these human remains measured countless times and have had their cultures analyzed, categorized, and alphabetized. Libraries are full of the findings of this research. Several years ago in a graduate level ethnographic research course, I listened as a fellow student, who had read all she could about American Indians, offered a narration on the Plains American Indian raiding cultures and the influence of the horse on the Sioux and Cheyenne. *And I thought, my God, if ever there was a raiding culture it was yours.* I remember having to ask the instructor to tell her to sit down and be quiet before I lost it completely. The skepticism I have toward some dominant culture research and researchers is shared by many American Indian educators I have talked to. This is not to say, however, that we do not read the research findings and find truth in much of it. We do, however, approach prior research with caution.

When it comes to learning styles, there is general consensus of the importance of knowing individual student's learning styles and adapting instruction to address each individual. This is particularly true with minority students. Banks (1994), Delpit (1988), Ramiriz and Castaneda (1974), and Shade (1989) recognized that the learning, cultural, and motivational styles of many minority students, including American Indians, differs from the teaching styles most frequently used in schools.

Teaching to a Variety of Learning Styles

There is no single American Indian learning style, nor is there a grouping of several styles of learning that fits all American Indians, either as individuals or tribal groups. This is the first and foremost finding from both existing research and from the voices of teachers in this study. The Indian Nations At Risk Task Force (1991) believed it was important to know and teach to all students' ways of learning (p. 16):

◆ Teachers should recognize that there are a variety of learning styles and adapt their teaching methods to the individual learner. At the same time teachers should build on and expand the individual student's approaches to learning.

Perhaps recognizing Gardner's (1983) work on multiple intelligences and the use of appropriate assessment techniques (Campbell, Campbell, and Dickinson, 1996) to identify and address them in instruction will ensure all students' learning styles are addressed. Gardner offers an expanded view of intelligences, indicating there are at least seven: linguistic, logical-mathematical, spatial, bodily-kinesthetic, musical, interpersonal, and intrapersonal. More recently, Gardner has suggested that there may be other intelligences, including naturalistic, existential, and spiritual intelligences. The task of schools, according to Gardner, should be to teach to all of them. The work of Gardner and others speaks to the universals in learning among all learners, regardless of racial or cultural backgrounds, and the strategies for teaching to multiple styles are included in "What Works" (Chapter 8).

Gilliland (1992) and Swisher (1991) have offered warnings about applying the findings of one small study to all individuals and all tribal groups, that findings must recognize that there are more than 500 tribal groups, 200 languages, and a variety of cultures. The voices of teachers interviewed in this study echo the concern of other researchers and our own fear of adding new stereotypes about American Indian students. The teachers spoke of two interrelated concerns, the danger of overgeneralizing and the need to individualize instruction to meet the unique learning styles of each student. Arlene, an American Indian teacher in the Southwest, spoke of the importance of this, especially when working with students from several tribes:

◆ I think rule number one is, you can't generalize. That's what I try to stay away from. I think the biggest statement I probably can make is that I would hope that they don't generalize all across and say, "this Hopi student would react in this way if I said this." I think individually you need to look at them first. I may be raised different. I'm Hopi. Mr. _____, who is Hopi, may have been raised a different way. So we may respond to this question differently. It's really hard for me to pinpoint one thing they should know. Again, it goes down to sensitivity, knowing that you have different cultural backgrounds in your classroom. As a good teacher, I would want that teacher to be sensitive, know something about your students. Again, I can't overstate that, that you can't set one rule—like you [may] have two different cultures in a classroom—you can't say that this one rule will apply to both cultures, and leave it at that.

Patty, a teacher in the Northwest, offered similar sentiments in approaching students' learning styles:

◆ With Indian kids, you've got to educate the whole kid. You've got to worry about the whole self. Not just whether or not they've got their math done, but you've got to deal with all these other things that they're bringing in with

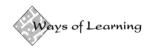

them—all this luggage that they're bringing in with them. Once you get that straightened out, and they know that they can trust you and they feel safe and nonthreatened, then they can settle in, and they learn exactly the way that non-Indians learn. You know there's this whole craziness that they're visual or auditory, all these kinds of things. But you've got to get all that other stuff taken care of before they can settle in. And once they know that they're not being threatened, basically that they're loved and that you care about them, they're exactly the same. I think we make too much about that they're Indian and they're different. They are different inside. Spiritually, they're different. The outside shell, the working gear, all the motor and all that kind of stuff. It's generic. It's like everybody else. The [spiritual] part that's inside is the part—and that part doesn't have to be touched very often. But we use that as a reason why they're not being educated instead of just going in there and saying, "Hey you guys are smart, and I expect the same thing out of you." Their brains work the same and everything. It's their heart that's different. But if you break their heart . . . .

How might the need to individualize to each students' learning style play out in the classroom? Teachers can begin by assessing their own personal learning (Campbell, Campbell and Dickinson, 1996) and teaching styles, followed by an assessment of students' learning style preferences. A variety of assessment measures are available through school counselors and administrators. Teachers can then diversify their teaching to address the variety of learning style preferences of their students.

The Influence of Culture on Learning

Recognizing that teachers must use a "teach to a variety of learning styles" approach does not mean that culture doesn't have an influence on learning styles. The differences in the cultures of home and school certainly impact the teaching-learning process, and these differences were discussed in "Ways of Being." The influence of home and community culture on learning styles was recognized by Swisher and Deyhle (1992) in discussing the cultural difference hypothesis; they attribute poor academic performance to the differences between the environment and teaching methods of schools and the environment and teaching methods of students' homes and communities. Difficulties occur, according to the research hypothesis, because the ways children learn at home conflict with the ways schools teach. Gilliland (1992) indicated that education in most American Indian homes is more casual, informal, and unstructured as opposed to the (rigid) formality of most schools.

How might recognition of this play out in practice? Classrooms need to integrate culture into curriculum to blur the boundaries between home and school. Schools need to become a part of, rather than apart from, the communities in which they serve.

The Need for Competence

The need to feel competent before engaging in an activity was found in several studies of American Indian students. Appleton (1983), Brewer (1977), Longstreet (1978), Wax, Wax and Dumont (1964), and Werner and Begishe (1968) studies of Navajo, Sioux, and Yaquis children found that many of these students were ill at ease and preferred to watch an activity and would not physically engage in it until they were confident that they could perform it. Non-Indian children, however, often try again until they succeed. Philips (1972, 1983) found similar characteristics among Warm Springs children, who seemed unwilling to engage in classroom presentations. They did not like to be put on the spot and preferred not to speak in front of class.

How might this play out in the classroom? Teachers can informally assess each student's comfort level with engaging in activities. They can design activities to encourage group performances and to ensure success for all learners. Teachers need to be cautious of calling on students to perform unless they are sure students feel comfortable with the activity.

Cooperative Rather Than Competitive Learning Environments

There is some evidence that classrooms having a cooperative rather than a competitive learning environment meet the unique learning needs of many American Indian students. Cohen (1986), Slavin (1983), and Stahl and VanSickle (1992) found that many minority students learn best when cooperative teaching is used. Philips (1972) suggested using cooperative groups when teaching American Indian children. For all children, the school rules and learning outcomes that accompany this methodology also must be easily understood, with clear and explicit expectations (Delpit, 1988). Leacock (1976) thought that some teachers may misread American Indian students' unwillingness to compete as a lack of motivation or passivity. Miller and Thomas's (1972) and Brown's (1977) research with Blackfeet and Cherokee found that American Indian children "are predisposed to participate more readily in groups or team situations." Both research studies seem to confirm that

American Indian children "avoid competition when they view it as unfair." Other research (Dumont, 1972; Wax, Wax, and Dumont, 1964; Havighurst, 1970) seems to indicate that in many American Indian cultures it is not considered appropriate cultural behavior to show yourselves as being better than others (more thoroughly described in "Ways of Being").

How might recognition of the need for cooperative learning play out in the classroom? Teachers can establish noncompetitive learning environments using cooperative groups, such as learning centers and noncompetitive games. They can assess their current classroom practices from the perspective of reducing the competitive nature of schooling. Classrooms using cooperative groups meet the fundamental needs Glasser identifies: power, fun, belonging, and freedom. Cooperative learning is conducive to student achievement for all students, regardless of cultural or racial background. Cooperative strategies should be looked on as universal teaching practice.

Visual Learning

There is some evidence that many American Indian students may be visual learners who learn best from observation. Swisher and Deyhle (1992), in summarizing American Indian learning styles, indicate:

◆ In summary, the body of research, although small, on learning styles of American Indian students presents some converging evidence that suggests common patterns or methods in the way these students come to know and understand the world. They approach tasks visually, seem to prefer to learn by careful observation preceding performance, and seem to learn in their natural settings experimentally.

This summation was supported by numerous other research studies done on American Indian children from various tribes (Appleton, 1983; Brewer, 1977; Gilliland, 1992; John, 1972; Philion and Galloway, 1969; Rohner, 1965; Wax et al., 1964; and Wolcott, 1976).

The voices of teachers in this study discerned that many of their American Indian students were visual, image-driven learners as well. Kevin, a non-Indian teacher in the Northeast, talked about the creative writing of one of the American Indian students in his classroom and the differences between it and that of the non-Indian students.

◆ The Indian kids are image-driven. One Indian, a junior, is just a wonderful writer. His writing is very evocative, imagery and pictures as opposed to abstract. Even his prose feels like poetry. He's a good writer. He's a talented writer. Whereas, for white kids, some of the best writers write poetry, but they write more theoretically. Something about that seems like there's a cultural difference there. Something about the way they see or experience.

Recognizing that there may be these differences in ways of learning and applying it in a classroom setting seemed fundamental for one of the American Indian teachers. Al, a teacher in a Northwest school, described how he had combined the visual and creative process with traditional content areas:

◆ I met an actor, a Nez Perce. He came with a theater group. He gave our students a lecture. When he was done he said, "You should get these kids into doing something, performing." And that kind of inspired me to start in the directions of doing a drum and dance group. Schools would have talent night, and we would get the opportunity to go out and do one or two songs. So from that we got our little drum and dance group going. And that's been just as successful as the art. I've always done artwork on the side as well as teach. It was a way to bring those kids together in the community and [for them to] express themselves. There was a tutoring program; that's what got us into this. A lot of kids were showing up and saying, "Hey, I'm having trouble with my homework." So I was bringing in art to teach them simple math or geometry or reading skills. So they were getting a little bit of math and a little bit of reading.

There are many ways that the visual learning needs of students can be met in the classroom. Teachers can establish a visual learning environment (Campbell, et al., 1996) with a variety of tools (paper, crayons, markers, chalk, videos, etc.). Classroom activities can combine the visual arts across the curriculum. Flow charts, visual outlines, pictures, maps, and unit charts should be used to decorate classrooms. The use of learning centers will allow students to change their visual and social perspectives. Moreover, teachers need to be conscious of the effect of their presence and body language as visual clues to students.

Oral Learning

A thorough description of the relationship between oral tradition and literacy is offered in Chapter 7, "Literacy, Thought, and Empowerment." This section focuses on the combination of visual and oral learning as the predominant way of learning most often described by American Indian and non-Indian teachers alike and the need to use multiple approaches in teaching. Many teachers thought it was important for each lesson to be described, demonstrated, and experienced for the teach-

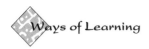

ing to be effective. Teachers also believed the strong oral tradition of American Indian tribal groups remains a potent influence on the ways many of the students learn, despite the fact that many of these students are first language English speakers or the fact that many have not been directly influenced by traditional storytellers. American Indian teachers thought oral learning was especially important for students from more traditional tribal backgrounds because many of the students who are grounded in their tribe's culture also preferred oral learning. One of the American Indian teachers from the Midwest, Beatrice, thought that her own traditional upbringing taught her the importance of listening. As opposed to Patty's beliefs that there is no real difference in learning, she believed this might even be genetic, "hard-wired" in many American Indian students.

◆ I think it's maybe genetic how we learn. It seems like we learn more with showing. Even in my growing up, I think I learned better by somebody showing me how to do things and then sitting back and listening. I was always told to listen. I'm really glad I was raised that way because it really helped me later on in life. You know how that is when you're growing up and you're always told what to do and then you don't want to listen. Kind of rebel against it. But I can remember what it's like back when I was growing up, and how I was taught. We were always told to listen to what they had to say, and listen especially to the elders.

We do not know whether such predilections toward learning are hard-wired. Researchers have not yet answered that question.

Another American Indian teacher, Anne, described the combination of listening and then doing:

◆ And that's why sometimes teachers won't get a response from an Indian student right away because they have to watch it and see it, take it in a little bit and relate it to a frame of reference and then see if it fits in there. And that's why I give them specifics. Like how to write a story, I'll say "Well, let's do the framework first." And this is how they learn how to do it. If we were talking about writing a scary story or a frightening experience, I'll tell them a frightening experience that happened with me. And that's how they can write theirs. By letting them know first. Something they can relate to, listen to, think "Ah ha, I can do that."

Listening is a skill that is prized in many American Indian communities, and children brought up in homes where they are taught its importance often model it in school. Linda, a Northeast school administrator, noticed how important watching and listening are in her community.

◆ Body language says it all for the _____ people. And listening is important.
How well we listen is almost more important than what we say, how much we
hear and how willing we are to articulate what we hear in a descriptive, non-
judgmental way. I learned that even with very young children. I began to hear
it from parents who would finally work up the courage to come to the school
and barge in with the demand that their child needs to be heard. So that "we
need to be heard" thing is crucial, I think. Almost all communication is verbal and physical. And there's very little communication of meaning, of substance, that's done in writing. Writing is just a documentation. I notice that
with students, the older students—in terms of how they present their learning to me or to their teachers—if it can be physical and verbal, we can learn a
lot more about what the children are really learning. When they have to put
pen to paper it loses its quality, its depth, its tapestry of deep understanding.
The other thing that I've noticed is, if I listen, if I interact internally and cognitively with their need to be heard, I think I'm more valued as a member of
that group of learners.

There are many ways in which teachers can address the oral learning needs of
students. Teachers can bring in traditional storytellers, use students as storytellers,
engage classrooms in regular discussions and discussion groups, listen to poetry,
read to students, teach listening strategies, encourage group oral presentations, and
have students interview elders or community people.

Need for Personal and Practical Applications

We found some evidence in the existing research for a preference for "hands-on"
learning among American Indian students. Gilliland (1992) cited Walker, Dodd,
and Bigelow (1989), who found that students need to find personal and practical
applications of schoolwork to their daily lives. Gilliland also expressed the need for
schools to employ active, relevant learning strategies and to use stories and legends
to reinforce traditional American Indian values in an indirect and informal way.

Some of the teachers we interviewed thought American Indian students
learn better if the lesson was practical and had real-world application. One teacher
thought that, although the ways all students learn is similar, there may be differences. She described her American Indian students:

◆ They needed to see it and visualize it and see where it was going. I think
young children anyway need a lot of that. I don't know whether we want to
say there's so much difference. Children are children. I think that the white
children are somewhat similar. I think our [American Indian] children do
better with hands-on or visual.

161

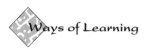

This sense was echoed by Jenny, an American Indian teacher from the Southeast.

◆ Most of these kids, they learn by doing, by the concrete. I've found that works the best. You can't tell them about a trip here or a trip there. You've got to take them, let them have the experience.

There are numerous ways teachers can engage students in practical, "hands-on" learning activities. Field trips need to be encouraged. Schools can sponsor or take students to pow-wows, museums, and local points of interest. They can encourage students to actively participate in cultural events (making dance outfits or learning traditional music) and extracurricular activities. One suggestion came from a northern Minnesota art teacher, who said, "The key to being an effective teacher is to be as active or be more active than your students."

Wholistic Learning

An expanding area of interest in the field of American Indian learning styles is some researchers' belief that many American Indian students are wholistic learners (those who see the whole rather than the parts) rather than being logical-sequential learners. Blakeslee's book (1980) *The Right Brain* is considered by many to be a definitive source for information on the subject. Whereas Gilliland (1992) cites many studies to indicate that Indians are wholistic learners rather than logical-sequential, he offers little evidence to support his assertion. Certainly Cajete's (1994) intriguing book, *Look to the Mountain,* offers educators a traditional, wholistic perspective on the direction he believes we should be going in American Indian education. Ross (1989b) offered a blueprint for reforming schools that educate Dakota children. They should move away from what he describes as a left-brain orientation to a more wholistic, right-brain approach.

Ross indicates that contemporary American schools are oriented for learners who use the left side of the brain, the side he maintains controls logic, linearity, reading and writing, time orientation, and masculine expression. He asserts that the right side of the brain is dominant in instinct, wholism, dance, art, spatiality, and feminine expression. The left side of the brain is dominant in analytical and linear thinking and can only see the parts of the whole. The right side starts from the whole. He maintains that the Lakota people are right-brain dominant. These traditional cultures, he asserts, used right-brain techniques in solving problems, including thought incubation (pondering a problem and letting it "cook" before acting on it) and dream analysis (the recognition that dreams have meanings and should be interpreted for their meanings).

Ross cites Blakeslee, indicating that a delivery method allowing the right side to function as a doorway to the collective unconscious is that of learning through discovery. By permitting the child to discover his or her own answer, the child's understanding and retention of that experience are much greater. Ross believes that this is also the Lakota way of using precept and example. Thus, he thinks discovery learning should be stressed in schools serving American Indian children.

Although there was usually a preliminary caution of the need not to generalize certain learning styles to all American Indian students, many teachers, including the American Indian teachers, did believe that the practice indicated by Ross worked with many American Indian students. Arlene told of her own wholistic way of learning when she described a tutorial program she attended in college to help her with science classes:

◆ This was a program that supported us in the science field—anatomy and physiology. After classes were through for the day, [for] one hour a day, we had a tutorial. The assistant went into the really difficult courses with us and took notes. I'm a visual learner, and in that classroom she would draw out pictures. There were two Anglo women [tutors], but they were so culturally sensitive. We could talk and not worry about our grammar; everything was out the window, and we could talk like friends. They would diagram for us what we were talking about, and you could relate it to this and this. In the class they start from the pieces, I had to see the whole picture as it was first, and then I could break it down. The way then we would work in the tutorial was to start with the whole picture and then break it down.

The idea that many American Indian students may be wholistic learners parallels the right-brain dominance theory asserted by Ross and others. Several other teachers concurred that there seemed to be a preponderance of creative, wholistic American Indian students. One Southeast teacher, Ingrid, believed that was even more true with more traditional American Indian students, who were more in touch with the natural world.

◆ Our kids are so right brained and so artistic. I'm kind of a right-brain [learner] myself, so I tend to really want to encourage that kind of thing, but we have artists and poets like crazy over there. Whenever I do my creative writing class, the kids write so beautifully. I mean, go into the art teacher's room. Kids with hardly any training in high school doing beautiful things. You couldn't possibly teach a kid that much in a couple of years in high school. It has to be a talent that he's helping to encourage. I mean we should have an art gallery here. We should be publishing books of poetry written by native kids.

163

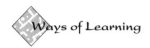

Although Ross and several of the teachers we interviewed make clear distinctions between left and right brain cognition, there is considerable evidence (Elliott, 1985) that many brain functions rely on synchronicity between both sides. We question left-right brain terminology. Our assertion remains that human cognition is inherently more complicated than the left–right terminology and distinctions can explain.

How does recognition of a diversity of student learning styles preferences play out in practice? Teachers can begin by self-assessing their own stereotypes about how American Indian students (or all students for that matter) learn. They need to start from students' strengths and build from there to learning styles that are not their strengths. Classrooms that adopt active, project-based experiential learning address learning from all angles and all learning styles. Teachers who lack up-to-date information on teaching to multiple learning styles need in-service and further training. These training experiences need to practice what they preach by modeling best practices, by doing things and avoiding the pitfalls of teaching only from a text.

Case Study

"The Great Circle of These Things" is an application in story form of a traditional Anishinabe (Ojibwe) way of teaching and learning. The influence of culture on learning is demonstrated in the story, as well as active learning that comes from inquiry and experience. One of the main characters, Ron, learns from his uncle in a traditional setting that relies on learning the whole of things, both the literal, practical application of things and the deeper layers of meaning—the subtle meanings. There is no mismatch between the teaching and learning process. Learning is wholistic and relies on observation, oral, visual, and practical hands-on experience.

The Great Circle of These Things

I.

On most days, he would lay in bed and listen to his mother getting up. It was early morning, and there were the familiar sounds that signaled the beginning of each day: the padding of her feet across his parents' bedroom floor, the close of the bathroom door and the click of a light switch, the whirring of the bathroom fan and the flush of the toilet. Then there would be the padding of feet and the transition to kitchen sounds: the opening and closing of cupboard doors, the running of water, and the brewing of coffee. Finally, he would listen as she approached the door to his room. It would open and she would say in her soft and gentle voice, "Ronnie, it's time to get up and get ready for school. You've got about half an hour now, so hurry up." With rare exceptions, this was the way Ron remembered each school day. These were familiar patterns for him. He could not imagine it any other way.

Each morning, he too would follow similar, familiar rituals: getting up, getting dressed, washing his face, and stepping into the kitchen for a quick breakfast. Then he would say goodbye, step outside, and take the short walk to the old dirt road that made its way down the hill to the main highway. Each day, he also left himself enough time to be alone outdoors before entering the noisy bus load of boisterous relatives, neighbors, and friends.

Each morning, the bus would come. It was affectionately called the "rez bus," by both Indians and whites alike, because that was its mission—to deliver kids from the reservation to school in the morning and then return them from school to the reservation each afternoon. It was always nearly filled with kids and almost seemed to dance down the hill each morning. Its door would open, and the bus would swallow Ron into a different world, a world of headphones and gum and hats on backwards, a jostling world filled with bus conversations.

Between conversations with fellow bus mates, Ron would peer out the window toward the lake. He always sat on the lake side of the bus and either traded places with someone or used his size and demeanor to force others to trade. From there he could sit and look out to the lake and the islands, and he would dream dreams of fishing. The big lake was special to him—special because he wanted to be a commercial fisherman, just like his father and Uncle Eddie. Since childhood, he had ridden along with them during the summer months and on weekends to set and pull the fish nets around the Apostle Islands. When school was in session, this part of his being would become inaccessible, so many times after school he would go down to the docks when the fish boats came in. There he could watch and listen as the men would emerge from the old trawlers with stories of the catch and storms, and of cold, hard work, and of long hours. Never once, though, did he hear them say they were getting out of the business because they didn't like it. It was the manner of their discussions and the look in their eyes that convinced Ron the work was something special. It was a necessary part of their life's journey.

Soon the bus would lurch to a stop in front of Bayfield High, and Ronnie would emerge along with the other kids from the reservation. Most would move in herdlike fashion into the school. There were a few minutes of noisy visiting. Then it would be classes. Then the changing of classes, and study hall, and lunch, and more classes. Bells would ring. Teachers would try to teach. Students would disrupt teachers. Principals would negotiate disagreements, shoo stragglers to class, and pick up gum wrappers.

165

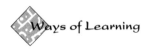

Each school day he would do this: get up in the morning, go to the bus, ride the bus, look at the lake, dream of fishing, go to school. And in the afternoon, the process would reverse and repeat itself. He could not imagine it any other way.

II.

One particular fall evening, Ron returned home from school after a typical day. Stepping from the bus, he saw his father sitting on the porch making repairs in a fish net. "Them d - - - northerns. Every once in while one of them will end up in a net and they just cause one hell of a mess. Just rolling over and over again, tangling and tearing it all to hell."

He set his work down and moved onto another subject. "By the way, Ron, are you very busy in school right now? I could sure use you out on the lake for a couple of days. Your mom and I have to go over to Duluth to help Auntie Marilyn move out to Fond du Lac. So we been thinking about heading down there tomorrow sometime and coming back on Friday. She has to be back Friday night because it's her turn to call bingo for the women's group."

This was one of those opportunities no sane tenth grader would ever pass up—a chance to do what he wanted to do and, with his parents' permission, to miss a couple of days of school in the process. A chance to have the house all to himself. It was just too good. "Sounds like a deal to me. Will Eddie come up and get me in the morning? I might need him to call and wake me up on Friday. Where do you have the nets set?"

His father just laughed and went back to his work. It was a gut laugh, one that knew exactly what a boy was thinking.

That night Ron was so excited about getting the chance to go out into the lake that he had difficulty getting to sleep. When he finally drifted off, he dreamed of the islands and fish, of the soft wind and smells of fall.

III.

"Ronnie . . . Ronnie . . . Hey, kid, it's time to get up." It was his Uncle Eddie standing over him, a cigarette in his mouth and cup of coffee in his hand. He was laughing. "What the hell kind of fisherman do you think you are anyway? We should be out on that lake already."

He was up in an instant, then down the hall to pee, then out to the kitchen, where his mother and father sat drinking coffee. His father dished him out some eggs and fried potatoes and poured him a cup of coffee. His mother reminded him that the lunch she'd packed had to last him all day. Uncle Eddie reminded him that it was time to get moving. Out the door they went.

It was a beautiful late September morning. There was a gentle breeze, and the sun sparkling off the lake made him squint. He helped Eddie load the net boxes into the old fish boat, "Megan," a name given by a long-ago owner. Fishing boat names, once given, were never changed. It was bad luck. Megan fired up, and out into the lake they went.

The first set of nets they lifted were out on the south side of Hermit Island, about four miles from shore. To get there they ran the boat along Basswood Island, the closest island to the village of Red Cliff at about a half mile out. From the lake, he could see the fall colors in all their brilliance of yellows and oranges. The wind was gentle in his hair, as he looked back toward shore and watched Red Cliff shrink into the distance. Wood smoke drifted from many houses.

"Time to get our butts in gear," Uncle Eddie reminded him. With Megan's hydraulic lifter, the 300-foot net came up easily. While Uncle Eddie kept the boat on course, Ron removed and measured the fish and folded the net into the fish box. Lake trout and whitefish smaller than fourteen inches were thrown back, but the herring were kept regardless of size. Then the fish were put into fish boxes by type. Always the boat was surrounded by noisy gulls, all wanting a taste of the action.

"You know, when we go to lift nets over on the other end of Basswood, you're going to see them two young eagles swooping down with the gulls, trying to get a free handout. It's funnier than hell seeing them do that. They're supposed to just sit in their nest and practice being majestic."

Uncle Eddie knew a lot of what he was talking about, and it was one of the reasons Ronnie enjoyed fishing with him. He would get a chance to hear some of his stories. Eddie was one of the few people left who knew the old stories, having learned them from his father and grandfather. He not only knew about the plants and animals that lived on and near the lake, he also knew the *why* of them. For over forty years Eddie had fished these waters, and he knew its corners and moods. He was familiar with its storms and shifting winds, with its gentleness and its unpredictability. He had seen many generations of eagles nesting on the south side of Basswood for over twenty years. He was a forgiving and good-natured man, easy to tell a joke and poke fun. His laughs were genuine. He had a kind and gentle heart.

"You know them birds and the other animals the old Indians called Elder Brothers because they were here before us. They were the third in creation after the earth and the plants. You know they're special because they know about things before they happen. That's something we ain't too good at yet." He laughed and went on. "Them young eagles that are always begging for a free meal. They come out to meet us every day because they recognize our boats. A long time ago, when the Creator first made eagles, he gave them strong wings and the ability to see a long ways. They can be gliding way the hell up there and then come down and pick a fish out of the water just like that." He made a quick sweeping motion with his arms. "And

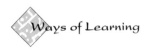

the Creator made most of them kind of aloof, like they have an attitude. So to see them begging for fish just doesn't seem right. They beg for them fish and still are uppity." He laughed and lit another cigarette.

Ron knew there was a serious purpose in his uncle's stories. He knew that this one had something to do with Eddie's dismay that others had been feeding the young eagles, when the birds should be learning how to fish from their parents. It was something about the fact that these two eagles were stooping down to partake in something beneath their dignity. It was the way Ron had learned to interpret stories.

As they passed the rocky outcropping that was the north end of Basswood Island and made their way down its eastern shore between it and Madeline Island, Uncle Eddie told him other stories. One he never tired of hearing was the story about the Great Flood of long ago and how all the animals had helped to create the new earth. Eddie always told the same stories many times, and Ron would not know of the reasons for this until many years later, when it would be his time to tell it to his nephews.

". . . When that sky-woman moved onto the back of that giant turtle, she asked the water animals to go down to the bottom of the ocean to get some soil. And the beaver and fisher and marten and loon, they all tried to help her get some of that soil, but they all came up out of breath. Finally, that old mushrat (muskrat), he tried, and he was down there a long time, and then he floated up all out of breath. But he had some soil in his hand. And the woman painted the turtle's back with the soil and blew life into it, and it spread and became an island as it grew bigger. And she let the big turtle swim away once the island was big enough, and soon the island became the home of all the animals. You know that's why us Indians call this Turtle Island. This whole earth, you see, it's Turtle Island."

Soon they reached the south end of Basswood. To the south, Ron could see the city of Bayfield, only two miles away. There, most of the other kids his age were in school. It could have been a million miles away. Much farther south, at the end of Chequamegon Bay, was Ashland.

As they rounded the island, the eagle's nest appeared at its southernmost shores, and the two juvenile eagles flew out to meet them and beg food with several hundred noisy gulls. Ron worked and watched them in fascination, these two young eagles not even in their adult colors, their bodies still dark brown and without the white heads of their parents. They begged food with such grace and dignity. When they found out the Megan and its crew were not going to provide them with a free meal, they returned to their nest and sat out over the lake and watched the two men work. They practiced being majestic.

Ron and Uncle Eddie lifted and set three 300-foot nets that day and then returned to the shore. As Megan chugged back toward Red Cliff, Ron hosed out the boat and got the nets ready and the fish properly boxed. They brought the catch in and took it down to Severson's fishery to sell. Eddie gave Ron $5, a 7-Up, and a small bag of barbecue chips. Honest pay for an honest day's work. When he was dropped off at home, it was only 2:30 in the afternoon, but Ron was tired and immediately took a three-hour nap. He ate popcorn for dinner and watched movies until well past midnight. When he went to bed, he dreamed of fish and eagles and turtles and muskrats.

"Ronnie. Ronnie . . . Hey kid, it's time to get up." It was his Uncle Eddie standing over him with a cigarette in his mouth and a cup of coffee in his hand. "Time to rise and shine, kid," he laughed.

He arose slowly this morning, his body aching from yesterday's work. For several minutes, he spent some quality time sitting on the side of the bed, scratching his belly and yawning. Then he got up, padding his feet to the bathroom to pee, then out into the kitchen, where his uncle was frying potatoes and eggs. He ate and gulped down two large cups of coffee. He'd need more. It was one of those four-coffee-cup mornings. They walked outside to a cool and misty late September morning. Eddie's old pickup coughed, and they lurched down the hill to the boat landing.

Megan was fired up. It was an old boat, but it purred like a kitten. They loaded the nets into the boat, and Eddie reminded Ron he was going to have to settle for his "commod peanut butter" sandwiches for lunch. Out of nowhere his uncle said, "One of them young eagles died yesterday. I heard it last night at the casino."

Ron didn't say anything. It was the way Uncle Eddie had said it, and the fact that he didn't offer any more of the story. This was the way some of these old Indians say things. They just say something, and then people have to think about it for awhile. They rode in silence out to Hermit Island to pull their first set of nets.

After the Hermit nets were lifted and new ones set, they started the journey down the east side of Basswood to its south end. Ron chewed on a peanut butter sandwich and watched his uncle steer the old boat through a small chop and misty day.

"I don't know how that eagle got killed. I've seen it before, though, you know. Some of them make it and some of them don't. Some of them get themselves shot and others get poisoned. Some of them don't come back from their migration. Most years there are eagles in the nest, though. Sometimes just one of the young ones makes it. Looks like it's going to be one of those years."

And on the journey down the east side of Basswood Island, an uncle told his nephew the story about life and the great circle of life, and about the four hills he must climb if he is so lucky to grow to be an old man. It was a story so beautiful and simple and profound that Ron would not consider it important until he was much older—until he himself had climbed the fourth hill.

"... some of them babies, you know, they don't make it over that first hill." He reminded Ron about several of his cousins who died as babies, and Ron remembered hearing about a baby who froze to death in a car one winter while the mother drank inside Bate's tavern.

"... and some of them young people, they don't clear that second hill. They have lots of energy, and most make it over that hill easily, but a few don't make it." Ron remembered a young cousin who was killed in a car accident several years ago, just south of Washburn.

"... and they come to that third hill, and now most of the women and men walk as partners, although there are some who walk alone. They aren't as frisky as they were a few years ago, but they keep moving ahead." Ron vaguely remembered Sara, Eddie's wife and his Auntie, who took an evil mix of pills and alcohol.

"... and some of us, we make it to that fourth hill. The lucky ones." He laughed and lit another cigarette. "We're old now, and it takes a lot of energy to climb that hill, and most of us don't make it. The top is always covered in mist. That's our afterlife. That's where we go when we die."

When they rounded the tip of Basswood, only gulls came out to beg for food. One young eagle sat in its nest and practiced being majestic. Uncle Eddie took a cigarette out of his front shirt pocket, crushed it, and threw it overboard into the lake.

IV.

His mother and father returned from Duluth that night, and after his father cooked their dinner, his mother went down to the bingo hall because it was her turn to be the caller. The women's group was raising money for the village Christmas party.

The weekend passed.

On Monday morning, he lay in bed and listened to his mother getting up: the sound of her feet padding the floor to the bathroom, the close of the bathroom door and the whirring of the fan, the flush of the toilet. Then the sound of feet, and a transition to kitchen sounds. Finally, she approached the door to his room and said in her soft and gentle voice, "Ronnie, it's time to get up and get ready for school. You've got a half an hour, so hurry up."

After spending some quality time sitting on the edge of the bed, he got dressed and went to school. On this day, he took a note, written by his mother, to the principal's office, which read: "Please excuse Ron as we kept him home from school for Thursday and Friday of last week because he was needed out on the lake to help his uncle pull fish nets."

The attendance secretary would not excuse his absence, and the schoolwork Ron missed during his absences could not be made up for credit. Ron wouldn't question the decision. He was too consumed with water and islands, with turtles and muskrats, with eagles and uncles. He was practicing being majestic.

Case Discussion

1. Describe the wholistic ways of teaching and learning found in the case. What does the story mean by "the whole of things?"
2. In what other ways does Ron learn? How does the uncle as teacher use observation, visual, oral, and practical hands-on application in his teaching? What evidence is there that Ron may be a visual learner who learns best through observation, who needs to feel competent in an activity before engaging in it, who learns best in cooperative rather than competitive environments, who may prefer practical, "hands-on," active learning and stories, or who may be a creative, holistic learner? In what ways might these ways of teaching and learning be incongruent with the ways Ron learns in school?
3. What unit of study or project might both engage Ron and allow him to develop skills he might need in the future?
4. Might there be dangers in overgeneralizing the ways in which Ron learns to all American Indian students?

Full Circle

There is a need to return to the story I began at the beginning of the chapter. I mentioned how I have used the anger and degradation I felt when my high school guidance counselor advised me not to go to college because, as an American Indian, I was "good with my hands." All of my life I have used that episode as impetus to change what is going on in the schools that endeavor to educate American Indian children. In the language of political correctness used today, I may have been told I had bodily-kinesthetic intelligence (Gardner, 1983) and should consider a career path that was a close match to my strengths. In today's world, I may have been told that I was identified by the Swassing-Barbe Checklist of Observable Modality Strength Characteristics as having a kinesthetic learning style. Or I may have been told that my records indicated a preference for a practical, hands-on approach involving active learning. It has made me realize how important it is that we recognize the power and meaning of the educational language in which we label children because, regardless of the sophistication of the label we give them, it is nonetheless a label. If history is any judge, labels, once given, are difficult to change. By the way, I did build my own house. Maybe that counselor was right . . . .

The common pattern that emerged from both existing research and the voices of teachers we interviewed was that there is no single American Indian learn-

171

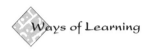

ing style, nor any combination of learning style preferences that fit all American Indian groups or individuals. Good teachers use multiple teaching methods to meet the unique learning style preferences of all learners, regardless of their cultural or racial backgrounds.

Things to Remember

1. There is danger in overgeneralizing the findings of limited research studies on American Indian learning styles to all American Indian students and tribal groups. Teachers should adapt their instruction to meet the unique learning styles of all students.
2. There was a strong sense from most every teacher interviewed in this study that students do not all learn alike and that all students (American Indian and non-Indian) enjoy the kind of learning that comes from inquiry and experience. These strategies should be regarded as universal teaching practice.
3. The ways of learning predominant in the home and community may influence the preferred ways of learning of the students at school. Culture has an impact on learning styles.
4. Some American Indian students may be visual learners who learn best through observation.
5. Some American Indian students may need to feel competent in an activity before they will engage in it.
6. Some American Indian students may learn best in cooperative rather than competitive environments.
7. Some American Indian students learn best from practical and personal application and stories.
8. Some American Indian students are wholistic, creative learners. Schools have generally been linear institutions and therefore may contribute to a mismatch between a student's preferred way of learning and a school's way of teaching.

References

Appleton, N. (1983). *Cultural pluralism in education.* New York: Longman Press.

Banks, J. (1994). *An introduction to multicultural education.* Needham Heights, MA: Allyn and Bacon.

Blakeslee, T. (1980). *The right brain.* New York: Anchor Press/Doubleday.

Brewer, A. (1977). On Indian education. *Integrateducation, 15,* 21–23.

Brown, A. (1980). Cherokee culture and school achievement. *American Indian Culture and Research Journal, 4,* 55–74.

Cajete, G. (1994). *Look to the mountain.* Durango, CO: Kivaki Press.

Campbell, L., Campbell, B., & Dickinson, D. (1996). *Teaching and learning through multiple intelligences.* Needham Heights, MA: Allyn and Bacon.

Cohen, E. (1986). *Designing groupwork: Strategies for heterogeneous classrooms.* New York: Teachers College Press.

Delpit, L. D. (1988). The silenced dialogue: Power and pedagogy in educating other people's children. *Harvard Educational Review, 58,* 280–298.

Dumont, R. V. (1972). Learning English and how to be silent: Studies in Sioux and Cherokee classrooms. In C. Cazden, V. John, & D. Hymes (Eds.), *Function of language in the classroom.* New York: Teachers College Press.

Elliott, P. (1985, October). Right (or left) brain cognition, wrong metaphor for creative behavior. *Journal of Creative Behavior* (October).

Gardner, H. (1983). *Frames of mind.* New York: Basic Books.

Gilliland, H. (1992). *Teaching the Native American.* Dubuque, IA: Kendall-Hunt.

Havighurst, R. J. (1970). *National study of American Indian education.* Washington, DC: Office of Education.

Indian Nations At Risk Task Force. (1991). *Indian nations at risk: An educational strategy for action.* Washington, DC: U.S. Department of Education.

John, V. P. (1972). Styles of learning–styles of teaching: Reflections of the education of Navajo children. In C. Cazden, D. Hymes, & V. P. John (Eds.), *Functions of language in the classroom.* New York: Teachers College Press.

Leacock, E. (1976). The concept of culture and its significance for school counselors. In J. I. Roberts & S. K. Akinsany (Eds.), *Schooling in the cultural content.* New York: David McKay.

Longstreet, E. (1978). *Aspects of ethnicity.* New York: Teachers College Press.

Miller, A. G., & Thomas, R. (1972). Cooperation and competition among Blackfoot Indian and urban Canadian children. *Child Development, 43,* 1104–1110.

Moore, A. J. (1989). Native Indian learning styles: A review of researchers and teachers. *Journal of American Indian Education, 28* (Aug), 15–27.

Philion, W. E., & Galloway, C. E. (1969). Indian children and the reading program. *Journal of Reading, 12,* 553–560, 598–602.

Philips, Susan U. (1972). Participant structures and communicative competence: Warm Springs children in community and classroom. In Cazden, C. B., John, V. P., & Hymes D. (Eds.), *Functions of language in the classroom* (pp. 370–394). New York: Teachers College Press.

Philips, S. (1983). *The invisible culture.* New York: Longman Press.

Ramirez, M. III, & Castaneda, A. (1974). *Cultural democracy, bicognitive development and education.* New York: Academic Press.

Rohner, R. P. (1965). Factors influencing the academic performance of Kwakuitl children in Canada. *Comparative Education Review, 9,* 331–340.

Ross, A. C. (1989 a). Brain hemispheric functions and the native American. *Journal of American Indian Education,* (Aug), 72–75.

173

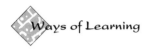

Ross, A. C. (1989 b). *Mitakuye Oyasin—"We are all related."* Ft. Yates, ND: BEAR.

Shade, B. J. (1982). Afro-American cognitive style. *Review of educational research, 52,* 210–244.

Slavin, R. E. (1983). *Cooperative learning.* New York: Longman.

Stahl, R. J., & VanSickle, R. L. (Eds.). (1992). *Cooperative learning in the social studies classroom.* Bulletin No. 87. Washington, DC: National Council of Social Studies.

Swisher, K. (1991, May). American Indian/Alaskan Native learning styles: Research and practice. Charleston, WV: ERIC: CRESS—Appalachia Educational Laboratory.

Swisher, K., & Deyhle, D. (1992). Adapting instruction to culture. In Jon Reyhner (Ed.), *Teaching American Indian students* (pp. 81–95). Norman: University of Oklahoma Press.

Walker, B. J., Dodd, J., & Bigelow, R. (1989). Learning preferences of capable American Indians of two tribes. *Journal of American Indian Education,* (Aug), 63–69.

Wax, Murray L., Wax, R. H., & Dumont, R. V., Jr. (1964). Formal education in an American Indian community. *Social Problems, 11* (suppl.), 95–96.

Werner, O., & Begishe, K. (1968). *Styles of learning: The evidence for Navajo.* Paper presented for conference on styles of learning in American Indian children. Stanford, CA: Stanford University.

Wolcott, H. (1976). *A Kwakuitl village and school.* Chicago: Holt, Rinehart and Winston.

Literacy, Thought, and Empowerment

One day well after our first snowfall in the winter, I went to listen to Amelia LeGarde, an Ojibwe woman who came to the University of Minnesota, Duluth, to tell some stories and to talk about story telling. During that winter, Tom Peacock and I were in the middle of analyzing the transcripts of the interviews, and, although we agreed that literacy was essential to the social, cultural, and intellectual health of American Indian children, we were surprised at how little teachers were able to say about issues of literacy. As a language educator, I had been disappointed; I had been looking for insights into literacy. The teachers knew what worked well and what did not work at all; they thought that literacy skills should be equally accessible for all children; and they hoped there was more that might work. They left us with more questions than answers. It was Amelia LeGarde who unwittingly offered me insight that day in Duluth, and I will explain her part in my growing insight into American Indian literacy later in the chapter.

Questions to Jump-Start Your Reading

1. Given what you have learned so far about differences in culture, about learning styles, about the remnants of oppression, and about native language, what problems do you think some American Indian students might have with reading and writing?
2. If you have been in classrooms that serve American Indian students, what have you noticed about the students' reading and writing?
3. If you went through school systems as an American Indian student, what difficulties did you have in school expectations in reading and writing and speaking?

A Chapter Road Map

We will begin this chapter with a discussion of what the sixty teachers said about issues of literacy, including some of their great tips to teachers for instruction in reading and writing. We will then discuss what both the sixty teachers and researchers have said about cultural differences in thinking. For readers to rethink American Indian literacy, we will then present the concepts of contextualization and decontextualization. Finally, we will look at the strengths of the whole language approach, delineate some of its limitations, and talk about strategies that can empower American Indian people through literacy.

What Teachers Reported about Literacy

At the time we interviewed them, reading and literature teachers in the United States were sincerely and laudably concerned about finding culturally relevant reading materials for their students. Many, many teachers talked about realizing how important the cultural background of the students was in their learning and in their self-esteem as learners.

Selecting Relevant Reading Materials

Rose Fleming, a non-Indian teacher from the Northeast, said:

◆ Eleventh grade books had collections of Native American poetry and excerpts from speeches that were given during different treaties, and there were selections from Momaday's *Rainy Mountain,* so I didn't feel I had to go out and try to supplement [the text]. But, about eight years ago, one of my Native American students slapped her book shut and said, "I'm tired of reading this." My first reaction was that she was reacting to all the white and black literature. And I was so wrong because, when she slapped her book closed, I said, "Mary, what's bothering you?" She said, "Never mind, you'll get mad." I said, "Please tell me." And she said, "I'm tired of reading all the literature by the money tribes." And I said, "Excuse me?" And she said, "All this book ever does is talk about the money tribes. How about talking about my tribe for a change?" Her whole anger was because books never anthologized her literature. And she pointed out that what little literature was there was from the Western tribes, and there was absolutely nothing about the East. So I said, you've raised a really good point. And I think that's something that we should maybe ask the publishers about. So she went back to the school at the reservation, and she signed out a few books and brought them in the next day to show me what her books look like. She read some of it out loud for the class, and she did that very, very proudly. And I was really pleased that she would do that. In following years, we got their literature into it. And when I do incorporate the literature with what we're doing in the curriculum, they are saying, "Where did you get that; where can I get more? Was that in our library or did that come from one of your books?" I have to work at really getting these students to ask questions and talk [in class]. And part of it is by, early in the year, introducing their own literature. Because once I've made that contact, it seems to have brought more success for me. There's another group that seem to be upset because attention is being drawn to them. And so I find that I'm doing a high wire act on not making it appear that I'm singling a group out because they're present in the class. But I don't mind doing that. My approach to literature is, the more you read by a group of people, the more you come to understand what they value, what they believe, and what their history has been.

We applaud teachers like Rose who find literature and other curriculum materials that will be meaningful to their students. Rose's students had perceptions that could be questioned concerning which tribes have more money, but what

Mary really wanted was literature connected to her culture. Literature of the Southwest tribes has been more highly anthologized, as publishers have attempted to bring multicultural literature into textbooks. If one defines reading as making meaning of text, then having materials that students of your region can relate to, materials connected to a world they can recognize, is an important support of the reading process, no matter what the age or ethnicity of the student.

Teachers' Explanations of Literacy Problems

Most teachers, as many American Indian as non-Indian, were simply confused about why a large number of their students were behind in learning to read and write. Nevertheless, a few were remarkable in their insight into issues of literacy and culture. They talked about:

1. the discontinuity of the culture of the school and the culture of the community in relation to literacy learning,
2. the differences between the ways communication was modeled in the school and community,
3. the effect of the students' native language or dialect on literacy acquisition,
4. issues of oral tradition and its effect on literacy acquisition, and
5. the ways in which students' strengths could be brought to literacy acts.

So here is what these quotable teachers were saying about American Indian students' literacy. Some interpreted the lower-than-average skills of many American Indian students as being related to loss of time in school. In some cases, they noted this to be the consequence of culturally different priorities, as we noticed in the case "The Great Circle of These Things" (see Chapter 6), when Ronnie's help in hauling nets was counted on by the family. Teachers talked about the toll of absenteeism:

◆ I don't think that there is anything different about them except that they, even the little kids, are gone for a week at a time, or they're sick. Their problems don't stem from the fact that they aren't capable and desire that knowledge, it's just they miss so much. I think it hurts them more and more the older they get, the further behind they get.

Some teachers found it useful to have ongoing reading and writing projects that students could continue independently wherever they were.

A Southwest teacher, Arlene, and several others talked about the need for a changing role of the home in literacy:

◆ Now we're encouraging a lot of these young parents to read to their children. That's something new. I can't say that I came from a high print home. We always hear that in research, "high print, low print," and children from low print homes will not do so well academically. And children from high print will do really well. I think that's changing, too. But in my time I don't think that we encouraged that.

Parents who want their children to do well in school may benefit from knowing that reading to their children at all ages helps them to acquire a sense of written language and to improve their reading.

"Remedial" Programs and the Problem of Labeling

Some teachers acknowledged that some of their colleagues had low expectations of American Indian students. Warner Wirta, an American Indian who taught for many years in the Midwest, talked of his concerns with "remedial" efforts:

◆ There are negative types of support courses that literally injure that student; they used to be called "remedial." "Now we're going to have some redeem-ial reading!" It is a legalized abuse, destructive behavior from a person who's in a position of authority. This subtle abuse is "bonehead English." Now it's got new names, but it's abuse because students are downright humiliated. I knew there was something wrong [back then], but I just could not really process it in my mind. But I would send them all down to the elementary level, where they would read books to the younger kids. You'd be surprised how fast they learn when they don't have a judgment placed on them for being stupid or dumb.

Wirta explained how it took him some teaching years to understand why his students were not doing well; he also talked about students' resistance to involving themselves in acts of literacy (see Chapter 3 for more on resistance), until their acts of literacy had real purpose:

◆ About half to about two-thirds had a resistance to reading and writing. And they did not cooperate that well. I knew that they had fairly good skills because when [I sent them] down to the elementary level in teams to read, they just whipped through books. There may have been a few things that they had some problems with, but I don't think it was significant. I think it was

179

more a resistance at having to participate alone or without group support of their peers. It is my theory to have the very poor adolescent readers read Alice and Jerry books to younger students to reteach the tools of reading. Learning to crawl again, then walk. So this was teaching me a lot of things as an instructor.

Some students can become resistant to literacy acts if they are continually corrected without understanding why they make mistakes. They interpret the blizzard of corrections as criticism of their intelligence when, in reality, intelligence has little to do with why teachers correct them.

Some of the less insightful teachers mistakenly used the term "language deprivation," an outdated term used to describe children who have little language use in their home before they enter school. However, true language deprivation can only occur in cases in which there is severe family dysfunction. Unless something seriously interferes with language acquisition, students will have competence in either their native language or in a dialect of English.

Dialect Interference

Many teachers were fully aware that their students did not have enough experience with the mainstream dialect of English. Students who have been raised with another language or dialect may take idioms literally. Therese Sullivan from the Southeast said:

◆ I pass off knowledge to them. Yesterday I said, "Oh, with my luck I'll be at the airport when my ship comes in!" That was the first time I learned that they didn't understand my idiom. They take everything so literally. Then there was the time I said, "You're pulling my leg." The student responded: "I didn't touch your leg!" So I sat down and did a whole thing on idiom. I wonder if they have idiom in their native language; [maybe] they don't know they're using idiom. I say, "A way of saying something that means something else." So they've learned "pulling my leg" and "when my ship comes in." Yesterday they had to ask me what "goals" were. They just didn't have the vocabulary. Their journal was three goals they had for the year. One of them whispered, "What does 'goal' mean?" So I said, "Does anyone else know what 'goals' are?" She wasn't embarrassed any more. No one in the room knew—one kid in the room knew that goals were something you tried for. Now you would think sixth, seventh, eighth graders would know what goals are. And I said, "Name some sports that when you make a point it's called a 'goal.'" And they came up with: a basketball goal, hockey, the person that protects is a goalie. I said,

"The person should be an anti-goalie because he's trying to keep it out." And we talked about the meaning of language.

This Southeast teacher was increasing the students' knowledge of the English language in the best way, in the context of what they already knew. Lots of exposure to and discussion of words or unfamiliar idioms in context will best help students to increase their vocabulary and ability to use standard English and to understand the workings of language.

Most teachers were aware of the "lack of correctness" in many of their American Indian students' language, and some had begun to see this problem resulting from the fact that their students "wrote their speech." Many American Indian students have been raised with an American Indian dialect or "rez talk." (For more about American Indian dialects, see work by William Leap, 1992). Karen Brown, a Southwest non-Indian teacher, saw "correctness" problems as being dialect-related:

◆ I've always told my students, "You write the way you speak. So if you say it, you're going to write what you hear around you as if it was grammatically correct, but it is not." I have not met all of their parents, but in most cases, what they hear is not correct, but it is what they accept as correct, and so that's what they repeat. And then when you want them to write it down, they write it down exactly how they've heard it spoken. And they have a much harder time correcting it here. The only time that most hear it correct is when they hear me talk.

Greg, a teacher who works close to a reservation in the Southeast, also saw non-standard English as being connected to the students' oral English and has found a way to work with students on it.

◆ This girl wrote this beautiful piece on the loss of her culture. As she wrote something down, I would say, "Hey wow, that's a good idea about your grandmother's story; I find that very interesting. Would you please expand on that, give me some more specific information, tell me what a couple of stories are all about?" And she would, and she liked it that I was interested enough to ask. But she has some trouble with standardized English. And I'll be honest, I've always questioned using the remedial exercises that we do in class; I really don't think they're going to help her at all. I think the oral tradition maybe of the Indian culture carries on to even their learning to write. "However I speak, that's how I'll write." But I just see that as totally separate because I hope I write a lot better than I speak! So I think that she's caught up in that, and whatever she's heard, like "gonna" and "ain't," etcetera, then she is just going to keep making those mistakes. I had to do a lot of the polishing up in her paper. I had to get her focused on trying to keep a paragraph together, and I think I was more successful in teaching her that way, by getting across to her the items that needed to be corrected rather than by using grammar exercises.

We will come back to the "write their speech" topic that so many teachers brought up later, but we can see that Karen and Greg are beginning to understand the complications that are brought about for these students by their home dialects. Greg's one-on-one explicit comparison of the students' home language to standard English is an excellent way to work with students who have difficulty with written English. Greg described this process later when he said:

◆ I'm going to have her compare, maybe make a list of mistakes. I think that's a good idea. You really do need a page that's formatted for the list because otherwise if you try to have them do it on their own, then they'll log it on a piece of paper, and even though they write the mistake up, look up the rule or come ask you, they'll not write it down with the mistake.

Instead of a list of "mistakes," another teacher had her students keep a "Grammar Log," with the heading "Home Language" in one column and "Written Language" in another to set up the explicit comparison. This less pejorative way of labeling language might allow students to begin to see the differences in dialects without feeling criticized for their written use of the oral language they would use at home. It is important for students and teachers to see this home language as a strength rather than as a deficit.

The Value and Influence of Oral Tradition

Greg's comment, "But I hope I write a lot better than I speak!" does not reflect the attitudes of many people who come from oral cultures where the art of fine speech is honored (see Fleisher Feldman, 1991), but it does reflect what mainstream teachers and the dominant culture will expect from students, which is correct writing. Other teachers as well were aware of issues of oral tradition and its effect on literacy. For instance, most non-Indian teachers were clear that the early learning of many children did not necessarily come from books. Kendra Ritchie, a Northeast teacher, said:

◆ I think they're used to hearing stories when they're little, not having books read to them. I think they don't have many books around. And we expect, in our own white schools, that if parents were good, they would have read to their children when they were little, and these kids would have familiarity with reading. And I don't think that's a fair expectation.

Some children who have been read to as young children come to school with many of the skills that they will need for reading already acquired. Children from oral homes have other language strengths that may be brought to bear on literacy.

The American Indian teachers we spoke with valued oral tradition (as explained in Chapter 2) and were keenly aware of its loss. Warner Wirta said:

◆ Most [of our] people would rather listen, in most cases, instead of trying to read something from a paper. And the oral historian can do a lot of things that can hold your attention [better] than just a piece of paper. I can still remember how these young kids would listen to an older person tell a story about something, and I've never seen eyeballs just like that. They're just completely glued onto it. Oh sure, you have to be able to read and write too. The clash of the societies. So that when the Indian child comes to school into a white world, he's got quite a few things to fight against. He has to fight against the fact that the other kids in the school system look down at the youngster because the facts have been so distorted in the textbooks, and these false things take book manufacturers such a long time to correct. It's hard to change those attitudes because the dominant society accepts things that have been written down that it's very difficult to weed them out. It's too bad.

The power of the dominant society is at once the most subtle and the most discriminating (in the worst sense of the word) when it comes to language use. Teachers who correct their students without being aware of the toll of correction on the self-esteem are perhaps as unintentionally harmful as the teachers who make no attempt to give their students explicit explanations of why they make mistakes in their writing. Without these explanations, students cannot understand an important means of their own oppression, and they cannot understand the power that standard language can give them in the dominant culture. Kevin Ritchie, who teaches both Indian and white students in the Northeast, was particularly insightful in trying to figure out the effects of oral culture on his students, and he acted on his insights:

◆ If I read aloud, the quality of the responses I get from the Native American kids is always better. And I think it also helps white kids, too, but they don't need to hear it spoken to make sense of it. If I can read a story, "To Build a Fire" for example, if I read it aloud, it makes a difference. Some of the kids may read the words—you know how you read a page and you think, "Did I read that page? I have no idea what was there." They'll read that way if they read silently. If it's read to them, they hear it and grasp it and respond to it, and understand the organization of it, and all that kind of thing.

Teachers can tap the strengths these students bring to literacy by reading aloud to them while they follow the printed text or by providing them with books on tape to go along with the text. To continue with Kevin Ritchie:

◆ But if they read it silently, and I ask them the same questions [seeking] linear connections, they have some idea of what was going on, but there's something they don't get. Probably for the same reason that if you are listening to a storyteller tell a Native story, their heads are nodding, and yours isn't. Because they're one step removed from the white experience of that writing. It usually isn't anything disastrous to their learning or to their grade, but the orientation is different.

Teachers can help students see the meaning in the act of reading by providing them with meaningful texts, texts connected with their own experience, or by helping them find relevance in texts they must read by helping them search for the universals in human experience.

Amy, a Midwest American Indian teacher, began to discover difficulties her students had with reading by doing a sort of miscue analysis. "They often read like they would say it; for instance, they'd cut out conjunctions or add them in if they're not there. I've made notes along the way when I've had them read aloud, and I notice they ad lib how they see fit." Students who make such miscues as they read aloud may actually be demonstrating comprehension of the material they are reading. Sometimes absolute correctness, connected with slow, belabored reading is an indication that meaning is not being made because students are so intent on duplicating the text perfectly. Correct oral reading in public situations may be important, but comprehension of text is essential.

The Need for Explicit Lessons in Writing

Moving on to writing, Kevin Ritchie said:

◆ Native American kids often don't feel comfortable writing things down. I'm sure part of that is not having that kind of emphasis culturally. Their organization seems to be different sometimes. Native American response to a writing prompt or essay question often will be kind of scatter-shot. I'd say it was poor organization if it was a white kid writing, but with a native kid it seems more like they write down the thinking that goes into the writing. In high school level writing, [if] you have a short story that you're writing, you have an essay that you're writing, or you have an essay response to a question in a quiz you're writing, there's a beginning, middle, and end. That notion of beginning, developing ideas, drawing a conclusion, or summarizing is hard for me to teach to those kids in a way that makes sense. One of the texts I'm looking at said that Native American storytelling tends to be very concrete. And that rung a bell. If my students have a character who they're telling a story about, they tell what the character does, but they don't really say much of what the character thinks or how the character feels. And sometimes it seems to me when I read Native American myths, they don't have a point. I don't get it. Symbolically I can do all this stuff with it that English teachers want to do. But I'm used to a story developing its plot and climax and insight. But their stories are filled with all these little equally important features, and then it's over. They don't tell a story as much as they give you little snapshots or episodes. Like there's some sub-text of the culture that you're not a part of, and so you don't pick up on the whole process. I feel almost uncomfortable talking about this, because I'm the farthest thing from authority. I've taught kids for twelve years, but I don't have any idea if this is accurate or not.

If I take my best white writers and my best Native American writers—I have two kids in my head right now—the best white writers are idea-driven, they want to develop ideas, or they want to explore ideas. They ask rhetorical questions. They ask specific questions. The Indian kids are image-driven. One Indian junior is just a wonderful writer. His writing is very evocative, imagery and pictures as opposed to abstract. Even his prose feels like poetry. He's a good writer. He's a talented writer. Whereas, for white kids, some of the best writers write poetry, but they write more theoretically. Something about that seems like there's a cultural difference there. Something about the way they see or experience.

Teachers can provide their students with explicit lessons about what the dominant culture expects from their writing. Indeed, comparing dominant culture written story format with the students' tribe's discourse style in telling stories could make quite a lesson. They need these explicit lessons about the need for introductions, development of ideas, and drawing conclusions if they want to write in ways that will win them power in the dominant culture. They also need plenty of chances to express their ideas in their preferred mediums, be they poetry, drawing, or whatever.

In concluding this section on what teachers had to say about American Indian literacy, it is so important to emphasize one result of this research. Although almost all teachers puzzled over many students' low literacy skills, not one teacher in any interview session cast any aspersions about their students' intellect, even when we went in search of teachers who might.

185

What Teachers Said about Cultural Differences in Thought

Related to these issues, the teachers interviewed gave some thought to differences in the way that white middle-class students and their indigenous students thought. Again, though teachers generally thought indigenous students to be bright, many believed that they were most comfortable with concrete thought. As we delved into this issue, we began to see how teachers might be confused about the kind of thought their students were comfortable with. We believe that, although these students can think well abstractly, they may be less comfortable in articulating their abstract thought. For examples of what teachers said about this topic, we will start with Carrie, a non-Indian who taught near a Northeast reservation:

◆ They do very well with creative writing, but not well with analytical writing. They do not like to write from a prescribed theme. If you asked them to go down through and analyze this story, they aren't going to do it. They need to be taken step by step. They're afraid they're going to get it wrong and won't try.

Another teacher, who had taught both on a Southeast reservation and in a border town, said:

◆ They still are some of the best creative writers I've ever had. Just beautiful metaphors, and they dig in deep, and they see things that other kids can't see, and they express thought so well creatively.

And over and over again, teachers came up with variations on two themes: "They write their speech," and "They use examples instead of statements to get their points across with as few words as possible." Kate, an American Indian teacher from the Northeast, said:

◆ One thing my students here do, they get right to the point. And if two sentences will do, why bother with six. I'm telling my students when they're writing: "Remember your audience doesn't know anything about the subject. Explain yourself." They've never heard it before. For example, on a standardized test, a writing prompt for an essay was given: "Tell about an experience that you had that didn't turn out the way you thought it would." And one student's essay was: "I thought this test was going to be easy. It's not, so this isn't what I expected."

Ingrid, from the Southwest, talked about the connection between language and thinking, which noted linguists have explored and still explore:

◆ They think in terms of different things than we do because their language is different. I've never really been able to analyze exactly what it is, but we just have some tremendously talented kids in our schools; they don't even realize how talented they are because it's not considered to be that different. These kids are natural poets. If somebody had asked me to write a poem when I was in high school, I would have looked at them like they wanted me to jump over the moon. And our kids are so good at metaphor, that's why they write such good poetry.

At the time I was interviewing, I was confused because to me metaphor is abstract, yet at the same time that the teachers talked about metaphor, most talked about the concreteness of their students' thought: "The abstractness they did not get. And the concreteness . . . they needed to see it and visualize it and see where it was going."

Metaphor does depend on an abstract leap. For example, to understand the phrase, "The test was a bear," a human mind needs to know the qualities of a bear, know the qualities of a test, and make an abstract leap between the two concrete images or items to construct the similarities between the two.

Metaphor: The test was a bear.

abstraction = shared but
unarticulated qualities

In trying to understand what American teachers told us, we have gone back to reexamine past and current literacy theory and research and are trying to build theory from both what teachers have said and from the standing literature. We will raise issues that come from our research and the research of others and then pose questions that will, it is hoped, make you think about teaching situations you know. We consider these issues to be among the most important, if not imperative, issues that are in front of teachers and teacher educators today.

What Researchers Say about Cultural Differences in Thought

In the last ten years, theorists and researchers in orality and literacy have amended the previous theory that there was substantial difference between the thinking capacity of people from oral versus literate traditions. Silvia Scribner and Michael Cole (1981) found that difference in thinking is more a function of schooling than it is of literacy. J. Peter Denny (1991) tells that all humans use rationality, logic, generalizing abstraction, insubstantial abstraction, theorizing, intentionality, causal thinking, classification, explanation, and originality. Denny summarizes research to state that "Cross-cultural differences in thought concern habits of thinking, not capacities for thought. . . . Different cultures make some of these thought patterns fluent and automatic, whereas the opposite patterns remain unusual and cumbersome" (p. 66). Current theorists and researchers have recognized one difference in thought of oral versus literate people. People from oral traditions contextualize their articulation of thought; they depend on shared knowledge of the people who will be listening to them and do not necessarily articulate what others already know. People from literate traditions tend to decontextualize thought, to add the context that a distant audience will need to make sense of speech or writing. Some researchers hold that literacy is not the sole cause of decontextualized thought. We will look further at issues of contextualized versus decontextualized thought more thoroughly in a later section.

Reenter Amelia LeGarde, Storyteller: Abstract Lessons from Stories

It is our sense that American Indian people think abstractly through story and metaphor, but this abstraction is not traditionally expressed in abstract words. Is the difference, then, in expressive habits rather than thought? Cultures vary; people differ in the way they are socialized to make sense of the world, differ in the theory that they have of the world in their head, and differ in the way they express what is on their minds. Worldview is perhaps a particular construct of perceptions of the world—not necessarily visual, but, in part, using visual information to form it (for instance, the gestures and expression of the storyteller), and aural (for instance, the words and noises of the storyteller), and messages from other senses of the perceiver. In schools of American Indians, those teachers who seem to be the most successful teachers depend on visual and experiential learning activities; they find the oral/aural language in instruction less effective, unless the language is in the form of stories; and they have learned to give explicit lessons if students want to use mainstream language and discourse structures. In more traditional Indian cultures, stories are the medium through which theories of the world are constructed. Stories are in many ways visual constructions of pictures and scenarios taking place internally. Listeners pull concepts/memories from the long-term memory, creatively constructing imaginary and visual representations of the oral stories. Ojibwe story teller Amelia LeGarde uses sound and silence, almost letting the listener create inner pictures before going on. She also uses gestures and expression so that the listener can almost see, for instance, a rapscallion raccoon wrenching itself away from Waynabozho's grasp. At the end of the first story Amelia LeGarde rendered for a gathering of university students, she told the audience that the story teller stops before there is full resolution of the plot and says: "Mi-i-iw" ("That's all"). And listeners go away thinking about the story. A Hopi woman told us the same thing about stories: "As children, we went away thinking." Tom Peacock, in a previously presented case, said, "This was the way some of these old Indians say things. They just say something, and then people have to think about it for awhile."

The thinking that children and adults need to do in connection with these stories is very abstract, yet it is acultural to articulate that abstraction. The mind has to work inductively to discover how to live by the values of the stories, but the morals themselves are rarely articulated; they work on metaphoric abstraction. The listeners need to make the abstract leap, connecting the unsaid message of the story to their own lives. For instance, there is a saying by Chief Seattle, "Man did not weave the web of life, he is merely a strand in it. Whatever he does to the web, he does to himself." There is an abstract, metaphoric lesson in that quote, but the lesson does not depend on abstract words. Learning from stories is an inductive and abstract process, absorbed and not necessarily articulated; nevertheless, the learnings guide life. We, as a white female author and as an Ojibwe male author, find that we write differently when we do not write for scholarly purposes. I, a white female author (who writes creative nonfiction on the side), often tell stories but will synthesize thematically from my stories and connect the synthesis with other stories, often articulating the abstract thematic connections. Tom Peacock, a male Ojibwe author (who writes educational cases, short story, and poetry on the side), does not put the themes therein into abstract language. In both cases, the articulated thematic ideas, or the raw stories, are still interpreted by the reader/listener, given shape on the basis of a thinker's experience and internal pictures, and both generate abstract notions about concerns in life.

A Return to the Chapter 4 Case: "The Storyteller"

At this point in the chapter, you should reread the case, "The Storyteller," which appears in Chapter 4.

1. Were any abstract words used in "The Storyteller"?
2. What two situations does Ronnie have to put together to get the lesson that his uncle intended him to have?
3. Given our own teaching experience, what lessons can we learn from the story, "The Storyteller?"
4. How does Ronnie need to think metaphorically?
5. Hypothetically, what should we, as teachers, do to help Ronnie with his writing given the following sequence of events: The Monday after his uncle's visit, we ask Ronnie to write in his journal about a meaningful weekend event. In a twenty-minute session, Ronnie doodles a picture and then in the last minute, he writes: "My uncle gave me a book."

The Explicit Lessons Needed for the Articulation of Abstraction

A problem American Indian students have in the dominant society (and most reservation schools mirror dominant society) is that most American Indian students are expected to respond to literature and other school materials in ways that have not been modeled to them in their culture outside of the school. The problem may not be so much that they do not understand school content, but that they are not called on in their culture to respond abstractly to what they learn. This sort of discourse needs to be modeled for them explicitly, so, if students chose to communicate in the way that the dominant society expects them to, they can understand the differences in expectations. Tom Peacock always warns prospective teachers, "Don't underestimate these kids; they may look like they're not following you because of averted eyes or a nonresponsive manner, but in most cases they're thinking all the time."

As Scribner and Cole stated (1981), we are still a long way from a complete understanding of the connections between culture and cognition. One of the strengths of our interview research is that it generates questions, and there are questions with which this study leaves us, questions that researchers and teacher researchers might further explore: Is there something unique in the thought of American Indian people—or is it in their expression of thought? Does not a construct of practiced thought patterns generate a way of thinking and a way of expressing thought that is connected with the culture of a people?

Issues of Decontextualized Thought

When teachers say things like "These children write their speech," we think they are referring to some American Indian children's difficulty in writing to distant audiences, to do what British author Margaret Donaldson (1979) calls "disembodied" thought, what some Americans have called "elaborated" thought, and what Australians (for instance, B. Gray [1990]) and current American orality/literacy theorists (Jerome Bruner and Susan Weisser [1991]) call decontextualized thought. It may well be that American Indian students, as well as other groups of children whose parents have not fully participated in or accepted middle class schooling and life, are used to talking and hearing talk that is contextualized, to only alluding to information that all those close at hand readily understand. Jerome Bruner and Susan Weisser (1991) note that "What binds people in a community is this shared recognition, this sense that 'I know that you know that I know what you mean.'" When a people need to express thought outside of a close community, expression of thought must be decontextualized. In the lingo of researchers, writers and speakers have to decontextualize their thought; they must articulate experience and information so that those out of the context, away from where they physically are, will understand what they mean. They have to figure out how to describe things so that people far away can understand. In a way they have to move out beyond their

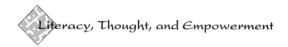

immediate community, to see things from others' perspective, to perform decontextualized thought and discourse. American Indians traditionally lived in small communities and in some cases practice subsistence farming. Denny (1991) notes:

◆ As the community increases in size with the development of agriculture, speakers cannot rely on hearers having such contexts available, so the context is specified in the utterance by relative clauses. Under such pressure the grammar slowly shifts to make more of the noun positions in a sentence modifiable by relative clauses. Relative clause formation amounts to decontextualization because it allows contextual information to be included in the message instead of being added from context by the recipient. (p. 74)

Because of the nature of communication in the United States today, white middle class people from literate communities have learned to write their stories, relate information, and persuade audiences distant from them. They decontextualize information. To do this, they have to develop something I will term "audience sense." Competent writers need to be able to look through another person's perspective so that they can determine what information that person, as audience, will need to understand what they write and what arguments or words will sway or win them. Without this audience sense, they will be disadvantaged. Teachers who give their students real audiences and real purposes for writing will help their students develop the ability to decontextualize their thoughts by giving them real people to have in their minds while writing.

There are many implications for this in the classroom. Teachers of Aboriginal children in Australia are trained to begin literacy learning by using materials and themes from their students' immediate context. They are taught to start with content that is familiar to the children. Many American teachers have figured out that this step is important in teaching all children. An Aboriginal man from the Pitantatjara homelands told us that he wanted the young people to learn the "secret English" because "students leave here with English, but they still can't talk the right way and get us what we need." I can't say it quite the way he did in his Aboriginal English, but that was the gist of it. Our belief is that students do need to start their learning with content that is immediate, but that, if they want to advocate for themselves in the dominant culture, they need to learn the "secret English," which we think is decontextualized articulation of thought. They not only must learn words or the reading or writing of words but must also come to know dominant society's discourse structures. In our interviews, John Nesbit from the Southwest was most articulate about these needs that students had because of the graduate work he had done in linguistics.

◆ I tell my [college-bound] students, "When you go turn this into your English professors, most likely they're going to be looking for this linear structure, saying what you want to say, the [examples/support] straight down, and do the stupid thing of repeating yourself at the end. If you don't, your teacher may thrash you for that." You try to get across to them that there's different kinds of writing, but that they may need a structured, well-supported essay to get by.

Students need to connect literature with personal experience and then be taught explicitly how to move toward analysis in abstract words, using conventional academic formats as a way of articulating their experience for a distant audience. Dale Holloway (1980) said:

◆ Presumed deficits in the logic and cohesiveness of minority student writers may actually result from the dominant culture's isolation of its minority cultures, the imposition of homogeneity in customs, cultures, and language, and inadequate recognition of cohesive devices and unfamiliar systems of logic, not from deficiencies in cognitive ability but from "differences in cognitive orientation" between some American minority cultures and the dominant white culture. (p. 6)

Thus, we are left with another set of questions for researchers and teacher researchers: Do American Indian people express themselves in writing and speech with fewer relative clauses? What is the best way for indigenous students to learn the "secret English" that will give them power in the world without losing their cultural uniqueness? (We will make a stab at answering this one in the next chapter). Should the dominant society have to learn "multiple literacies"?

Whole Language Is Not Enough in Empowering American Indians

Perhaps the strongest method by which the dominant culture has maintained power has been to construct schools that replicate the value system and language system used in the culture of the middle class home. Younger children in these homes are well on the way to literacy before they even get to school. They learn inductively by being read and talked to. For years, school-age American Indian children have been taught using texts that represent white children's experience and that separate them from their own experience and context. Children outside the dominant society have been handicapped; lack of success through education has been perpetuated. For this reason, whole language is a big breakthrough in literacy for children who are not white and middle class, and this may be precisely the reason that whole language instruction has incensed the political right in our nation. Whole language gives children of color a chance.

◆ At the same time as whole language sees common strengths and universals in human learning, it expects and recognizes differences among learners in culture, value systems, experience, needs, interests and language. Some of these differences are personal, reflecting ethnic, cultural, and belief systems of the social groups pupils represent. Thus teachers in whole-language programs value differences among learners as they come to school and differences in objectives and outcomes as students progress through school. (Goodman, 1989, p. 209, as cited in Willis, 1995)

The problem that our research brings up in connection with whole language/ language experience models is that although teachers interviewed were very willing to value differences amongst their learners, for instance, to search for literature that represented the culture of the child, they could not always see subtle cultural differences that got in the way of their students' learning. For instance, teachers' training did not help them see native language or dialect interference in standard English, or the differences in cultural discourse structures, or contextualized versus decontextualized discourse, or the relationships between power and language. Most were committed to enable their children to survive in the white world without understanding the complexity of culture and of the child's culture.

Arlette Ingram Willis (1994), a black educator, has recognized the subtle problems that whole language instruction, albeit any instruction, can impose on African American children. "Only the packaging is new. . . . If you want to advance you must learn to play the game" (p. 44). But, we might add, children of color do not know the rules, and as Willis points out: ". . . Institutionalized racism is something we all know, but see as an unavoidable part of education in US society" (p. 44). "Educators have not effectively built upon the culture and language of every child, and have set arbitrary standards of acceptance and defined them as normative" (p. 47). As teachers, we must constantly clarify for ourselves cultural differences that get in children's way. Teachers will need to better see and act on the inequity that comes when children from one culture have to operate in the schools of the dominant culture. Whole language is a huge step in the right direction, but it is not enough.

Empowerment of American Indians through Literacy

◆ The problem lies also, some have long recognized, in the very structure of society itself, which is mirrored by, reproduced in school, and ordains the success of some children but the failure of others. . . . Young people resist socialization into docility—and rightly so—but in the process forfeit the learning they need in order to mount any effective challenge to the system. (Glynda Ann Hull, 1988, p. 2)

The scary question for us in terms of reporting our research has to do with the almost "racist" actions that teachers might unknowingly get themselves into by asking children to change their habits of thought or their way of expressing thought, empowering though it may be. Some teachers who wanted to do well by their American Indian students actively sought their assimilation. We are convinced that there is a possible danger of teachers being unconscious agents of "assimilation" when they advocate the changes necessary for children to find a purposeful place in society. What is necessary and what is not?

It would be nice to think that there are not major differences between literate and oral ways of being and to think that asking children to be able to learn two ways of expressing themselves is not a form of assimilation. Getting along in two cultures requires complex code-switching and a tugging of values. Many American Indians can do that smoothly and with integrity. Tom Peacock calls it a kind of "acting" that he does. He is an actor when he operates in a white society "play," when he functions at the University of Minnesota and in Minnesota educational leadership. Tom Chee talks about the added strain it brings if your construct is not the dominant construct: "There is constant shifting, 'double clutching'" (Harvey-Morgan, 1994, p. 10). "If you know who you are and maintain your world view, you can go through all the hoops of the dominant society and come back and reconnect. It becomes easier with age to shift gears" (p. 10). Is it with age or with an evolved consciousness of what you are doing and why?

Lisa Delpit (1988) discusses these issues in relation to other minorities when she says that schools should not change homes of children to match homes of those within the culture of power. She equates that with "cultural genocide."

More than one teacher in our study said, "You have to help them to learn a good handshake." Often, harm is borne from the best intentions. If we were to take the high moral ground, perhaps we should teach white children that Indian people are apt to have a gentler handshake. But discussions of critical literacy have evolved beyond advocating that the language and culture that a child brings into the classroom should be seen as legitimate and important aspects of learning. For American Indian students, we need expanded notions of literacy because if these students want to construct meaning from print, they will need to find reasons within themselves for doing so. Acts of reading and writing will need to be those in which students can understand themselves and their relationship to the world, acts that help them to examine power relations in society and the connections between knowledge and power. "Central here is the need to engage voice as an act of resistance and self-transformation, to recognize that as one comes to voice one establishes the precondition for becoming a subject in history rather than an object" (Giroux, 1991, p. 22). These discussions assume that human beings can be fully bicultural and bilingual. We have been convinced that is possible, but we are not sure that is possible for a group of people that have been so thoroughly oppressed for so many years. Indigenous people around the world are severely disadvantaged because they do not naturally articulate abstraction, because they do not communicate with decontextualized thought, because they do not fare well in the school situations of the dominant culture. Their traditional lives have been taken from them, some have been forced into purposeless lives, some have developed the chemical dependency that comes from despair, and ever so many still resist assimilation.

John Ogbu says that the passiveness and recalcitrance that teachers believe they see in some students may be in reality a form of resistance. Tom Peacock says that passive resistance is not traditional but is a trap in which those who cannot see how to move find themselves. It has to do with the lack of power, purpose, and hope that comes from oppression. Those who are literate, reflective, and articulate can get up and leave any time they want. People who have social consciousness and are beyond powerlessness and hopelessness can think their way past the anger. These people are able to act on their world. If American Indian people are to be empowered through literacy, as teachers we should teach indigenous students to see how reading and writing can be used to serve their own purposes and those of their communities. When teachers in our study reported that students became excited about reading and writing, it was most often when students were reading to find something out that was important to them or when they were writing to accomplish something that they wanted to accomplish. In the next chapter, we will look at how teachers can construct situations so that their students can learn and see the importance and power of their knowledge and skills. Amy, a teacher from the Midwest, described the excitement her students experienced as they interviewed community members about the services they wanted from their reservation. They wrote up their results, developed charts and graphs, and presented the results in writing and orally to the reservation council. If Amy were to be lucky enough to work with Ronnie, she might want to encourage him to investigate fishing, its traditions, the modern issues it involves, its connections with his family, its environmental and biological considerations, etc. She might help him act to better his future while maintaining his cultural dignity.

There are things to be accomplished; there are disappearing languages and oral histories and stories to be protected, rights to be protected, and purposeful and hopeful futures to be found. If students in groups use literacy to work on these community issues or work as individuals to further understand their own personal worlds (literacy for the real purposes of their community and for real audiences beyond their community), they will maintain the intrinsic motivation for literacy that comes with acts of self-determination. (For more about literacy for real audiences and purposes see Miller Cleary [1991] and Chapter 8).

*C*ase Study

A Short But Historical Case Study: Literacy for Real Purposes

Almost two hundred years ago, James Evans, a missionary in northern Ontario, introduced the Northern Ojibwe to a Cree syllabic system (Bennet & Berry, 1991). There were no writing implements, no paper. But ten years later, other missionaries a thousand miles away found Northern Ojibwe using written syllabic language. They had been used to signification; they had used trail signs for centuries. But two centuries ago, they passed the Cree syllabic system from one person to another to keep touch amid isolation. It served their needs. It is still used today, but its use decreases with the number of satellite disks set up amongst smoking houses and outhouses.

Case Discussion

1. How did the Cree syllabic writing system get used for real audiences and purposes?

2. Why might its use be decreasing today?

3. What kind of reading and writing for real audiences and empowering purposes might teachers encourage today?

Things to Remember

1. The reasons why some American Indian children have difficulty with literacy (reading and writing) are highly complex. They may involve any or all of the following:
   - ◆ Attendance issues (children do not have as much time practicing literacy acts)
   - ◆ A late beginning (children are more apt, because of coming from an oral tradition, to come from a "low print" home and to be read to less at an early age)
   - ◆ Less impetus to acquire standard English, the language of power (children are often raised speaking a different dialect or language, using different discourse strategies)

2. If teachers are to work toward improving the literacy of American Indian students, they must:
   - ◆ Understand and help parents understand that reading is acquired when children see its usefulness, the potential fun in it, and when they practice it
   - ◆ Find reading materials that will have real meaning for the children, materials they can connect with their experience
   - ◆ Engage students in writing that will have real purpose and audience, which will show students the usefulness of writing for themselves in the modern world
   - ◆ Give students the explicit lessons that will help them define their difficulty with standard English dialect as connected to their early learning of another rich dialect that also had rules (but different rules). Help students to see the difference in the rules of each dialect.
   - ◆ Give students explicit lessons in the difference in structures between their traditional story telling and fiction from the dominant culture
   - ◆ Give students explicit lessons, lessons connecting their writing to real purpose and audience, which will show them the need to decontextualize language so that those out of their immediate environment can understand their thoughts

◆ Engage students in literacy acts that will empower them or their communities

◆ Above all, let students engage in literacy acts that draw on or connect to their strengths (creative strengths or any strengths)

References

Bennett, J. & Berry, J. (1991). Cree literacy in the syllabic script. In D. Olson & N. Torrance (Eds.), *Literacy and orality* (pp. 90–101). Cambridge, UK: Cambridge University Press.

Bruner, J. & Weisser, C. (1991). The invention of self: Autobiography and its forms. In D. Olson & N. Torrance, (Eds.), *Literacy and orality* (pp. 129–148). Cambridge, UK: Cambridge University Press.

Miller, Cleary, L. (1991). *From the other side of the desk: Students speak out about writing.* Portsmouth, NH: Heinemann.

Delpit, L. (1988). The silenced dialogue: Power and pedagogy in educating other people's children. *Harvard Educational Review Writing, 58* (8), 280–298.

Denny, J. P. (1991). Rational thought in oral culture and literate decontextualization. In D. Olson & N. Torrance (Eds.), *Literacy and orality* (pp. 90–101). Cambridge, UK: Cambridge University Press.

Donaldson, M. (1979). *Children's minds.* New York: Norton.

Fleisher, Feldman, C. (1991). Oral metalanguage. In D. Olson & Torrance, N. (Eds.), *Literacy and orality* (pp. 45–65). Cambridge, UK: Cambridge University Press.

Giroux, H. (1991). The politics of postmodernism: Rethinking the boundaries of race and ethnicity. *Journal of Urban and Cultural Studies, 1* (1), 5–38.

Goodman, K. (1989). Whole-language research: Foundations and development. *Elementary School Journal, 90,* 207–221.

Gray, B. (1990). Natural language learning in Aboriginal classrooms: Reflections on teaching and learning style for empowerment in English. In C. Walton & Eggington, W. (Eds.), *Language: Maintenance, power and education in Australian Aboriginal contexts.* Darwin, Australia: NTU Press.

Harvey-Morgan, J. (Ed.). (1994). *Native literacy and language roundtable proceedings.* The National Center on Adult Literacy and The Native Education Initiative of the U.S. Department of Education Regional Educational Laboratories. Distributed at AERA in San Francisco, April, 1995.

Holloway, D. (1980, March). *Cohesion in English: A key to the way our culture thinks.* CCCC paper, Washington, DC.

Hull, G. (1988). Literacy, technology, and the underprepared: Notes toward a framework for action. *The Quarterly of the National Writing Project and the Center for the Study of Writing, 10* (3), 2.

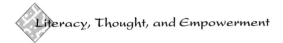

Leap, W. (1992). American Indian English and its implications for bilingual education. In L. M. Cleary & M. Linn, *Linguistics for teachers* (pp. 207–219). New York: McGraw-Hill.

Scribner, S., & Cole, M. (1981). *The psychology of literacy.* Cambridge, MA: Harvard University Press.

Willis, A. I. (1995). Reading the world of school literacy: Contextualizing the experience of a young African American male. *Harvard Educational Review, 65,* 30–49.

What Works

Student Motivation as a Guide to Practice

"What works?" Amidst the quandary and frustration in their work, teachers had a lot to say about this question. As what they said evolved from interview to tape to transcript, they collectively had thousands of pages of things to say about what works and what does not with American Indian students. These were the real gems in their collected wisdom, and we have saved many of them for this last chapter.

As researchers, we experienced equal quandary and frustration in our work of figuring out how to organize this chapter for our readers, but while drafting Chapter 7, I began to see a pattern in what teachers were saying about effective practice. Before the study we are reporting here, I, Linda Miller Cleary, had done a study of the motivation eleventh graders had for writing and had uncovered six innate characteristics in human beings that motivate language acquisition. In a moment of insight, we saw how those same universals fit with our data. With very few exceptions, all of our coding connected with effective practice slipped right into these categories. What works with American Indian students seems to work because humans have by nature: curiosity, an inclination toward self-expression, an inclination toward imitation, responsiveness to feedback (Frazier, 1982), a desire for self-determination, and a desire for feelings of competence (see Ames & Ames, 1984, 1989; Deci, 1975, 1985; Stipek, 1988). We remembered hearing teachers say

again and again that, indeed, what was working for their American Indian students were just the things that worked with all children. What we report here is not simply good practice for American Indian children, it is good practice because of the very universality of human motivation.

Questions to Jump-Start Your Reading

1. What incentives for learning are currently used in mainstream schools?
2. What kept you wanting to go to school as a child?
3. Was schooling valued by your family?
4. How might this be the same/different for American Indian children in schools today?

A Chapter Road Map

In this chapter, we will first examine why current mainstream school systems' incentives for learning are not apt to work for many American Indian students, and we will also examine the difference between extrinsic and intrinsic motivation. Then, after seeing how a Midwest American Indian teacher, Amy, worked with her students, we will begin to see how innate human attributes play themselves out in effective teaching. We will focus on methods that foster the following innate intrinsic motivators: the desire for self-determination, curiosity, responsiveness to feedback, the desire for feelings of competence, an inclination toward self-expression, and an inclination toward imitation. While focusing on these, we will also examine how interpersonal relations between teachers and students support these sources of motivation for American Indian students.

Why Mainstream Schools' Incentives Do Not Work

Carrie, a non-Indian teacher from the Northeast, said:

◆ They keep saying: "This is stupid." "I find it impossible to follow." "Every time you give us a rule, there's always an exception." "There's no rhyme and reason for this, so why do we have to know this?" And then I get the "Aw, I'm not doing this" attitude. And they'll just sit there. We're doing a grammar unit in that class where I have a lot of my Native American kids, and I have this kid that's taken four zeros rather than do the work. It's worse than with other kids; I only have two white kids that are doing that. Whereas with my Indian students, the percentage is much higher. I'd say at least a third of the Indian kids are not doing any of the work. In fact, I have this one student, I think he's going to be a freshman for four years. He has done two homework assignments since September. He did the creative ones. He wrote a short story, really getting into it. And another one was a description of their ideal world. He did wonderfully on those two assignments. But an opinion paper—"Nope." "We're going to write an eight-page composition research paper." "Nope." But this kid's articulate, he's bright, he's very verbal. He comes in before class begins, talks to me, understands what's going on. Call on him in class . . . same type of attitude. Like some of the Indian kids here, you ask them a question, and even if they know, they don't want to say in front of anybody else; they don't want to be laughed at. Last year there was a class leader who is at Dartmouth now. Others fail, and say, "Well, so what? I'll come back next year."

Carrie echoes what other teachers said about the difficulties of motivating their American Indian students by the traditional grading system. In Carrie's quote, we see students who spread widely across a continuum, from the successful Dartmouth student to four-year freshman student. Some American Indian students are as successful in mainstream schools as their "best" mainstream peers; many get along, but many more hang around at the bottom of the continuum waiting to drop out. As teachers, it is our challenge to nudge students up the continuum.

So far in this book, we have heard possible reasons why a number of American Indian students are not successful: lack of parental support for schooling and the understandable lack of respect some parents have for it, different priorities in life, a curriculum that is not relevant to students' lives or foreseeable futures, a dialect that causes them difficulty with standard English, a level of discomfort with analytical writing, discomfort in competitive systems, the need to be somewhat accomplished before performance, the need not to "shine" in front of peers.

The incentives that work for many students in mainstream schools (a beckoning college career, attention accorded by the family for good grades, rewards that are meaningful, enjoyment of competition, potential shame in failing grades) are simply not there to pull many American Indian students along. These extrinsic motivators, motivators external to the individual, just do not work for students who have been marginalized by society, who rarely see how academic endeavor has served/rewarded the adults in their community, who do not see real purposes for the knowledge and skills they are supposed to accumulate. Few of these students

203

have bought into the rewards the dominant culture has to offer. Indeed, teachers reported that rewards, public praise, and grades are not effective motivators for many American Indian students.

Rewards

◆ We have incentives, like if you're working in all your classes, and you have good attendance, then at the end of the week you'll get a five dollar gift certificate to MacDonalds, and there are very few who want to do it. The exterior rewards aren't that effective. Trying to force the student doesn't work.

—Mary, a non-Indian Midwest teacher

◆ Every year I try something a little different to see what works. The ones that are really good, I give them something special. I give out pencils for their spelling tests, bringing homework back, and they're glad to have anything, but I think it's really the attention that they are craving.

—Jenny, an American Indian Southeast teacher

Grades

◆ Kids carrying books and doing homework were ridiculed. And still today we have problems with kids doing their assignments and not turning them in. They don't care enough about the grades. The Indian way of behaving is: you watch and you observe before you act. You never want to show off because it's not good taste to pound your own drum.

—Jeb Beaulieu, an American Indian Midwest counselor

◆ My daughter came home one day and said that one rule that she learned is that you are not to exceed a certain grade because if you do, you might as well not have any friends. So she would rather get a C versus an A any day.

—Arlene, an American Indian Southwest teacher

Reward of Going to College

◆ White kids come in with this whole attitude that school is part of the game you play to get in college. Where Indian kids see it as a chore, going to school is a chore, a place I have to go, where I'm put.

—Patty George, an American Indian Northwest teacher

Public Praise or Criticism

◆ You don't withhold praise, but make sure that you do it discreetly. Sometimes you find a student who won't do anything until they check with the teacher first, afraid of doing it wrong. They've really gotten hooked into wanting to do it exactly the way you want, and they lose their creativity, their spontaneity. Growing up here and being here as an adult, I can see that if one person gets too much recognition, then other people have a hard time dealing with that, and you set up that one person to become almost an object of scorn.

—Kate, an American Indian Northeast teacher

◆ And I can criticize them, but I do it one-on-one. And I laugh a lot when I'm criticizing. Because that's the only way to keep it painless. You can't do it out loud in class because it's too destructive.

—Karen Brown, a non-Indian Southwest teacher

With few exceptions, teachers noted that extrinsic motivators did not work well with American Indian children. Research notes that although most mainstream students strive to be successful in school and therefore respond to extrinsic motivators, those same motivators actually decrease even mainstream children's intrinsic enjoyment of the activity that they are being rewarded for (Deci, 1985). So, again, although the methods that we will advocate in the rest of this chapter are methods teachers reported that worked well with American Indian children, because they are based on intrinsic human motivation, they will work well with all children.

Instant Success May Be Unlikely

Some American Indian students, like Carrie's Dartmouth student, are successful in systems in which they compete for grades, rewards, and college entrance. Some students even feel uncomfortable if they aren't "doing" school "correctly," if they aren't duplicating what they think is occurring in mainstream school or if they aren't experiencing what their parents experienced. Anne, an American Indian teacher from the Midwest, had students who wanted to be studying what they heard white students read in the border town high school: Shakespeare.

◆ They chose *Julius Caesar!* And I said, "*Julius Caesar* sounds great. We can work with that. You are as capable as many of those public schools students,

and many of you are more creative." So anyway, I sometimes do things like that because the students give me the impression that they are really insecure about their abilities.

And some students, like the one below, won't respond immediately, even to what would seem to be obviously common sense lessons for life.

◆ Like today, he just kept replying, "I hate math. I'm not gonna to use it." I told him it was required. He came up with the answer, "Oh, I'm just gonna live on the rez." I asked him about his goals. "All I need to know is how to add and subtract for the store." I kept trying to persuade him that he could use it; he kept trying to persuade me that he wasn't ever going to need it. I told him I was trying to teach it to him in a way so he wouldn't be basically ripped off when he was older. So those are some of the things that kind of make work difficult.

Some students may have failed for so long in school that they will be initially resistant or even feign boredom rather than instantly turning around to be an enthusiastic student. They may be irresponsive for some time even to the most relevant curriculum. One can not expect instant miracles with students who have had a history of disenchantment with school. With this warning, we will turn to a teacher who found a way to connect with innate human dispositions toward learning.

A Profile of Amy, a Teacher Who Builds Instruction on Intrinsic Motivation

Amy is a very reflective, committed, and perceptive young teacher. I would like to think that it was because I prepared her for teaching, but if you've read our introduction, you will know that I began this research precisely because I hadn't done such a good job in the past with Amy's peers. As Ketron does with his talented students, all I do with Amy now is to cheer her on. I have highlighted the ways in which Amy taps students' intrinsic motivation

In Amy's first interviews, she talked with concern about the lack of hope her students felt in their futures:

◆ I love teaching, and I love teaching the students that I have. A lot of times people say, "Oh that kid's such a problem." The kid's not a problem; the kid has problems. The kid is often an innocent victim. And when I look at some of my students, I see a powerless, almost hopeless, look in their face. And I believe that a lot of times they act out because when they get to school that's the only power they have in their lives. Maybe saying no to doing a worksheet is the only power a student has. As human beings, we all need to feel some sort of power and ownership in our life. I think for some of these kids the only place they get that is the school, and unfortunately it's sometimes being a behavior problem. When I have success with them, it is almost like we're the underdogs, and when the underdogs pull out and rise above and succeed, it's like an incredible high. For a teacher it is an incredible high.

In her final interview, she talked directly about one of many successes she had with her students.

◆ We took on the task of looking at the reservation services that are currently offered. We wanted to find out what the community wanted or needed. I was hearing from the kids, "There is nothing to do," and I was hearing negative things about what's not being done. So I thought, "Let's look and see what is there" and "Maybe there's lack of knowledge about what is really out there."

As a teacher, Amy connected with students' concerns about their immediate world. She helped them by tapping their desire for self-determination, showing them ways to collect information about their world and give it to those who might affect it.

◆ It directly dealt with them and their families. What they were looking at was a big piece of their existence. They really get excited when they talk about what we did and that something came of it. We started out with a brainstorm about the services the tribe offered: buildings, groups, etc. And then we went and asked some people in the community and in the school whether we had missed anything that was offered. And we created a survey on computer to ask people what services they used. We asked them their age and whether they were an enrollee or not, and then we had them rank what they felt was the importance of what was offered, and then we asked them what things they would like to see offered, and we gave them some examples of longer school hours, computer classes for parents, language classes. Once we got the survey completed, we looked at it, had some people review it, and it was ready. [At a community gathering], the kids set up a table to give the people the survey. We gave them an extra ticket for a drawing for prizes if they filled it out. And the kids went down to the mall in town; a lot of them lived in

town and knew what was a good time to go to catch people there. And the kids that live on the rez did their neighborhood and community. Some called the clinic and asked if they could set up in the lobby there. We ended up with 150 surveys completed, which was more than our goal of a hundred. The excitement was there right in the beginning and then there was a lull: "Okay now we have to figure out how to do those results." When they were getting real answers, the kids got excited about them. Some [respondents] were writing a full page on the back about what they wanted, what they were willing to do. The kids felt that someone else really cared.

Another reason why humans want to learn is that they have an inclination to imitate those whom they respect. In this case, Amy thought that they learned most from observing and imitating each other.

◆ They became role models for each other. There was one student who volunteered off the bat. "Oh I'll take twenty-five surveys home with me." And others did too. And we had deadlines. There was a deadline when we had to get this done. If they didn't have their surveys completed, they couldn't get to point B. Once you put it on them, then they're responsible. "Here's what's happening," I said to one student who kept forgetting, "You're a big piece of this puzzle; without you we're not a puzzle." "They're in the car; they're not at home." Then the rest of them got on him, and the peer pressure made a lot of difference. I divided them up into groups once all the surveys were completed. I have never seen a group of kids who respect each other and work together as male and females better, ever, than I have with these kids. They're all in the same kind of boat, and nobody judges anybody here. One kid made a comment to another student about kind of teasing each other about t-shirts or something. And another student observing that said, "We don't tease. We're an Indian school. We're just who we are here." They all know that they've got stuff in their life and nobody meddles in that. They just come together like a little family. They remind me of just a whole big group of brothers and sisters.

In groups, we sort of did a coding system. The groups were according to services. What the clinic offered, one group had the school, other areas too, what services the people wanted. So they went through and manually marked, tallied, then we had a computer program that we used that tabulated all the results, and they made some graphs and grids that they thought were really cool. A gal [that had worked with this computer program] came in one day and [instructed] the students and me about how to run the program, how to put in our data, how it kicked out. We had all kinds of graphs, and [she helped] with what they meant. They had to figure that out. They thought it was really interesting.

Amy's students started realizing that they were doing, writing, and graphing for a real audience and a realizable purpose. She capitalized on their natural desire for self-determination.

◆ They had too much on the survey. "People don't want to fill out a three-page thing. We want to make this quick and painless for people." They had to re-vise the questions so that those surveyed would do it. There were things the people really wanted. Ojibwe language was a really big one. The community also wanted the school open more hours, the gym and what not. That was ranked second. So then when that was all done, we had to figure out what to do with this information. They went ahead and talked to the principal, who suggested that they send the findings to the (RBC) Reservation Business Committee. They felt really connected. And our results went to our educa-tion division, and they did implement some of the results. The kids reported their findings, and now we do have longer school hours, gym hours into the evening, and language classes, and they opened up a house out in Mahnomen [a reservation housing project]. That Mahnomen House is a positive place for the kids to be. They have various things that go on there. One night a week they work on their dance outfits, other nights on language and com-puter classes. It's just a real safe, healthy place for the kids and their parents to go. They really, really accomplished something. The kids see it as a result of the survey, and that was a clincher. I had the kids who were in other classes ask whether we were going to do something similar to that.

Amy found that the project relied on the curiosity of some and developed curiosity in others.

◆ It sparked some curiosity. One thing I was leery about was that some of the kids, maybe less than half, don't live out on the rez. I was worried that they would think, "Well what do I care, I don't live out here," but they found out that there were things that were open to them, like they could go to the clinic. And from there they got more curious because a lot of them have formed and shaped opinions about where the rez spends its money. They all have their concerns, opinions about whether they are getting a fair shake. If you don't use something, you have no idea it is even out there. So I think that helped them realize, "Hey, maybe we aren't so bad off. There's a lot of stuff here I don't use, but it is available." Once they started digging, it sparked curiosity, and it was good for them to hear what others thought.

209

Amy thought about their lack of feelings of competence and how to raise their confidence.

◆ A lot of them are afraid to fail. And having them go out onto their own, venture out onto their own, is asking them to almost expose themselves in a way that they are uncomfortable with. And by me giving them a guided ladder, I call it, if they follow that, then they feel there's no room for them to fail on that ladder. But if I just ask them to develop their own ladder, it's tough for them to do.

Students enjoyed the new feelings of competence that they developed in writing and computer analysis. Amy was concerned that all the students would show competence in the areas she had designated.

◆ I did a lot of checking, assessing them, and we did a lot of reflection. I was thinking, here I'm supposed to be an English teacher and what are we doing that is English? I am the only English teacher there. I have to be sure I am getting across to them things that are important as far as the writing and the computer skills. And I had to make sure I knew what it was all about because I had to check their ability. I would rotate them around so that they all got a chance. Some people excelled at the computer, and some shied away from it. I made sure that they all did a graph and that they all put the data in there and could show me how to do it. So I would sit with one at the computer while others were entering data and said, "Okay, make me this kind of a grid." I checked their competence that way. If they didn't know how, I'd say, "So and so, come here; we need to know how to do this," and then I'd have another student teach the both of us. Some excelled and others didn't: "You go and help so and so because they need your help." And I did some other checking. Is this meaning anything to you guys? Do you just want to bale on it? They were pretty receptive to that; that's what helped finish it. Checks like that. Writing out memos that related to the survey helped their writing skills. And I had in mind human skills, P.R. skills: What do you do when you approach someone about doing a survey like this? Sometimes we overlook social skills parts of education, and this was a great thing. Going out into the community, a lot of them haven't had that experience. So we'd do pretend type things. [Role plays were part of her guided ladder and depended upon imitation]. And when we had to call someone, we'd do a pretend type of thing on the phone. Everybody did that, everybody did the memo thing, everybody did the how-to-approach thing. If you're going to call over to the RBC, know who you're going to ask for, that type of thing. I wanted to make sure that they felt like they could do it.

Students are also motivated when they feel the power in their own voices, the project tapped their inclination toward self-expression:

◆ They designed the survey, the sole ones responsible for the entire project. I just stood in the background to help them edit, review. They'd make up questions. We'd put down our objectives. They created something that was tangible that showed what they wanted. At the end of the project they had to do a written report, there was kind of some technical writing in there, but also they reflected on what they felt about what they did. Everything that came out from them was real positive.

Motivation theorists also believe that humans learn because by nature they are responsive to feedback. Amy described how she orchestrated feedback for her students' work:

◆ I kept questioning what they were doing. If they had a survey question that got long and drawn out, they'd say, "Okay how does this look," and I'd never cut them off at the knees, but I did want to make them aware of what they're doing, so I would read it out loud and ask, "How does that sound to you?" "Well, that's too long." They'd try to edit. I kept asking them:
    "If you got this survey, would you fill it out?"
    "No."
    "Then why?"
    "We want to make sure that we aren't a bug to people."
    I kept questioning along the way. That allowed them to give themselves and each other feedback.

Amy recognized that students are purposeful and hopeful when they feel what they do matters:

◆ It's empowerment for them; it's powerful that they have the ability to care for their own people, and I think when they start seeing things that way. They get excited because they think: wow, I do have something I can do. I'm not going to let the dominant society, you know walk all over us, take advantage of us. I think that's neat, but it needs to come from somewhere nice. I think schools can be like that.
    Every so often I see a little flicker, like a flame of potential, and it could just be a full-blown fire that's just burning, but there's always something that has to go and smother it, and it drives me nuts. I go back to my attendance problem a lot, and I know that there's so many things that get in the way of

kids getting to school, but I really believe, if there is an ember there, it could be turned into a burning desire with a hook. These kids are survivors, and if there was something [in school] that was really, really exciting, that punch in there that they needed. . . . They're survivors, and they're tough, and they could get there [to school] no matter what is going on at home or what they went through the night before.

We will look individually at the things that we think help students to have the desire to get to school.

Need for Feelings of Self-Determination

Amy was able to see her students' need to feel like they had some power in their world, that they had some purpose. We recognized in this research that breaking away from the remnants of oppression can pose huge challenges to those who have felt hopeless and purposeless in the larger society. Connecting to the human need for self-determination can provide motivation for students and, as argued in the last chapter, can allow teachers to avoid being agents of assimilation while still helping their students to acquire skills.

Norm Dorpat, a non-Indian teacher from the Northwest, described students who felt no purpose or hope in their situations:

◆ If they don't find meaningfulness and a method of instruction that is responsive to their growing edge, they turn off, and tune out, and drop out, or get pushed out, or they end up being "behavior problems." Kids don't come that way. We make them that way. I think the system has a responsibility to be more responsive to kids. The curriculum is so linear and structured, and you look into our classrooms, even as young as kindergarten, and you go in there and the desks are in rows, columns, and kids are doing ditto sheets, and this lock-step curriculum doesn't fit where they are as people. They ultimately get squashed, and give up, or they rebel, or they become like little zombies going through the system, and that's the worst-case scenario.

Even though many classrooms do not feature desks in rows, American Indian children may still exhibit the behavior that Dorpat describes. When students experience a vital curriculum and see real purpose in school endeavors, especially when that starts at a young age and continues, it can help them break out of the cycle of feeling hopeless and purposeless.

There are two ways in which teachers can connect with the motivation that comes from students' innate need for feelings of self-determination. First, they can help students develop strategies by which they can understand the world they live in, and second, they can help students learn strategies to act on their worlds.

Community Needs for Feelings of Self-Determination

Barry Dana, an American Indian teacher from the Northeast, described the kinds of needs his tribe has and the necessity for students who will be prepared to meet those needs:

◆ With their skills, of reading and writing and math and science and all that, they won't be able to take control of their own government. There's got to be a system that believes in that. We don't have big money at the tribe, but we have enough [to prepare students]. The need is saying, "This is what we need, this is what we want, this is what we're going to honor in our tribe." And then the kids will come forth, the high school kids, and go [on to school]. But I find, with my own tribe, that if the tribe itself does not set a priority, then there is no priority. It's not a community thought that this is what we need, and this is what we should be working for.

The kind of curriculum that Amy tactfully devised was one that helped further the tribe in a view of what it needed and wanted. Lena Mann, a Southwest American Indian teacher, also saw the need for tribes to develop skills in self-determination.

◆ Some other tribes are completely lost because they have lost the basis; they have nothing traditional to live for. But somehow they need to pull together. We have something to live for. My father always said: "You drive your own wagon, you get off course, you have to learn how to get back to the road." With drugs and alcohol and all these things that are supposedly fun that lure you away from the main road. If you're not strong enough, if you do take a path like that, you've got to be strong enough to get back to the main road.

Students need to understand their world and to learn strategies to act on their world.

Reading the World, Understanding the World:
A Step toward Self-Determination

Ingrid, a non-Indian teacher from the Southwest, found some strategies to help students understand their world, and in the process she found strategies that helped to counteract resistance. In relating with students, she has found that direct demands don't work.

◆ Our students' grandparents remember being forced to go to school and forced to not speak their languages. And so that hostility factor is there. And you're less likely to want to learn a language if you have bad associations with it. English teaching is all associated with the coming of the white man. The freshmen this year were just awful. To think that they were as old as they were, and they couldn't put together a paragraph. And they weren't really interested in learning about it either. If I had started preaching topic sentences, they would have just ignored me. And so that's a really powerful thing, too, about this culture, is that if they don't like something, they just ignore it. But what I started doing was just having them write journals all the time. And I'd give them topics, or I just let them write. And after a while they just wanted to write about what they wanted to write about. They've started to have opinions.

Ingrid's students found a method to explore and understand their world. A step toward self-determination comes from observation and reflection. Teachers reported their students were good at the observation but often needed time and space for reflection and practice in articulation of thought in written and oral form. Students needed to see beneath the layers of human behavior, to see clearly. Talking and writing about experience can be a first step in self-determination. Mike Rabideaux, previously an American Indian teacher in the Midwest, said:

◆ We told the students why we were going down there to protest and [asked] if we should go down there. And the students said, "Yeah." And we went down to the historical society down by the capitol and protested NSP [Northern States Power]. The kids had fun, sang, and walked around bouncing signs around, and came back. I told them to write about what we did. Couple of them said, "We went down and protested." Couple of them said we went down there to try speaking out for a larger part of the Indian community, and we protested. And a couple more went as far as writing a whole page on what we did. They saw a little bit more.

If teachers seek to understand students' points of view and actively engage in exchange, they will model aspects of understanding the world.

Self-Determination through Acting on the World

As Amy pointed out, students may not have much control in the rest of their lives, but they can have some feelings of self-determination in a school setting. Amy orchestrated her classroom so that students were making group decisions to get something done, and many teachers told us of the effectiveness of activity-based learning, or project-based learning in which there were real products and results. Dorpat, a non-Indian, noted that even in teacher-centered instruction, students could take some responsibility in setting goals.

◆ Our goal [as a class] was, by the end of the school year, we were all going to know how to do fractions. That meant everything, like denominators, mixed fractions, adding, subtracting, multiplying, dividing. We're all going to be good at that. We focused on direct instruction for getting through those fractions: quick pace, quick checking for understanding, quick review, stuff that is real efficient, teacher-centered, but we agreed to do that.

Shared decision making and goal setting alone increases ownership in instruction and models self-determination, but the advantage to having real audience and purpose in student work can also be a powerful motivation force.

Real Audience

Jane Hatfield, a non-Indian teacher in the Southeast, discovered the powerful presence of peer and other student audiences to help students grow to believe in their own voices. Students who know that there will be audiences they care about, audiences beyond the teacher, endeavor more in their work.

◆ I had two Indian boys in my class, and I had them write an end to this Indian Legend that we were studying out of that anthology. It ended with these two Indian boys getting stranded on top of Devils Tower out in Wyoming, and I wanted them to tell me how they got down. Because in the myth, it just says that the boys got down off of Devil's tower. Everyone else was making up these crazy endings. One girl said that they bungy jumped off the top. Tommy wrote that the boys didn't really get down, but they stayed up there without food or water, and the sun dried them, and they died, and they turned to ash and then the wind came like a giant broom and swept their ashes off. That was one of the most beautiful things I've ever read. And I read it to the class, and they were like, "Wow!" And I took all of them, and we read

the legends and their endings to the fourth and fifth graders. Some of them were really funny, and the fourth and fifth graders were sitting there giggling, but it really was a successful little lesson that we did. Before I had students retell legends, and even the shyest boy I had in there, who would never even look up, though he was a wonderful artist, retold a legend. Whenever I was trying to get him to read, he would hardly do anything for me. But he just got up, and I was just blown away by how great he retold the story.

Amy generated a real audience for her students' work by helping them generate a survey for community members and helping them decide to take their resulting report to the Reservation Business Committee. As indicated in the last chapter, if students have a more distant audience than the teacher or even fellow students, an audience beyond their immediate context, they are more apt to develop audience sense, to decontextualize their writing so that those who are not in the immediate area will understand. Kevin Ritchie had his students practice this skill of writing to audiences that do not have immediate knowledge of the topic.

◆ About halfway through sophomore year, I found a project using tinker toys, a writing project. I divided them up into four groups, four kids in each group. Each had a box of tinker toys. And I took the directions away. And I said, "You can't design anything you see on the container, but what I want you to do is a series of things. I want you to design something, some product, imagine that you need to teach somebody how to assemble it and how to use it. I want you to write a technical manual for this. Organize it appropriately, table of contents; you need to be able to show how to put it together, and explain a function for it in the world, as if we were going to take this into production. Half your grade will be based on the narrative. You can draw pictures and diagrams and all that stuff with it. But when all four groups are finished, I'm going to take group A's project and give it to group C. And group C has to use only the written work. And they have to put it together. How well they put it together, how quickly, how efficiently your instructions allow them to put it together, part of your grade will be based on that." We spent two weeks in there. Every day they'd come in and get working. And I noticed that the Indian students, Sam especially, took charge. Sam is not a kid who cares at all about being in charge, but pretty soon people were looking to Sam for direction. Like, "Okay, we've got this subassembly together, now what do we do?" "Well, we gotta make it spin somehow. Why don't you guys work on that?" Since that time, it's been three years now. I've found a couple of other things that are similar to that. It's very task-oriented. One of our math classes is using a applied math concept, too. It's been real effective. It made it clear to me that I can give up some authority in the classroom and give structure for kids to figure out what they're doing themselves, and put a component in there that allows them to be in control of what it is they end up writing about, or explaining or solving. That was real engaging to the Indian kids, and the white kids. I think I realized that if I really do want to be a teacher of Native American kids, and if I really do want to reach white kids who don't care about school, I can't be a teacher in the way I've been taught. Being able to speak clearly and write fairly well and understand what you read and understand how to maneuver in the world of ideas: I need to help Native American kids feel like those things are all done in their culture, too.

Ritchie allowed his students to be self-directed and hence self-determined in their activity, but he also provided them with audience for their work. In all disciplines, if students have real audiences for their work, they will begin to be able to articulate (oral or written) ideas, and they will have reason to do so.

Real Purpose

Like Amy, Warner Wirta, a retired American Indian teacher from the Midwest, told of curriculum he developed that gave students both real purpose and real audience for academic endeavors:

◆ We used to develop symposiums dealing with community issues. We probably spent only about two days a week working out of the textbook. I used to say to myself, "Why in the world am I lecturing out of this social studies textbook? It's meaningless. That's not motivating kids. They just come in there just to wallow away their time. What's the use of talking about social movements if you don't put some of this into operation? What's the use of talking about the legal system? So that's what we started to do. The kids were writing letters. They would contact various people in the community to come and talk. And one of the best symposiums we ever developed (or I should say the kids did it; I mean I just guided them) was the wolves. That was the biggest issue in the community; everybody complained about those wolves killing everything! But then the kids started to do research and contacted people. And finally we got this doctor, Dr. Mech, from the University of Minnesota, who conducted this study of the wolves on Isle Royal, and we had him come up and talk at a symposium, and we must have had about 300 or 350 people from the community in the gymnasium. Those kids were just enthralled. It was just a beautiful experience; they had community involvement. We had a lot of these symposiums. We had attorneys come in to talk about the law. Very inquisitive these kids were. I tell you, they just threw questions left and

217

right. Fact it developed to the point that we were about to get somebody from the prison to come and talk, and that's when the principal put his foot down. Once you get them all working together, when they give each other responsibilities, they start working pretty good together. They cease to be judgmental of each other because they're in it together. And this seemed to have more of an effect on Indian students because it seemed like they had involvement, instead of the isolated types of experiences.

When students learned from being involved in projects that had real audiences and real purposes, they understood how to read their world, how to collect information, and how to act on their world.

Career

Career exploration has the possibility of bringing students to the deepest sort of self-determination, devising a future. Teachers should develop ways to have their students see possible careers, all the way through their schooling and well before high school, by which time students might have cut off options. For many mainstream children, the future is there to grab, yet all students deserve to feel hopeful about a future. Teachers talked again and again about the lack of hope that many American Indian children exhibit. Carrie, a non-Indian teacher from the Northeast, said:

◆ We did a section on life skills, and we did resumes and applications and career assessment. And the majority of the Indian kids could not identify what they wanted to do, and they're seniors. I have one young man who didn't know, so he decided to go in the service as a last option, just to get some direction on the task. I had another one who told me that he wasn't going to do anything next year. He was going to go live with his parents. His brothers did the same thing.

It is clear that senior year is too late, and that a resume, practice at job applications, and a career fair thrown in for good measure are just not enough. A major problem for American Indian children is that because of the remnants of oppression and resulting unemployment or underemployment, many are not exposed to adults with a variety of careers. Brad Hibbard, a non-Indian teacher from the Northwest, said:

◆ If they could see where they could be in ten years, a lot of them might see a place they'd like to be. They say, "Why do I need this?" The best answer I can give them right now is, "Well you don't know where you will be in ten years.

Let's just try to make sure you're ready to be somewhere." A lot of kids just don't know what options they have in life.

Career investigation needs to provide many visible possibilities for students, and students need in-depth exposure, exposure beyond a career fair or two. Amy developed a unit she called "Get a Life." Students chose five careers, investigated them in the library to find out (1) what work each entailed, (2) what reading, writing, and math skills they would need for the work, (3) what budget they might live on if they did that work, and (4) what working conditions they might have. They visited a career fair, interviewed people with three of the careers they had chosen, and shadowed one or more of those interviewed.

Every human being has the right to look to a future that doesn't have a ceiling; they should dare to dream. For this to happen, children need to think about the future, starting at a young age, before life tempts them to cast off choices. They need to be conscious about the possible consequences of their choices, for instance, a decision to avoid college preparatory math or science. They need to believe that they have some power over the course of their life; they deserve these feelings of self-determination.

Some students, because of a disability they have, do have a limit on their possibilities. Arlene, an American Indian teacher from the Southwest, however, believes that even students with severe disabilities can find purpose in their lives.

◆ The children who need a communication board are issued a computer, but out in the village, in the hogan, if you give them a sophisticated computer, they will put it away in a drawer for the summer; the family would feel intimidated. So there is a whole nine months lost of what you have been working on. [Instead] they need pictures on a board to help them communicate. I'd like them to even be able to make things themselves. And there are other possibilities of things to make: it could be an adaption of a TV, a blender, using gross hand movements. Giving them decisions in their life, do I want to watch the TV or listen to the radio. Now I have a supervisor who is supportive of an idea I have, a Native American, and now in the fall we will have a workshop. It's happening. He said this is the first of its kind. If we can teach these students skills like splicing, making low tech equipment, and we can employ our own students. The elderly use a lot of this equipment. Students would be contributing. When you go out to the village, how many of those people will use computers or synthesizers? There are some things that they will use. My job is not only speech, but vocational. I have identified a need that hasn't been addressed yet; it is not happening yet. I am going to give it a shot, and I want to make sure it goes through. I want to have workshops, so we can teach high school students these low tech skills.

219

Jeb Beaulieu, an American Indian counselor, has a way of letting his students know that more is riding on their choices than their own futures:

◆ The community has a multitude of problems, and we need doctors, we need lawyers, we need all these kinds of people to come back and help out. And I tell them, "I'd like to have you be a teacher or a principal, so when my kid gets to be your age, you will be his teacher." And I tell them, "You can't be just as good as other people. You have to be better because as an Indian you're going to face racism and discrimination." And so I tie it back up to the tribe, helping the community, and bring it back around again.

Teachers talked about the fear of getting children's hopes up when experience had taught them that dreams are often smashed. But teachers should not cut off possibilities on that basis, nor should they be discouraged when their hard work does not pay off on graduation. Because of the complexities involved in American Indian life, because of those remnants of oppression, there may be a delay between graduation and the beginning of a career or career preparation. If adolescence is delayed, it is important that students have something in mind when they find themselves ten years down the road looking for a future.

Retaining/Renewing Culture

At the community level, the school can support the tribe in retaining or renewing culture. Although this was the subject, in part, of Chapter 4, we would like to return to that theme while thinking about what works in the classroom. First, educational endeavors can engender self-determination at the tribal level. Arlene, an American Indian teacher from the Southwest, describes a community educational project that brought pride to those involved in it:

◆ A comment was made that the center used more light bulbs than anyone on the whole reservation. And that's how it was. From the interest of the people, a whole new stone building emerged. Students had a part in building it out of our own native material. And it was an art building. They had just about everything you can imagine. They had auctions to sell off their paintings; these students were artistic and talented. They sold their pottery, their weaving, and people would bid on them. I mean they advertised it all across the country, and then we had teachers from New York who read about our school, and they wanted to just volunteer, but some stayed on. And it was one thing after another. All you could see once you entered the hallway were just walls covered with students' work. And in the evenings, the families. Mothers would come over there to the school, and they would make pottery at night, and we went there with our mothers and our fathers, and we'd build things. It was a real community school. Then they had weavers who came in and taught students how to weave. And then as a math project, the seventh grade and eighth grade boys went out into the village and made those bread ovens out of rock. That was their math project. And they had students write their own books, and they used those to learn. And they had, like Scott Momaday and other people like that.

Many teachers told tales of such school-related programs that instilled cultural pride and self-determination beyond the school. Zantua, a Northwest American Indian teacher, described a school program that instilled pride within the community and respect from those without. By performing, students acted on their world, to real audiences and with the purpose of improving intercultural respect.

◆ My students want to do well because they are in the public eye. And the majority of the performances are for non-Natives. We used to go to other schools, and the students there used to do that little "whoop, whoop, whoop" stuff. And a couple of times when we were out at like military base [schools], and there were kids that threatened to shoot us. "I'm gonna shoot you Indians. I'm gonna shoot you." When you hear little kids like that . . . it's really absurd. And after the presentation, I've just said, well, "Weren't you the one that wanted to throw rocks at us? How do you feel about Indians now?" "Well, I want to be one." Now we don't hear that "whoop, whoop, whoop" stuff. When we started we had four kids that had outfits. Now we have maybe twenty that are ready in a minute and have full dress. If they don't have an opportunity to perform, at least they have their outfit, and they can go out in the community and do pow-wows.

These are only two of many school-connected programs teachers talked about that involved students and community members who were motivated by doing things for real purposes and sometimes real audiences; the programs helped to renew or maintain the culture, and they dispelled negative attitudes in the mainstream culture.

Interdisciplinary/Thematic Projects

Many teachers also talked about the success of interdisciplinary thematic projects, though some added some cautionary remarks that we will focus on after a brief introduction. Although this type of curriculum development is nothing new, it is

particularly consistent with the ways of learning that many teachers described their American Indian students as having. These projects permit students to learn while seeing the wholeness of the topic and of the endeavor, and while seeing the way different disciplines fit together to accomplish real end results. Real purposes and real audiences for student work will help student motivation for these projects because through them they can often learn about their world and learn how to act on their world, giving them feelings of self-determination. Bernita Humeyestewa, an American Indian teacher from the Southwest, said:

◆ Right now we're into a cluster on "Bold Journeys" that has to do with the Southwest. And the first reading selection started out with how land is created, the making of California. And it's an Indian legend, so the kids really responded to that, and I just took off from it and got them into other legends, we did some reading and they did little summaries as a skill. They made maps of California, mapped out the routes that the animals took. They got into it; that's what makes it exciting. The other thing is using—there's a lot of terminology for it—holistic language or whole language, hands-on, activity-based. That's the kind of teaching that I find works while integrating a lot of the subjects. And what I started out doing this year, a lot of which I didn't do a lot of years before, was to *not* block off my time and say "this is a reading period" and "this is a math period" and "this is a language period," but to bring them together. That works a lot better for me.

Many teachers talked about the difficulties that absenteeism, short attention spans, or low skills can pose to interdisciplinary projects. We will quickly summarize solutions that other teachers posed. It is useful for each student to have an individual endeavor going on during a project, be it related to a students' strengths (a book to read, an art project connected to the theme, or a challenging math endeavor) or be it related to a student's weakness (independent math exercises, a book selected because of its interest and because it will not pose frustration for the student reading independently, extra independent work with a concept or skill covered in a prior unit that the student had not mastered). In this way, there is always something the student knows he or she can be doing if absent or if a class or group activity is distasteful for the individual for some reason. Teachers also can plan so that many facets of the project can be going on at once so that if some students are out of sorts or have low attention spans, or if others need the nudge to follow their curiosity, there are alternative activities: copying relevant material from a text students had found the prior day, reading, writing, computer work, CD-rom searches, art work, collecting information, running an errand. In short, make sure that each student can be purposeful. Many reservation schools and mainstream schools have been experimenting again with flexible scheduling. As long as teachers plan to meet the attention spans of their students and to keep them engaged, longer blocks of time than fifty minutes can support project-based learning.

Other teachers talked about the difficulty of assessment. It is useful to generate a list of outcomes that are either appropriate to the content of the unit or that indicate skills, dispositions, or knowledge that your students particularly need. You can track individuals' progress in the study unit or in the year, perhaps with an individual record for each student, including the individual's personal goals for learning. This kind of authentic assessment puts the emphasis where it should be, on progress in skills and in accumulated knowledge. If grades are necessary in your situation, contract grading in project situations may help both teachers and students track progress. We will come back to assessment issues at the end of the chapter.

Students' Curiosity: Making It Relevant

A very strong intrinsic motivator for schoolwork is a student's own curiosity, but it is only when the world of the student has some overlap with curricular content that we can tap the student's curiosity. Making the curriculum relevant is a first step in capitalizing on a student's curiosity, but only a first step. Thus, in this section we will start with the importance of relevance, moving closer to curiosity as we move on.

Over and over again, teachers told us that it was important to find connections between students' lives and the content to be covered. Thomas Smith, a non-Indian teacher from the Southwest, said:

◆ Every period is a struggle to get the kids on task of what you want them to do, and I just am really weary of having to try to force children to want to learn. My own little kids and what I see when I go down to the lower-level schools is that little kids have such enthusiasm for learning. Such a tremendous curiosity. And they go into junior high school with that. When they come out of junior high, it's gone.

Curriculum has traditionally changed when students enter the secondary sector, and I think it particularly interesting that Smith identified curriculum in the high school as "what you want them to do." Elementary teachers are generally skillful at

delving into realms that children find intriguing (what they want to do), but when a child rounds the bend into junior high school, their worlds are too often disconnected from the curriculum. Amy talked about this in relation to her own high school experience.

◆ I remember these guys sitting in class, and they hated reading *My Fair Lady*. And they failed English because they hated *My Fair Lady?* What good is that book going to do them when they're out ricing, hunting, living? Those things are real to them, not *My Fair Lady*. They would tell us stories about the things they would do or make. I just think that had we had the opportunity to learn about that, if somebody would have tapped [our interests), that really would have been something for us. But it's that fear the teacher has of reaching out, being out in new territory. And I understand that, but you have to let yourself go into the student's territory.

The challenge for the teacher seems to be finding the overlap between your students' worlds and the content you project the student will benefit from in their future. Some responsibility for this task will go naturally to the student if teachers permit their students choice in what they learn.

Choice

Students who are allowed choice in how and what they learn bring two kinds of intrinsic motivation to their work. First, they have feelings of self-determination linked with a task because they have had some control over its selection and perhaps its development, and second, they are more apt to have a natural curiosity connected with a task or topic if it is chosen. Linda, a principal in the Northeast, recognized the necessity of choice and relevance.

◆ Kids have got to have some choices in what they learn. And we as teachers, absolutely, **must** develop the skill of not teaching the basics in isolation [from their interests]. Teaching the basics in integration, we've **got** to do that. It's the only way that we're going to manage schooling for these kids with any success, and I define that success as connecting the kid to the reality of his community so that education means something to him. It's got to become an integrated, project-based approach.

A non-Indian teacher in Linda's school thought that reading scores improved because of allowing choices:

◆ When I identified that the reading textbooks were at the grade-three level even though the kids were at the middle school level, I knew something had to be done. And at that time, I wasn't exposed to reading or writing process. I had this gut feeling that there was something more, but I just couldn't articulate what was missing. So now I negotiate. "You have your interest, great, but you also need to do the things that I need to have you do in the curriculum as well." So that's what I mean by negotiation. Kids pick out what they want to read, novels, trade books. I hate to use scores as an indicator of success, but each year, progressively on the California Achievement Test, you could see the progress in the reading scores. And I know that has to do with allowing the choices.

Be aware, though, that students who have had no choice in school material may feel overwhelmed when they do get to choose. They may be so out of touch with even their own interests that they may not be able to see possibilities for connecting those interests with course content. Gradual transition from having no choice to having unlimited choice is best. Furthermore, some students are so keyed into pleasing the teacher that having no view of what the teacher might prefer can be scary. Finally, other students who have taken up resistant behavior to have power in their world may need to be tantalized with a deep interest before they will change their behavior. Initial passivity or resistance must not be mistaken for lack of curiosity or interests.

Real-Life Interests/Relevance

Once learning had become connected with a real-life interest, some teachers said that American Indian children were self-starters who followed their own curiosity. Brad Hibbard, a non-Indian teacher from the Northwest, can introduce this section because he recognized himself in his students.

◆ One math teacher got me interested in relativity. By the time I finished tenth grade, I'd gone through every physics book in the public library. That's why I understand a lot of our students. They're basically self-directed if you catch their interest.

Starting with students' own ideas for learning is even better than giving them choice. Linda, a principal from a Northeast reservation school, described how one of her teachers had done that:

◆ This teacher said, "Now, this is what we mean by a fraction. Now, kids, what kinds of things could we do to investigate what fractions are and how they work in our lives and everything?" And the kids are all talking at the same time, and they're coming up with different kinds of projects. The teacher's running around getting materials for the kids, and when I say to the teacher, "What's your learning objective?" that teacher is one of the ones that knows.

David Winsky, a non-Indian teacher who teaches in a Northeast public school, warned about focusing all instruction for college-bound students and their interests:

◆ When we do an activity outside, it just seems that every one of my Native American kids relishes that sort of thing, take more of a leadership role than they normally do. Paper and pencil and textbook stuff: they may do it or they may refuse. One of my students, some time after we were done with our forestry unit, said that when he walks through the woods now it's a whole different experience, he's looking at the trees and identifying them. And I thought, great. Of all the students that walk in the door, only 25 percent are going to complete their college degree. So what about that other 75 percent? So how important is it that I go into great depth in the chemistry of photosynthesis? I've been looking at things with a lot more keener perspective lately: what's the pay-off here? Even a college graduate may not remember the dark reactions of photosynthesis. I'd rather that years from now they can walk through the woods and identify a dozen different trees. There are tons of things like that in biology. I think, the more we can do to get them to connect, the better.

Winsky's student, the one who walks in the forest differently now, may also be nudged to do independent work to follow up on his new interest. Nudging students from an area of interest to more sophisticated knowledge in that area is an important next step for all learners; this student may be one for whom the "dark reactions of photosynthesis" would stick. Nudging is what this kind of teaching is all about. John Nesbit, a non-Indian teacher from the Southwest, has a simple rule for himself about teaching English:

◆ Everybody who is successful in working with the kids here in English finds ways to get the kids actively engaged with language and then things happen. And it's that simple. It boils down to that. I make sure they are doing something with the language, that they can't just sit and kick back and be passive. Every year my class changes, depending on what's going on in the world, and I bring a lot of current things, whatever I can find, to try to get the kids engaged in things.

Tapping Cultural Interests

Some teachers found that connecting material with a student's culture helped students who were otherwise not engaged in what was going on. Kevin Ritchie, a Northeast non-Indian teacher, said:

◆ The Indian kids require that you be a little more real. Sam's hand was up, he says, "Mr. Ritchie, I don't got any idea what you're saying." That's kind of sobering, and he means it; he's not trying to disrupt class. What he's saying is: "Keep talking if you want to, but I don't have a clue. If you want to help me, good. If you don't, go ahead." I appreciate that kind of honesty from kids. So I think, "How can I do this differently?" And now I take special pains to search out literature that is relevant to them. I take special pains to make those connections whenever I can, and to normalize them after making those connections, too. Not like, you're Indians and you're special. There's none of that to it. It's more like, we're all part of this whole process, see if we can get a different perspective, "What do you think?" So I think by the time they're juniors and seniors they feel like their culture and their thinking and their experience has a place in the classroom. And their literature, too, because we read Scott Momaday and read Joy Harjo.

In some tribes, American Indian teachers and teacher's aides found that it was useful to have the children collect and write down oral stories; in other communities it was decidedly forbidden. Terri, an American Indian teacher's aide from the Southeast, said:

◆ I've been doing that with my class. We write down legends. We tried to do a legend in our language, but most of them don't know it. Some a little bit here and there they do, but they don't speak it fluently, and I had to tell them the words most of the time, but it was worth it.

And although some students have deep and developed cultural interests and curiosity, other students do not find motivation in such curriculum. Anne, an American Indian teacher from the Midwest, warns us not to assume that a cultural connection will provide motivation:

◆ I try to bring in the cultural aspect of it, but this boy wrote to me, "This doesn't relate to me. In fact, I hate it. Indian culture doesn't mean anything to me." And he thought I was going to be angry about this because he came up to me. And he said, "Anne, I answered how I felt." And I said, "Well, that's great. That's what I wanted from you." And what I found out was, 'cause I

227

was wondering about this, that his dad was Indian but his mother remarried someone caucasian, and they don't follow the Indian way of life. And he doesn't participate in anything Indian. And he's a very capable student, but he comes here, and he doesn't get very involved.

Anne also told about the work she does in helping students to compare cultures:

◆ Today in tenth grade, we were reading a story, and it was a Native American story called "The Man Who Sent Rain Clouds." I said, "What was their burial ritual?" And so the kids said, "Well, they put pollen out, and they put corn meal out, and they would paint certain marks on their faces, and they wrapped them in blankets." "And what was the ritual that the Catholic priest expected?" "Well, to mark it with the holy water." "Okay, now let's bring it to our experience; how do we traditionally bury our people?" And many of them knew. They knew how we did it, what we put on the body traditionally. And then I asked, "What were the two different perceptions of the water?" "It was for drinking water on the journey. It wasn't to wash away sins."

Anne helped her students be analytical about cultural difference, and to be analytical of literature about cultural difference. A next step might be to have them investigate different cultures' burial traditions. She might have taken them from insight to further inquiry, a next logical way to tap curiosity in the classroom.

Inquiry

Curiosity is based on questions that a human has about their world, and to fully use the inclinations that humans have toward curiosity, school curriculum can be organized so that students can search for answers to their own real questions. And finding answers to real questions, as Amy's services project demonstrates, loops back to be a step in self-determination through acting on the world. Students can ask the questions, see situations more clearly, and then they can find a way to act on what they found out.

Brad Hibbard, a non-Indian teacher from the Northwest, found a way to get students to ask questions:

◆ I've got all kinds of these books and things I pick up and leave around, just weird things, because I know they'll be picking them up and looking through them and then asking questions about them. How does that work? How does this work? All kinds of neat questions.

Neat questions can come from real life circumstances as well. A middle school in the Northeast asks student to write down questions about themselves (Bilodeau-Jones & Bossie, 1993), about the world, and questions about what the world expects of/from them. They take everyone's questions and build units of thematic study around the intersections of the students' questions.

The library is one source for answers to students' questions. Warner Wirta, a retired American Indian teacher from the Midwest, said:

◆ I would have the kids get together in various groups, the so-called smart ones and those that were not the best of readers, and have them work together as teams of maybe five or four. And I would have them learn to use the library. That's more important than classroom work because that's where it's going to happen when you leave this place. You have to learn how to use these particular types of educational tools that you will use in the future.

Rose Fleming, a non-Indian teacher in a public school in the Northeast, has students start by researching aspects of their own culture and bringing something in to describe to the class:

◆ Basically, you can talk about how you spend a holiday; you can talk about if there's something that marks a passage, like a particular birthday because your parents feel that it's an important day. It could be a recipe that's passed down from generation to generation, or it can be an art form. So last week Diane came in and she shared the making of Indian bread with the class. So she read the recipe to the class and said, "I can't tell you how much to use of the ingredients because I do it all by eye." She talked about what the dough would feel like in her hands. And she made some bread for us. And she had a piece to give to everybody in the class, and talked about finding out all the different ways that it's been adapted. Her mother told her that many generations back, they would dip it in molasses; it was a sweet Indian bread then. Over the last few years she said she noticed that other families use jam, some put maple syrup on, and some just sprinkle brown sugar and confectioner's sugar.

Fleming likes Ken Macrorie's concept of I-Search (Heinemann Educational Books, 1988) as a way to get her students started on research:

◆ The students pick a topic that's important to them and then search out the answer using a lot more private sources of material than encyclopedias. I like it for early stages, and I wish that in the younger years, like in the ninth and tenth grade, other disciplines would handle it that way. Really, as far as a full-

229

fledged research paper, there's a very small percentage of our students that are going to use that again. The rest just need to know how to go about and get information.

In I-Search, students pick a question they really want to know an answer to, they write about (1) what they want to know and why they want to know it, (2) what they already knew about the question before their search, (3) how they went about their search, and (4) what they found out. All this is done in the first person after students search beyond the secondary sources that libraries hold: interviewing people, phoning and writing letters for information, observing, searching the Internet, and using many other forms of primary research that serve their ends. If teachers want students to learn citation and footnoting, that can be done in the context of this more engaging kind of paper, just as it might be in a more formal research paper.

Teachers can also have classes work in groups modeling the cultural journalism of the sort of research that Eliot Wiggenton developed for *Foxfire* (Wiggenton, 1985). Cultural journalism creates a sense of urgency that stems from a strong sense of the community as audience and a strong sense of purpose—to preserve culture before it disappears. Students write articles in a magazine format for their community. This unites students in the spirit of collaboration and in a sort of collective self-determination, resulting in the preservation of culture. There's potential for this kind of writing in every community. Students collect information about an aspect of culture by interviewing elders, examining artifacts, and/or observing the cultural events in progress. Students also can develop photography skills to record the search that they have made. There are cultural events that are appropriate for such research (such as wild ricing or certain kinds of dancing or feasting), and there are events (such as religious ceremonies) that are not appropriate. As a teacher you will need to know or find out which is which.

The Teacher's Role in Connecting Students with Their Curiosity

Teachers who want to encourage student curiosity as a motivator for learning will need to support the student in reconnecting with their interests. Interest inventories may be a useful way to begin a school year, no matter what a teacher teaches. Above all, teachers need to be good listeners, seeking to thoroughly understand the student's inclinations and questions about the world. Teacher interest in student topics further fuels student curiosity; teachers who believe they can learn from their students are in for a real treat.

Responsiveness to Feedback

Teachers can enhance student motivation by the feedback they give. Amy talked about just how responsive her students could be to her one-on-one feedback:

◆ If only there could be one of me for every one of them—they are definitely receptive to that one-on-one situation. I sit down with one kid and go through something that they just might get. Maybe it's just because I'm right there on them that they feel like they need to get going. I've pulled things out of kids that they thought they couldn't do; they've been able to develop beyond [their expectations]. We've been working on essay writing—that abstract kind of writing—and they're shocked that they are doing it. At first it was this two-page thing where they just [went], "Forget it, here's a page and that's it," and I said, "No, that's not it; we're going to sit down together." I had one kid who at first said "forget it" but then couldn't stop writing; the bell's ringing, and he's sitting in there. But definitely I pull things out of them that I couldn't do if I had a huge class. I can approach each one of them differently. I can sit down and say one thing to her that I wouldn't say to the whole class, something I've observed related to her own life. It kind of hooks them. A little bag of tricks that teachers carry around.

Feedback is a little bag of tricks that teachers carry around. Research tells us that students who are used to failure tend to perceive success as having little to do with any effort they put forth. We need to help these sorts of students to redefine success as directly connected to effort. Tom Ketron tells about the bag of tricks that he carries around in his very large classroom. He works to keep them trying.

◆ The kids have to realize they're going to get better with effort. I always tell them that. "I like this; this is good; this is why I like it." Or if there's something that's wrong, it's not that it's wrong, it's: "These are things you could do that would make it better. These are the next steps." I work from the top back down. I tell them, "You are only in one stage. And don't worry about your grades because when you go to a gallery, they're not going to ask to see your grades or transcripts; they want to see your artwork. You are constantly going to improve. You're going to get better; you're going to get faster; you're style's going to change. This is just one stage. And that's why everything doesn't have to be perfect. And you're going to make mistakes. And if you know why you did it wrong or why it blew up, or why it collapsed, [all the better]. You're just working on learning." The one thing I don't grade on is talent. Talent doesn't mean anything. 'Cause I have some who are very talented, and they don't work. I grade on, "You work, and you try, and you put out an effort, and

you are learning, and you are improving. It doesn't matter where you are on the scale, on the ladder, as long as you're moving." I'm constantly going around, circulating, watching them, telling them things I see in the different stages.

Tom's process of feedback helps students to be reflective about their work so that they need him less and less as they improve. At that point he is only there to rejoice with them in their success. He builds students up until they are receiving real world feedback from others, from colleagues or artists judging contests or shows. Teachers need not be their students' only source of feedback. Peers, even elders, or other real audiences in the community or beyond it can become powerful sources for feedback.

American Indian students may have come from classrooms where feedback hasn't been as careful as that of Tom and Amy. Public criticism of students is disastrous, and if that has happened, students may prefer to do no work at all rather than put themselves in a potentially humiliating situation. These students need to rebuild trust in the giver of feedback. We will learn more about building trust in the next section.

Feelings of Competence

Amy, the teacher we profiled in this chapter, said:

◆ Their lack of believing in themselves is what's difficult. So many of them just don't believe in their ability to succeed, and it's so sad to look around and see how different ones have fallen off the wagon for whatever reasons. So much wasted talent. And I think, "How did we fail these ones? And I go through the roster, one by one, and I go, "How did we fail them. How?"

Human beings by nature like to do things that they do well. They desire feelings of competence. It is not fair for schools to set up situations that make children lose the feelings of self-respect that come from feeling competent. Ketron called his technique to keep this from happening "guaranteed success."

◆ They can be successful. I help them be successful. And they like to be successful. It makes them feel good. That's why I take things to school board meetings and to shows and around the community. And people praise the work they do. It reaches a point where success brings more success. When they feel success, we can just talk art. I don't even touch [this one young man's] projects anymore. He's getting better than I am.

Teacher Acceptance and Belief in Students

When teachers believe in students' ability to be successful, they often begin to believe it themselves.

◆ When I was in fifth grade in town, I remember this one teacher, she asked me to read one day in front of the class. And I got up and started reading, and her eyes got big. Later on, after class, she asked me where I learned to read like that. And I said, "From going to school." So, the next day, she bought me a whole bunch of reading books and told me, "If you can read, you can do anything you want in life." She knew my parents couldn't afford books, so she bought me books, and those were mine. And she told the other kids that I was the best reader in her class. And I got a ribbon for that. And I used to have that ribbon, but I don't know what happened to that.

—Anne, an American Indian teacher from the Midwest

Teachers can help students turn around their belief in themselves by finding the things that students do well and encouraging them. Teachers also can help by setting up situations in which small success is possible, pointing out these small successes, and nudging students along a ladder to improvement. Even the very best students need this nudging. To do this, you simply must accept students for where they are at the moment, and start from there.

Establishing a Safe Environment

◆ You have to do it so it's nonthreatening because if you don't they'll yack back at you mean, really mean. And when I talk to them, I don't do it in a threatening way. I just go up to them and say, "Hey, you know, we have to do this. So let's do it." And so that gives them the option to say, "Yeah, I can decide to do this, I'm not being really threatened." So its still cool for them to say, "Well, maybe I can do it." You have to let them have power to [get themselves in that position].

—Anne, an American Indian teacher from the Midwest

Some students may transfer into your class because things have not gone well elsewhere, or they may hardly ever be in your class because things have not gone well in the past, and they have given up on school. Or they may be successful students who are in your class but nervous about showing their success because they have been in prior situations in which they were humiliated because of success, for all the complicated reasons explained in prior chapters.

To begin to take advantage of your knowledge, whatever it may be, students will have to drop defensive strategies and recognize your classroom as a safe place where learning will take place. So many teachers told us that anger or frustration directed at American Indian children can cause great harm. Anger quickly destroys the beginnings you have made to establishing a safe environment. Patty George, an American Indian teacher from the Northwest, tells how he sets up a safe environment:

◆ The way you lead up to teaching them is different. You have to gain that trust. Where they believe that you believe that they can do it. You expect the best, you get the best from them. And that's a process you have to go through with them. Basically what I do when I get a group of kids is I treat them nicely, I ask them nicely to do things. I don't tell them to do things. I talk to them a lot, even though they look like they're not listening and they're turning away. I tell them how I really feel, and I do activities to build their self-esteem. I talk a lot about how important they are, how special they are. I do a lot of build-up.

In an inner-city situation, Norm Dorpat has discovered that he needs to be very clear about limits and consequences to establish a safe environment.

◆ You have to make sure there are clear limits and clear expectations within that classroom. I have to think about power; what does this situation demand, and it's my job, as a representative of the tribal community, to make sure that happens. There are consequences, not the kind of wishy-washiness of trying to massage the situation. And if you are firm, fair, if you show that respect to the kids through that consistency and fairness, they'll fight it initially, but they love it eventually. They just love that, almost without exception. Many are crying out for that kind of clear limit setting. They want to know where they stand, and they want to be able to predict what's going to happen. If I do this, this is going to happen. [As a teacher], if you do it based on how you happen to be feeling that day, you're doing a disservice to the kids because they don't know where they stand.

Clear, Reasonable, and Growing Expectations

◆ So we have students that expect more of themselves because we expect more of them, and they've increased their expectations of themselves because we've increased ours. And they're more than capable of doing it, they can do it if you modify their program somewhat [to support them].

Teachers agreed with this non-Indian teacher from the Northeast that, after investigating how skilled students were and accepting students for where they were, it was important to have high expectations of students. Thinking ahead to where you want them to be, setting up goals, outcomes, results, competencies, or objectives (whatever the currently appropriate word for them is in your state) will help you to maintain discernible expectations. It is very important that you do not assume that because some are behind, they need to have less expected of them in the end. Kate, an American Indian teacher from the Northeast, said, "You have to look at what your goals are in being a teacher. They shouldn't be any different for one group of students than for another group of students."

Teachers varied in the amount of flexibility they used to get students to meet goals. A non-Indian teacher from the Northeast, who also wanted to be called Anne, had students who knew what to expect if they didn't get their work done:

◆ Do you water down the work so they can pass? It's something that we struggle with all the time. I have a ground rule: "When you come to my classroom, you come with your homework completely done, or you have to stay after school until the bus comes at 3:10." They tried for a long time to give me every excuse in the book why they couldn't stay; I didn't buy it. They need consistency.

The tough love approach seemed to work well for some teachers; other teachers found that if they didn't budge on goals but were flexible about where or when the work was done, they still had pretty good results. As previously stated, teachers talked about the benefit in setting up contracts or independent work with their students who were prone to absenteeism.

Teachers recognized a point of conflict between setting high expectations and maintaining the feelings of competence that generate motivation. As a teacher, one has to do a careful balancing act. Anne continued by saying:

◆ Once they open up and they've had success, then if they reach a point where they can't have success, they shut down again. If they come to a point where they can't go beyond where they are [without support], you have to be careful about how you approach it, or they'll shut down on you. Small successes, small steps, over a long period of time.

Small Steps

Many, many teachers talked about the necessity of, even used the same phrase, "small steps." It's important to recognize that these teachers were talking about the students who were having trouble being motivated because they lacked the impetus that past feelings of competence might have brought to their work. Teachers,

however, noted that other American Indian students were already motivated by feelings of competence, and that they were ready for the highest of expectations—giant steps.

There are symptoms that can identify students as the ones who are low in feelings of competence, and teachers need to learn to read these. These students are often highly defensed: they would rather be seen as recalcitrant, angry, resistant, stubborn, bored, or apathetic than admit that they cared about their competence in schoolwork. Some students who feel incompetent are the ones who hide in the back of the classroom, hoping that the teacher will pay no attention to them. Indeed, many who have felt bad about themselves as a learner for a long time actually do stop caring. Why should they care, if they never had success?

Bart Brewer, an American Indian teacher from the Northwest, described how he needs to work with the more defensed of these students:

◆ Some kids want to try to take the easy road out, basically get by with the least amount of work, and I try to throw in little road blocks. I try balance—I push them and yet I try not to push them too much. It's kind of intuitive. There's some people that you can push a little bit, but if they start pushing back, you have to back off; otherwise, they'll start escalating to where I'm fighting with the student.

Matt, a non-Indian teacher from the Midwest, has learned to emphasize forward progress rather than focusing on how behind students are:

◆ Give it to them in small pieces. Rather than laying it all on them, "Okay, you're 450 pages behind," you say, "Okay, you're one page behind today." Small doses so they can handle it, because if you give them too much at once, they tend to back away. I found out that it helps to set up daily expectations, something they can complete in one day, rather than extended projects. A lot of independent work has actually worked well with my math classes; everyone's at such different levels, everyone's on a different contract with me; they work at their own pace, and that's successful. I draw up a contract based what they feel they can do. We go week by week with the contract, and at the end of this week, we'll evaluate what they've done, and then we'll set up the next contract for next week, especially with the older students. This way they're responsible for it, whether they're here or not; they can be caught up by Friday. That way has worked out well.

Amy has learned that in some subject areas students need step-by-step coaching to establish feelings of competence:

◆ They have a very hard time making the transition from that abstract level [of their thought] to the written word. Things that work well with their writing are very detailed and small step instruction. I can't just say to them, "Here's the assignment: writing a one-page essay on something you feel strongly about." Maybe I could do that down at the public high school with the same grade level. But here I might get one paragraph without support; they need to see the process, step by step. We need to go through the whole brainstorming, outlining, that entire process together. A lot of times what works is going through an example, and building in small successes over a long period of time. Give them something they can be successful at.

Building Confidence in Groups

Many students can build feelings of competence by working within a group situation. This builds on the strength in collaboration that many American Indian students have, as noted in Chapter 6, "Ways of Learning." Carrie, a public school teacher from the Northeast, said:

◆ I noticed that they don't like doing individual projects. They like being part of a group. They know how to do the work, but if you give them an individual task, every five minutes their hand will go up. And it's not that they don't know how to do it; they just want reassurance. 'Cause if you stand right there by the corner of their desk, they'll go right down through it, and they'll get every single answer right. But it's just the uncertainty. And you have to be constantly walking around the room. The Indian kids for some reason seem to need that verbalization more than the other kids. Just to assure them that they're on the right track. But they can do that for each other more in groups.

Arlene, an American Indian from the Southwest, noted that sometimes you have to help the students identify obstacles and help them eliminate them so that lack of confidence doesn't get in the way of collaboration.

◆ "The way you are going with that guitar," I said, "You could teach that to H. "What's stopping you? Tell me and I'll challenge you [to teach him]." "A guitar," he said. And I said, "Okay, let me ask the music teacher for the guitar." And the teacher said, "Oh, I have one at home." "Okay, bring it." [And to the student], "Okay, you have the guitar, you have the student, you have the talent, that's all you need. What else do you need?" And then he said, "Nothing."

"So you can't tell me you can't do it; you have the talent." And then he goes, "Okay," and he was beaming up. And he's known as a troublemaker, and I don't think anyone has given him the time to do a positive thing like that.

Collaboration builds feelings of competence as those with lesser skills have the chance to observe those with greater skills, learning that they, too, can use them. It also builds feelings of competence in those with the greater skills because they emerge in the role of teacher, solidifying their learning through an articulation or demonstration of the process. Lev Vygotsky (1978) discussed what he called the "zone of proximal development," the zone between what an individual can do in collaboration with those who are competent in an act and what an individual can do independently. Social interaction over learning helps students grow more independent in their ability because solutions and the small steps of a process are modeled to them.

Feelings of Cultural Competence

Children's feelings of competence can connect to the feelings of pride that they have in their culture. We all know that self-esteem positively affects learning. Having pride in culture can lead to feelings of self-respect and self-esteem, and, hence, heightened feelings of competence. Activities that enhance students' pride in their culture can increase students' feelings of competence in other areas. Warner Wirta, an American Indian from the Midwest, said:

◆ One thing white society knows is that you always have to write things down on paper. And see, for Indian society, history has always been carried on by storytelling. What I'm saying is that a lot of these thoughts on the contributions of American Indians have to be written down; then a white kid or non-Indian starts to believe it. I suppose it's psychologically that's how they've been raised. When the instructor knows about all the great powerful things that Indians have contributed to the greatness of this country, the Indian kids are all ears.

Pride in cultural identity can raise self-esteem needed for success in other areas. Furthermore, doing something for the tribe may give students the impetus to move beyond a place in which they are stuck. Zantua was able to establish enough pride in culture to help students develop social skills and feelings of competence that they otherwise might never have gained. He did this by putting them in front of real audiences.

◆ What made me laugh was two of these students had never, ever spoken in front of people, and they were so nervous. This one little girl was chewing gum, and I had to have her spit it out, of course, before she went on stage, but she was going at it so hard, I thought her jaw was going to collapse. It was hilarious. I said, "Are you OK?" "Yeah, yeah, yeah." She's really a beautiful person, but no speaking skills at all. But she tried so hard it made my heart feel really good. She got up there and she was so nervous, and she said a few good things to those kids about being from her tribe, and I thought, "Wow, what she did then probably made an impact on her whole life." I've seen her now. She was in here yesterday, and she was not afraid to walk up to somebody and give them a hug, or shake their hand and say, "Hi, how are you doing?" And I think it was from that moment on, she decided that, hey, "I'm going to talk to people." She was real introverted and quiet, and it just blew my mind [that] she got up there and she spoke in the microphone. To see a kid go through that change is really something; they want to do well because they are in the public eye.

Feelings of competence are powerful. They set humans up to be what they are capable of being.

Inclination toward Self-Expression

Zantua's student in front of the microphone was a young woman who was finding her voice. The inclination toward self-expression is universal, but those who have been oppressed or those to whom voicelessness has been modeled by elders who have been oppressed, may need to have powerful reasons to stand in front of a microphone, draw a sketch, perform music, or even to write on a piece of paper. Once students realize that their ideas and feelings are important, they usually want to express them to those around them. As a teacher, you may be the first to view or listen to students' budding self-expressions. You may be part of their first audience, and from there you can orchestrate ways for their voice or expression to hold power. American Indian teacher Anne, from the Midwest, tells how tentative early voices are:

◆ When I ask them for writing, I give them physical examples and talk to them about what I expect because they say, "Geez, I don't know what to do." Because they're really insecure, fear that maybe they won't do it right, I give them something they can relate to, so that it can click, "Oh yeah, I can write about this."

Ketron throws hunks of clay at his students and might even rough out a sculpture. Ingrid talks about how journaling is another way to get students started in self-expression. She provides herself as an audience.

◆ It's sort of my job to make sure that they are better writers when they leave than when they came in. And the most rewarding part of everything that they do is their journals. Writing a full page was like writing a novel for them, but now they can all do it. They just figure, "Oh, she wants us to write a full page, so we'll do it." And it's really fun to read. I'd read the journals, comment and give them back, and they write more. It's human. And a lot of things about teaching are not human enough for the kids or for the teachers.

Ingrid went on to note how traditional means of self-expression in the community are undervalued:

◆ We have kids who could end up as unemployed, depressed people when they could be painting, and writing poetry, and doing these kinds of things that have never really been considered really legitimate pursuits of Anglo culture. That's one-way thing I have come to see. The things that most people think of as arts and crafts here, like rugs and sand paintings, are things just sort of looked at as knick-knacks.

Self-expression does not have to occur on the written page; it can take place in art work, in movement, in music, and in speech.

Let us come back to Warner Wirta's symposiums, because they hold the key to how a human's inclination toward self-expression is connected to self-determination. This combination permits a double dose of motivation. Wirta rehearsed his students for self-expression, which, in turn, helped his students have more power in their world.

◆ We had this Society of Redman's American Club [SORA], and for the first time the Indian students were able to get together as a group where they could talk together and intellectualize, instead of always being busy hanging out in gangs to survive and fend off the other kids. At least there was an organized group where they could bring their grievances up instead of fighting, piecemeal, as when they were alone. We felt good about talking about these grievances instead of fighting, and finding out "Hey we've got this grievance; we can present it to the principal." Boy, that, they enjoyed. It eliminated a lot of the bad things that used to happen between the Indians and the whites.

The SORA negotiating group found an audience. At last they could give strong expressions about themselves instead of defending themselves piece-meal.

Wirta rehearsed his students, helped them find their voices, found them a legitimate audience, and capitalized on their oral strengths. Amy helped students find the Reservation Business Committee as their audience. Self-expression and feelings of self-determination go hand in hand.

Role Models: The Inclination toward Imitation

◆ My students say, "You're cool because you're a teacher and you've got money." I said to them, "What you guys have to understand is that inside of every one of you is me." I said, "I was you. And our hearts match. And whatever you see in me—non-drinking, helping my own people, doing those things—that is inside of you. You can do those same things."

—*Patty George, American Indian teacher from the Northwest*

In Patty George's very existence is proof to her students that a purposeful life is possible. Many teachers have told us stories in which we saw them acting as role models for their students: Tom Ketron continually let his students know that he was an artist who was also a teacher, and he brought in his own Chinese ink drawings for them to see. "And I use myself as a model. 'I messed up here. You will too; how are you going to handle it?'" Amy provided models when her students had to do the analytical writing that is so hard for many of them, "I'll actually have one all written out so they can read and then follow that," and she also told them about her own struggle in school and how hard she worked to make it.

◆ They can't believe I had to struggle. My students always ask me, "What's college like?" but then they always say, "But that's easy for you because you can fit in." But that's painful for me to hear that even from my kids because they have the ability to do that too; they have the ability to accomplish everything I've accomplished, even though I may look less Indian than they do. All of them do. And I shared similar stories with them. It really opens their eyes, makes them think about what they're doing. A lot of them use race as an issue; I just try to reinforce that they never use race as an excuse.

American Indian teachers also talked about the people in their lives who acted as models for them. Barry Dana from the Northeast said:

◆ If I had to look back and think who, as a teacher, taught me how to be a teacher, my uncle was probably the only person that really gave me some skills. It was mainly enthusiasm for what you're doing; he had that. Now, when my kids leave the room, I'll continue working on my canoe or drum or snowshoes, or whatever we're working on. The kids know that. So that's what I mean by enthusiasm, because you have to model that this is exciting stuff, no matter what it is you're teaching. And people shouldn't go into teaching if they don't have it.

Children learn a lot about reading and writing and its purposes from seeing those purposes modeled by family. Mike Raideaux, an American Indian from the Midwest, discovered how his father and grandmother modeled social responsibility and real purposes for discourse. He said:

◆ My Dad said, "Mike, I've always wanted to write stories." He went to school, too. For whatever reasons it didn't work. I always heard that he was intelligent. Not from him, but I heard it from other people. And he was articulate, and he always liked writing. He wrote beautiful letters. He would write grammatically correct letters. And that didn't dawn on me until I thought, "I like writing, too." And he'd read all that interesting political stuff. I kind of got interested in reading from what he talked about. He said, "You better get out and do something about that." My grandmother would say it, too. "You better go up there [to the tribal government] and do something about that."

Warner Wirta described how it took him awhile before he could feel like a worthy model:

◆ The school system was brought fame by my running. I made the Olympic trials, and if I hadn't had a leg injury, I may have gone farther. That stopped me cold in my tracks, but I had to learn to look at things more positive because I became more comfortable with who I was. I tried very hard, and I didn't make it, but instead of faltering, the feeling was growing quite strongly to work with other fellow Indians in the community. I did get the job in the school system, so I started to work with these youngsters to make them feel better about themselves. And the only way I could do that is to start to feel better about myself. Then, when I was able to start unfolding who I was, these youngsters started to identify more and started to follow that role model. It doesn't mean that they improved overnight; it takes many years to identify

with a role model for these young ones. But I was more than an Indian like
these novelty things wearing head dresses. They knew that this Indian person
struggled through a system that is racist and became a teacher.

Throughout this chapter we have shown you how teachers "helped" students, or
perhaps better provided the circumstances, audience, and materials so that students could help themselves; but being a role model for them is a different thing altogether. As role models, teachers provide views of their life and their struggles,
showing their students instead of telling them how to meet the struggles and challenges that will come for them. Those American Indian students who are keen ob-
servers, who learn in part by observation, spend time looking up to their teachers.
Teachers will do well to tell their stories and exemplify their courage.

Assessment

Because grades seem counterproductive for many American Indian students, performance assessment seems a much more productive way to go. Reservations that
have their own schools may have some autonomy over this process. When a community decides what they think it is important for their students to know before
they leave school, there can be a list of outcomes (or whatever the appropriate word
is in your locale [results, goals, objectives, standards, competencies]), and assessment of whether students have met school expectations can be authentic, shown by
the end results of students' endeavors. What you see or hear students do is what
they can do. When such lists are publicly available, the mystery of grades and of
lack of success no longer exists. What students can do and what they need to be
able to do is abundantly clear.

Portfolio assessment (in which students collect evidence of their competence) or rubric assessment (in which students and teachers keep checklists of competencies met) may be much preferable to grades. Some schools, districts, even
states have made or are making transitions to such systems. They make a lot of
sense for systems where many American Indian students attend school. Some systems will keep on requiring the kind of grading that can be destructive to the motivation of some American Indian students. In these situations, contract grading
procedures, if carefully developed, can provide evidence to students that effort can
bring about competence. If such systems provide a vehicle by which students can
declare their own learning goals and evaluate their own progress, students can have
some feelings of self-determination in the assessment process. (See Appendix B for
information that will support teachers in developing assessment through portfolios, rubrics, or contracts).

Transition to Mainstream Situations

◆ All I know is that if they want to be successful when they leave here, they need to know that they have the power within themselves to do what is necessary. So we try to communicate that to them.

—Anne, non-Indian teacher from the Northeast

◆ I was really afraid for them, especially the ones who would write in their journals that they wanted to be lawyers and doctors. And they couldn't write a paragraph that anybody could understand really what they meant by it. Most of us can only do what we think we're supposed to be doing with the particular group of kids we have.

—Ingrid, non-Indian teacher from the Southwest

If students' education is based on intrinsic motivation and if an institution that they will be going to is not, students may need help with transitions. Actually students who go from situations where they have had joy in learning for some years do pretty well in such transitions. A transition may occur if American Indian children will be attending K–8 in a reservation school then transferring to the public sector for high school, or if a student is moving, or if students will be going to a college or university. Mainstream schools may be different, but they may be no more rigorous or demanding. The intention here is to empower students to still be successful if they need to go from a non-mainstream setting into a mainstream setting. It may be that in the last half of eighth grade that students need to "play" high school, with bells and grades. Contract grading systems, as described above, can make a good way for students to get used to grades while maintaining the concept that success comes from effort. Students entering vocational schools or college may need to develop support systems before they go, they may need to interview students who are present in those situations so they see clearly what they will need to be prepared for, they may need to brush up on the kinds of skills that will be demanded of them in those particular situations. Transitions with thoughtful support can go quite well.

Caring Is Absolutely Essential, But It Is Not Enough

Just before this book went to press, Tom Peacock had his son Beau as a speaker in a class, "Teaching the American Indian Pupil." He asked him, "Who was your favorite teacher when you attended the Ojibwe School?" It took Beau only a moment to identify Amy. His reason for choosing her had nothing to do with what he thought he had learned in her classes or what activities she had planned. His reason was simple and straightforward: "She cares." Hence, the first of two last things to remember about what works: The relationship between students and teachers is probably more essential than what is taught and how it is taught. For many American Indian children, learning cannot begin until the teacher is perceived as safe and caring. We discovered many, many caring teachers out there, not just Amy and Tom Ketron. When that caring is present, the lessons will roll.

But just as caring about students is essential, it is not enough. Students also must learn. And this brings us to the final thing to remember before you begin or continue your work with American Indian students. Seeing students on a continuum between where they are at the moment and where they are capable of being or where they want to be is a caring and essential way to think of students. Then the teacher's job is simply to nudge them along the continuum. The nudge can simply offer up enough of a step to them so that they can take it and still have feelings of competence, or it can be dangling just the right book or individual project in front of them that will reattach them to their curiosity. A nudge might be encouragement to students who are trying to find things to say to people whom they want to have an effect on; or it can be connecting them to feelings of success in self-expression; or it can be helping them to find the feelings of competence they will need to operate in whichever world they choose to operate in; or it can be connecting them to just the right role model; or it can be helping them to do things that will make their lives more self-determined and the circumstances of their community better. Long live the nudge.

Full Circle: An Activity

Pick either an American Indian student that you know, or Ronnie from "The Great Circle of Things" (Chapter 6) and "The Storyteller" (Chapter 4), or Jessica and Marila from "They're Acting Really Squirrelly" (Chapter 3). Write a week's lesson plan for the student you picked. You may want to reread the cases so that you have a strong sense of the character. As you are planning, decide:

1. What will give the students feelings of self-determination?
2. What will tap the students' curiosity or interest?
3. What will help the students' to express themselves?
4. What will help the students' to have feelings of competence?
5. How will you give the students feedback in a way that will feed their desire to learn?
6. How might you act as a role model for this student?

References

Ames, R., & Ames, C. (Eds.). (1984). *Research on motivation in education: Volume 1, student motivation.* Orlando, FL: Academic Press.

Ames, C., & Ames, R. (Eds.). (1989). *Research on motivation in education: Volume 3, goals and cognitions.* New York: Academic Press.

Bilodeau-Jones, M., & Bossie, J. (1993, Fall). Integrated studies in a multi-age classroom at the middle level: You can get there from here. *Journal of the New England League of Middle Schools,* 8–11.

Deci, E. L. (1975). *Intrinsic motivation.* New York: Plenum.

Deci, E. L. (1985). *Intrinsic motivation and self-determination in human behavior.* New York: Plenum.

Frazier, L. (1982, Fall). [Lecture in course, "Language and Brain Processes"]. University of Massachusetts, Amherst.

Macrorie, K. (1988). *The I-search paper.* Portsmouth, NH: Boynton/Cook.

Stipek, D. (1988). *Motivation to learn: From theory to practice.* Englewood Cliffs, NJ: Prentice-Hall.

Vygotsky, L. (1978). *Mind and society.* Cambridge, MA: Harvard University Press.

Wiggenton, E. (1985). *Sometimes a shining moment: The Foxfire experiment.* New York: Doubleday.

Epilogue

Full Circle

As writers, we realize that the "doing" of research often affects the researcher more than the other way around. As a result of the countless hours of conducting interviews, having them transcribed, and reading them over and over again, several related yet dissimilar conclusions have come into focus. Each of these respective conclusions was related to our differing experiences as American Indian and non-Indian educators, and we believe these different perspectives strengthened our findings. We certainly found agreement on all of the concepts described in each book chapter, but we each came away from our work with our own lasting impressions.

Both of us were struck by the universality of issues in American Indian education with those of other colonized indigenous people. Linda Miller Cleary saw this universality through a seed metaphor she heard throughout America, Costa Rica, and Australia. Thomas Peacock came away with a renewed sense of hope in the tenacity of culture and the ability of American Indian people to triumph against all odds. Finally, both writers concluded that the complex issues presented by teachers of American Indian students could only be addressed by looking at and working on them using an integrated approach.

Linda Miller Cleary: The "Nurture a Seed" Metaphor

Sometimes while interviewing, you know that you are hearing something very important. You may simply feel a sense of excitement in the discovery of an insight you have been looking for. That happened in many interviews, but there was a succession and intensification of such moments that came to me when interviewees started using the same metaphor even though they sometimes lived thousands of miles from one another.

It started on a walk with an American Indian woman. I wish I had my tape recorder at the time, but I might never have heard what she said if I had. We were walking along a back road past the dump area where gawky turkey vultures were plucking at garbage, along a canal studded with heron, to an airstrip, and then back. The woman told me of her fear for her people. She said something like this: "The third grade this year is out of control, and they were born in the year after crack hit the reservation. The seeds being sown are not healthy seeds here, and the care that they need is not being given to the young seedlings." I was moved because I had seen for myself the younger, almost frenetic, classrooms in the school. There was a decided difference in the third graders' ability to concentrate and in the tenor of their classroom when compared with those of older children, those born before crack was present on the reservation. The difference was not explicable by students being at a certain stage of development.

When I moved on to the Southwest and was interviewing a Navajo woman, she told me:

◆ In today's society some of these kids are growing up like weeds. That's my father's words. All you think you have to do is feed them, water them, and they will grow. But my father said you cannot grow weeds. You have to grow a nice plant. You have to prune it. You have to nourish it. You have to love it. All these things. Weeds can grow anywhere, but they are unwanted. Now we are getting too many weeds in the school. I tell my students, "You need to grow straight, not all over the place. You have to have a purpose so you aren't just spread all over the place. Life is short and you can't play with time like that."

A few days later I felt the prickling of hairs on my arms, which often accompanies the uncanny for me, when a Hopi woman continued on with another version of the same metaphor:

◆ We have teachers in the community. My dad is one of them who can teach something so inner that it would be worth more. My dad is a scholar in his way. My dad doesn't have the textbook and the diploma, but he is a very wise man. He said that when you're planting, you have to look at the soil [to see] if it's fertile. You've got to take care of the plant. You've got to nurture it. You've got to sing to it. You have got to pray. When it is rooted it is strong that it can grow on its own. If corn is not strong in the very beginning, then you have to put ten times more work to get it to produce. He says that about education.

It was then that I began to understand that the depth of feeling all people have for their own children is the same as the deep feeling I have for mine. It wasn't a surprise to me. It was just that I hadn't thought about these things before.

I went to the Midwest. There an Ojibwe woman just wanted a positive experience for the students about whom she cared so much.

◆ I just think, had they had a positive experience, that seed would be planted. A teacher could plant it, even a non-Indian teacher. I just think it takes a spark from somewhere and then once they gain some success, even if it was just a small portion, that would start growing. Maybe I can plant that seed. School [could be like] a greenhouse, getting the seed going. We're like the little pots. And you know if that doesn't get done, there's violence and gangs when the seed starts growing the other way.

On that occasion, and not because of Minnesota's frigid temperatures, the hair raised straight up on my arm.

A Passamaquoddy man, unlike the women from the Southeast, talked to me with some hope:

◆ I believe that the children are not listening to elders telling stories around a lamp anymore. So what do you do? I really do believe, based on what I've seen—in terms of my teaching respect for the drum, and the dawning of the drum roots, and becoming more aware of ceremonies—I really believe that there's a real hungry audience out there. And once you've put seeds into them, they will carry it further. That's my vision.

By the time I reached Australia, my legs got involved. The hair rose on my legs when an Aboriginal woman said (I was without a tape recorder again, so I will not be able to replicate her Aboriginal English): "You know, we have trouble growing things here, and the children now have not learned how to gather. We try to take them on tucker hunts, but they couldn't survive on their own. But in the outback, when it finally rains, seeds germinate and bloom that haven't bloomed in years. I have the same hope for these children."

And finally, sitting under some trees at an Iguana Farm on the Caribbean coast of Costa Rica, I listened to two Bribri teachers talk of the children on the reserve. As the translator forwarded the words to me, the hair rose on the back of my neck and on my head, as well as on my arms and legs, and that was in the heat of the day, sun blasting all around me. It was the same metaphor. "We worry about our children, they are like corn that hasn't been planted and cared for, but the corn comes up because people didn't fully harvest last year's crop. And the weeds are not removed, so the corn is stunted." The women noticed that I was intent, almost unnerved. With a flurry of translation on both sides, I told the Bribri women about the Hopi woman and the Navajo woman and the Ojibwe woman and the Passamaquoddy man and the Aboriginal woman. And one of them responded with a serene smile, "You know we are all the same; we teachers care deeply about these children who are removed from their connection with the land and with their culture. We are all in similar situations."

And through the accumulation of this metaphor, I have become aware of the universality of the problem, of the great disservice that oppression has done to so many children and the need for each and every child to be nurtured by the community and by the teachers. Feeling the involuntary emotional response that the accumulating seed metaphor set off in me, is just that—a feeling, an emotion only. "Caring is not enough," I heard Paul Hughes, the Director of Aboriginal Education in South Australia, tell a convocation of teachers.

Now that I personally have come to a better conscious understanding of the complexity of these problems, I have begun to see the universality of the seed metaphor as a sort of imperative. I have to act on what I know. As one who prepares teachers, I know that I must let my students understand the complexities of cultural difference, the remnants of oppression, and the loss of language and of literacy. I must orchestrate ways to get my students, while they are still in training, into classrooms where there are Ojibwe children, and I must also help them process that experience. But that is still not enough. I must actively recruit American Indian prospective teachers and support them through becoming what they want to become because I now understand what a hard journey that is.

Hearing the collected wisdom from these teachers, we will all find things that we must do. We must all live up to the collected wisdom set before us.

Thomas Peacock: The Strength and Tenacity of Culture

My reservation recently held its third annual veterans' pow-wow, honoring all men and women tribal enrollees who served in the American armed forces. This year the planning committee chose to give special honors to the Vietnam veterans. After a grand entry, an honoring song, and a fly-over by two F-16 jet fighters, the master of the ceremony introduced the Vietnam veterans one at a time and had them come forward for a presentation of jackets, hats with beaded rims, American flags, commemorative knives with turquoise inlay, and eagle feathers. It was a special day for my family because three of my brothers were being honored. The oldest (Sonny) had been in Chu Lai in 1965 to 1966, serving as a Navy corpsman (medic) to the Marine Corps. The next brother to be honored was Mike (Pnuts), who had spent his combat time near Da Nang in 1967 as a Marine Corps anti-tank special-ist. Finally, my younger brother John (known on the rez as "Skin") stepped forward to receive his salutation, having served in the Marine Corps at the Saigon airport in 1975 during the evacuation of Vietnam by U.S. personnel just before its fall to the Communists.

Those who know the history of the colonization of America might think it odd that American Indian people would be honoring soldiers who had served in the same military forces that had marched through and dominated their ancestors' tribal nations. A similar American flag to the one that flew over the pow-wow grounds had also flown during the U.S. Army's massacre of American Indian men, women, and children at Wounded Knee, South Dakota. A similar American Flag had flown when thousands of Cherokee were force marched to Oklahoma Terri-tory, a journey that claimed thousands of American Indian lives. But the service was one of the few options for young reservation men until a few years ago.

As I looked around the pow-wow grounds, I saw many of the veterans' rela-tives: brothers and sisters, cousins, spouses, parents and grandparents, aunties and uncles, children and grandchildren. As with most pow-wows, there were very few non-Indians present. As each name was read and the veteran stepped forward, sec-tions of people in the stands would burst into applause. I noticed that many in the crowd were having difficulty maintaining their composure, as their hands would go to their mouths as expressions of their emotions.

Most of us were at the pow-wow that day to honor our veterans, our war-riors. The Ojibwe people have been doing just that for many thousands of years. We weren't necessarily there to honor war and its madness, including the millions of Vietnamese civilian casualties. After all, our American Indian ancestors had ex-perienced many of the same atrocities suffered by the Vietnamese. After all these years, we were there to finally honor our veterans' safe return. Standing in front of us were warriors who had survived the horrors of that war with their bodies still intact and, for most, with their sense of being at peace.

My children were at the pow-wow that day, and seeing them there reminded me of the continuity and tenacity of culture. The circle of the dance area repre-sented the cycle of these things. Pow-wows remain unique community celebra-tions, and they also serve as deeply spiritual gatherings to renew our souls. Rela-tives come from afar to these events. One of my cousins whom I hadn't seen in years came up from Omaha. My granddaughter was at the pow-wow, and at one point I walked her over to the mini-donut stand to make sure she had her fill of sugar.

Just several days later, possibly reflecting back on the pow-wow, she would proclaim to me at one of my summer cookouts, "Grandpa Tom, I'm an Indian."

"You sure are," I replied, wondering what a three-year-old was thinking when she said such a thing.

"Indians don't wear any clothes," she said.

"But you have clothes on, and you are an Indian," I told her, wondering again where she would get such ideas.

Both the pow-wow and the conversation with my granddaughter reminded me of how far we have come, as Ojibwe people, to retain our tribal ways, and of how far we have to go in educating others about who we are and of the struggles to convince this country to include American Indians in the American story. Somewhere deep in my soul, I know that my granddaughter will be fighting many of the same educational wars I have fought over the years. Although my generation has come a long way in addressing the educational issues facing our children and the schools that purport to serve them, we still have a long way to go. To ready my granddaughter for this continuing struggle, both her family and her schools need to ensure that she has a strong grounding in her Ojibwe culture—she needs to know that Ojibwe women wear clothes. I will have to feed her a lot of mini-donuts so that she has the energy to continue the struggle. Someday she may step forward at a future pow-wow to receive her salutation, surrounded by proud children and grandchildren. And when she dances her honor dance, she will dance for all of her ancestors and their descendants. That is the circle of things.

A Shared Impression: An Integrative Approach to American Indian Education

As this generation of educators works to improve the education of our children and grandchildren, including American Indians, we need to occasionally pause and remind ourselves of where we have been. As writers, our sense is that although we have made advances in lowering the dropout rates and increasing student achievement, the educational system continues to fail a disproportionally high number of American Indian students. Read on if you are willing to face some of these issues.

In the recent past, we have had a program approach to American Indian education. I, Thomas Peacock, remember writing my first federal "Title IV-A" proposal (then the Indian Education Act) for a local school district and using the funds to offer cultural classes to our students in maple sugaring and crafts and cultural field trips. Looking back at that period, I realize that most of the things we did for the students made little difference in their school success because the students who were going to be successful became successes regardless of whether they made maple sugar. Conversely, the at-risk students who went out to the sugar bush primarily benefited because they got a reprieve from the perceived oppressive nature of their classrooms.

As a tribal school administrator, I implemented a variety of programs that did little to help ensure the overall success rate of my students. I wrote a large grant to install fiber optics interactive video classrooms between our community college, the tribal school, and several area public schools. Another large grant was used to purchase cellular phones, thousands of dollars in the latest computer technology, and to offer professional development training in the writing of educational standards. Yet another grant was supposed to link us to the world via the World Wide Web. I don't think that ever happened. Meanwhile, students were still not coming to school on a regular basis, or they were dropping out of school altogether. Many of those who remained in school continued to lag behind their non-Indian peers in achievement measures.

As American Indian educators, we are constantly searching for the magic pill or the messiah to solve all of the problems of American Indian education. One year our conferences hail parent involvement and the next year they tout gifted education. Then the following year, the magic pill becomes right-brain learning. To be sure, each year a would-be messiah steps forward saying he or she has all the definitive answers.

This book is not the magic pill, nor are we as writers the latest messiahs of American Indian education. The recommendations we offer as possible solutions to the problems may be more difficult to implement than solving the problems. Put another way, the solutions may be more painful than the problems. Nonetheless, we offer you the following summation of the problem and solution:

Problem: The program approach in American Indian education has failed for a variety of reasons. Most of these programs were either too little, too late, or not enough, or simply bad ideas. Generally speaking, programs attacked an issue and ignored a whole set of other issues. The piecemeal nature of programs has not been able to break through the nearly impervious nature of institutional and overt racism in this country. In the meantime, today's American Indian students have been dropping out of school and achieving at rates strikingly similar to 1968, when the Kennedy Report on Indian education called American Indian education a "National Tragedy: A National Challenge." The truth is in the numbers, and the numbers have not changed significantly enough to say the program approach has been successful.

Solution: There is a need to look at the **whole** of American Indian education, to consider integrating issues and solutions. Using this approach, we simultaneously recognize and deal with issues in their complexity. For example, students cannot be prepared to live in both worlds (their tribal cultures and the mainstream society) if they suffer from characteristics of internalized oppression, such as anger, hopelessness, or passive-aggressive behavior. Similarly, making wholesale improvements in instructional methods and curriculum (as we suggested in Chapter 8) will have little positive effect on graduation rates or achievement if teachers and other school staff do not possess the interpersonal skills necessary to interact with students. American Indian language maintenance programs will have little effect on language maintenance if there are no natural uses of the language in the communities and if schools cannot find other ways of lessening the discontinuity between schools and homes. Problems in need of long-term solutions, such as literacy issues, cannot be addressed in malfunctioning institutions if teachers, administrators, policies, and priorities change at the turn of a dime. Schools cannot be expected to deal with all of the social, psychological, and educational needs of children if the communities in which the children come from are out of harmony and balance. Schools cannot effectively integrate American Indian culture and language into the curriculum or hire more American Indian teachers and administrators if racism in schools is not confronted.

Again, only when we have confronted all of these issues and solutions in their complexity will we really make progress in alleviating the educational problems in our schools. This integrated approach should consider the roles of communities and other agencies, in addition to schools. Compare the approach to the war the human body wages in fighting disease. Typically, there is no magic pill. But orange juice might do its part. Sleep offers its assistance. Mini-donuts give the body quick energy.

Finally, these issues need to be confronted with a sense of urgency. Each year that we fail to deal head-on with these issues means another year of failure for many American Indian students. Each year that we deal with these problems of the program approach means we fail to acknowledge that maybe people, not programs, are solutions to problems. We remind readers again that, at least initially, the solutions may be as painful as the problems: Schools need to become so integrated a part of the community that there is little discontinuity between them and the homes of American Indian children. Schools, communities, tribes, and individuals need to deal with the remnants of oppression. Schools and communities need to build bridges between the two that go both ways. Schools and communities need to determine responsibility for maintenance of tribal languages. Schools need to address issues of literacy (Chapter 7) as a crucial component of school achievement. Schools need to use the instructional and interpersonal strategies suggested in Chapter 8 and teach in multiple ways to address the learning styles of all students (Chapter 6).

A critical element of Paulo Friere's education for critical consciousness (described in Chapter 2) is that before we can be free we need to realize we are enslaved. Friere wasn't only speaking of awakening the critical consciousness of the oppressed; he was also speaking to the need for educators to confront themselves and their own practices, which have sometimes enslaved the schools that purport to educate children and have ultimately enslaved us as educators. The first step in giving American Indian education a "good solid kick in the ass" (suggested in Chapter 1) begins with confronting ourselves:

◆ In this life we prepare for things, for moments and events and situations. . . . We worry about wrongs, think about injustices, read what Tolstoy and Ruskin . . . have to say . . . Then, all of a sudden, the issue is not whether we agree with what we have heard and read and studied . . . The issue is us, and what we have become.

—Robert Coles

Appendix A

If You Are Interested in the Research

We realize that not every reader will be interested in the more technical aspects of our research, but the information in this appendix will augment that which is already in Chapter 1.

In-Depth Phenomenological Interviewing

The data generated for this study came from in-depth phenomenological interviewing based on a method developed for a study of community colleges by Irving Seidman and Patrick Sullivan and later described by Seidman in *Interviewing as Qualitative Research* (1991). This method was adapted for a study of eleventh grade writers by Cleary (1991) and has been adapted again for this study. The theoretical underpinnings of this method stem from the phenomenologists in general and Alfred Schutz (1967) in particular. In this model, the researcher deems the experience of the participant with regard to the subject being studied as important in coming to an understanding of that subject. This interviewing strives to maximize the participants' rendering of that experience. A series of three interviews provides enough time, privacy, and trust so that the participant can relate his or her experience, reflect on that experience, and, to some extent, to make sense of it. The three-interview sequence allows one interview to build on another so that a deepening understanding of the experience is developed with every interview. The data are

the words of the participant. In this study, the phenomenological approach to research assumes that the experiences teachers have had as American Indian and non-Indian teachers affect the way that they go about their work. Tom Ketron's response to his teaching situation and his experiences in the past affect the way he goes about his work in the present.

Implicit in this methodology are certain assumptions. It is assumed that we, as researchers, can learn and understand things through the words of the participant and that those words were a reconstruction of the participant's experience as they understand it.

Participant Selection

Another assumption in the research design of this study was that "human behavior is not random or idiosyncratic" (Bogdan & Biklen, 1982, p. 41). In selecting participants, we sought a broad range of teaching experience with American Indian students so that common experiences might show the dynamics in the teachers' work and the issues that concerned them. Hence, diversity was a major criterion for selection. We looked for diversity in gender, in race, and in the types of schools attended by American Indian students. We selected participants from five areas of the country, and within those regions, we selected reservation schools and public schools that were congruent with the schools serving American Indian children. We tried to select an equal number of American Indian and non-Indian teachers, although that was not possible in each area. We also interviewed some teachers' aides when American Indian teachers were not available in an area. Because we sought equal numbers of American Indian and non- Indian teachers, American Indian teachers are overrepresented, given their scarcity in some schools.

Data Analysis: Analytic Induction

To analyze the data collected in our study, we used a technique called analytic induction (Bogden & Biklen, 1987; Ely, 1991; Glaser & Strauss, 1967; Seidel, Kjolseth, & Seymour, 1995), to sort interview material into emerging themes and issues based on the juxtaposition of what the different teachers said. In this process, we first developed category codes based on themes and issues we heard in preliminary readings, and then both of us read through thousands of pages of interview material, coding them. It involved revision and re-re-vision of category codes as our understandings developed and as we ran into discrepant data that we needed to make sense of. As themes emerged from clustered category codes, we began to see an organization of the book that would hold the themes.

In using teacher quotes and profiles in this text, we have edited the raw interview material using the following rules for ourselves: We took out interviewer's questions, unless they furthered meaning of the quotes or were essential to context from which the teacher was talking. We allowed ourselves to take out the repetitive comments and material that were extraneous to the topic being covered. We wove material from different parts of the three interviews when they were on the same topic. Finally, we changed the tenses of verbs so the material from these different parts of the interview would work together. Most important, everything that is quoted is the teacher's own words, and we have committed ourselves to present them in a way that is in concert with the integrity of everything the teacher said.

Authors' Voices

We believe the "doing" of research probably affects the researchers more than those who read the results. Hence, the writers' voices have been added to the "collected wisdom" that is presented in this text. Furthermore, we believe that research is shaped by the researchers and that researchers owe it to their readers to declare their connections with the topics being studied. For this reason, we have included our own experiences and have made it clear when we are speaking from our own opinions rather than from the data of the text.

Bogdan, R. C., & Biklen, S. K. (1982). *Qualitative research for education: An introduction to theory and methods.* Needham Hieghts, MA: Allyn and Bacon.

Cleary, L. M. (1991). *From the other side of the desk: Students speak out about writing.* Portsmouth, NH: Heinemann Educational Books.

Ely, M. (1991). *Doing qualitative research: Circles within circles.* Bristol, PA: Falmer Press.

Glaser, A. & Strauss, B. (1967). *The discovery of grounded theory.* New York: Aldine.

Schutz, A. (1967). *The phenomenology of the social world.* Evanston, IL: Northwestern University Press.

Seidel, J. V., Kjolseth, R., & Seymour, E. (1995). *The Ethnograph: A program for the computer assisted analysis of text based data.* Qualis Research Associates.

Seidman, I. E. (1991). *Interviewing as qualitative research.* New York: Teachers College Press.

Appendix B

If You Wish to Change Your Method of Assessment

If you are looking for a way to change your method of assessment, we have included some tools to help with the preparation of contract grading, portfolio assessment, and rubric assessment. These are lists of questions that you might ask yourself to guide you through setting up what may be a new system of assessment for you. It may be useful for you to seek in-service assistance and models to help you in this change to more authentic assessment.

Questions to Guide Preparation of Contracts

◆ What outcomes/term objectives do you want your students to meet?

◆ What content and experiences do you want your students to have?

◆ How much do you think is necessary for your students to accomplish during the term?

◆ What level of competence do you expect at this age? What will make you and the student satisfied with progress? Quality? Quantity? Correctness of written language, features of format, depth of thinking, ideas, progress in developing specific skills, number of pages read or written, number of problems solved, number of drafts, intensity of endeavor?

- How will you monitor quality of the work accomplished?
- How much will you involve students in constructing the contract (to give them feelings of self-determination and ownership)?
- Will you permit students to show multiple indicators of success at a certain task?
- How much will you personalize the contract with individuals (permitting individual goals or concessions to individual strengths or weaknesses)?
- How will you keep track of student progress on the contract?
- How will you establish deadlines?
- How will you or will you build room for negotiation into the contract?
- What will you ask a student to do for each grade? What will you ask them to accomplish to pass the course? What additional things do you want them to do for a C? a B? an A?

Questions to Guide Portfolio Plans (inspired by Routman, 1991)

- Would the portfolio contain finished pieces as well as works in progress? Will you distinguish between a display portfolio and a working portfolio?
- Would reflective writing be included? Attached to each piece or to the whole portfolio?
- How would the pieces be selected?
- Who would select them? Teacher? Student? Student in consultation with teacher?
- How many pieces would be selected?
- Would pieces be polished for the portfolio? Selected from what's available?
- What else in addition to written or artistic pieces would be included in the portfolio? Personal goal statement and progress report? Statement of quantity and content of entire work? Rubric marking progress in skills?
- Would the portfolio be used to demonstrate progress on certain predetermined outcomes?
- How would the portfolio be used in the total evaluation process? (reading records/logs, journals, conferences, discussion groups, collaborative projects, etc.)

- On what criteria would the work in the portfolio be evaluated?

- How can the portfolio become a profile of the student, their progress, their needs?

- How can the portfolio put the student in charge of the learning process, allowing them to look at their progress over time?

- Will the portfolio be a term-only portfolio? Or will it contribute to an ongoing, career-long portfolio? Will it reflect work in classes in other disciplines?

- Will a conference be connected with the portfolio evaluation process?

- If you install portfolios for your whole program, will you design assignments collectively? Will you work individually or in teams when you evaluate the finished products? What kinds of information shall you attempt to extract and summarize for institutional purposes? (from Yancey, 1992)

Routman, R. (1991). *Invitations: Changing as teachers and learners K–12.* Portsmouth, NH: Heinemann Educational Books.

Yancey, K. B., (Ed.). (1992) *Portfolios in the writing classroom.* Urbana, IL: National Council of Teachers of English.

Questions to Guide Preparation of Outcome Rubrics

- What outcomes do you want to check progress on in this unit of study, on this rubric?

- From what shall you draw evidence to track progress on outcomes? From authentic tasks in which students demonstrate significant outcomes? From culminating exhibitions or project presentations? From demonstrations across the curriculum? From oral interviews/conferences? From reflective journals/ learning logs? From engaging tests? Student observations? From student self-appraisal? From peer assessments? From review of products? From anecdotal records? From checklists? From portfolios?

- Do you want to include a student's personal goals as outcomes to be assessed?

- How will you designate the degree of accomplishment of the individual outcomes? Satisfactory/Unsatisfactory? Accomplishment Evident/Development in Skill Evident/Initial Signs Evident/No Skill Evident? Excellent/Okay/Needs Improvement?

263

◆ How will you set up the rubric so that (1) it will be beneficial to you as a teacher, (2) it keeps students positive (not defensive) about growing in skills, and (3) parents will understand the purpose and their child's progress?

◆ How does this rubric meet the assessment demands of the state, district, school?

Index